BLUNDERS

CHARLES N. TOFTOY

Cover & Interior Design by Cindy Bauer

ISBN: 9798580021270

(Amazon/KDP)

Printed in the United States of America

Quoted lines from the poem, *In Memoriam*,
the greatest poem of the 19th century:

"I hold it true, whate'er befall;
I feel it when I sorry must;
'Tis better to have loved than lost
Than never to have loved at all."

Alfred, Lord Tennyson, 1849

In Memoriam

"To all those who have died or suffered due to mistakes that should never have happened. I think of them every day."

Charles Toftoy, 2020

Dedication:

To Patty, my wife of 56 years. She gave me the idea to switch genres from mystery thriller to self-help. She told me that I should write to inspire people. Actually, she was tired of me meeting with homicide detectives and studying serial killers. So, Amazing Fireside Talks was published.

In this new novel, I have carried Patty's suggestion even further by enlightening people to the many blunders that have occurred and could have been avoided—for the good of us all. And she agreed that this is a need for those people who might not realize mistakes made that shouldn't have happened.

Patty fits the Libra sign perfectly: appreciates art and nature, all for harmony and justice, shares with others and cares about people, honest and sincere, keeps a lovely home, and likes fresh flowers, especially my favorite: sunflowers.

As a perfectionist (and *Yes* you are—to some degree), she maintains a fine balance for our lives.

In short, I'm a lucky man to have her as my wife and excellent friend—my *one and only*.

CNT

A Special Dedication

This book is dedicated to those who are the most important people in our country: teachers, police, firefighters, first responders, doctors, nurses, and those who serve in the military.

God Bless them all

A Note From the Author:

This novel is not necessarily based on my viewpoint, rather it is an attempt to show you how many events in history did not have to happen. Many of these blunders were due to poor decisions, inept communications, and lack of able leadership.

It is set in logic, supported by sufficient facts, probably unknown to you. It is not *Monday morning quarterbacking, hindsight, 20/20 vision, afterthought, retrospect, or See... I told you so.* Those are all cop-outs.

Instead, this is about terrible, chilling, horrific events in our world's history that could have been avoided.

The blunder chapters are random. No order. I purposely want them to be off balance, and not an engineer project.

So hang on to your seat—this ride will open your eyes to a fresh look at unforgivable historical blunders.

"Those who cannot remember the past
are condemned to repeat it."

George Santayana
(1863 to 1952)
Spanish-American philosopher, essayist, poet, novelist

INDEX

CHAPTER 1

The Beginning

Suddenly Doris slipped off her chair and hit the floor extremely hard. Brenda shrieked, "Oh my God!"

Everyone in the pub heard the dull sound when her head smacked into the floor. It sounded like when a baseball meets the bat's sweet spot and everyone in Nationals Park can hear the crack... clearly a home run into the bleachers.

Tiger gasped and rolled Doris over on her back. Quickly, he wrapped two linen napkins together and pressed down firmly on the wound... a 2-inch gash which was bleeding profusely over her right eyebrow.

Hands shaking uncontrollably, Brenda grabbed her iPhone and dialed 9-1-1. She explained the situation.

"You know where the Celtic House Irish Pub and Restaurant is... off Columbia Pike? (pause) You do? Great... that's where we are. Hurry! She's still unconscious! (pause) Yes, I'll stay on the phone. (pause) Yes, she does have a pulse beat. (pause) OK. Please hurry! Someone will be in front to wave in the rescue crew."

Lars came out of the men's room sashaying leisurely and singing *Danny Boy*. Seeing Doris on the floor, covered with blood, he lurched forward and rushed to her side. He got on the floor behind her, placing her between his legs, and leaned her upright into a sitting position at about a 45° angle to keep her head above her heart.

Tiger began applying direct pressure to the wound.

Brenda grimaced at the splatter of blood on Doris's blond hair and her nice blouse. Doris, with her best buddy Brenda's help, had just purchased the blouse online three days ago, and Olivia had complimented her on it when she first sat down. An asymmetric hem roll tab sleeve lace panel, forest green. It looked beautiful on her, complementing her long, blonde *Veronica Lake* style hair.

"Of all things to be thinking about at this time!" Brenda chided herself. She would take it home later and try to get the stains out, and if that didn't work, she'd take it to Hurt's Cleaners on Wilson Boulevard.

Doris was still unconscious when the rescue team arrived. They carefully placed her on a stretcher and sped away like gangbusters. Lars rode with her inside the ambulance, heading for Virginia Hospital Center.

Tiger and Brenda waved goodbye outside the pub, hearts pounding... like the sound of a DJ drummer's loud thumps. Squeezing their hands tightly together.

"Hope is all we have," said Tiger. Both wiped tears from their eyes.

CHAPTER 2

Afterwards

Three weeks later, the Alpha Team: Lars, Doris, Brenda and Tiger, met for breakfast at the Metro 29 Diner off Lee Highway in Arlington. After everyone was seated, Doris sprang to her feet, confessing, "I ruined it. I ruined it. It's my fault. Dammit! Sorry everyone."

"What are you talking about?" Tiger asked.

"I ruined our start on the discussion of blunders. Really upsets me."

"You got it all wrong, Doris," chimed in Brenda. "The pub party was just to celebrate our start on the blunders journey. Remember? It's here at Metro 29 that we planned to have our weekly discussions."

Lars pointed out, "She's right. Every Friday at 0800 hours (8 a.m.) for breakfast at our favorite table, #98, back here in the far corner."

Tiger added, "And with our favorite waitress, Anita!"

Doris smiled. "OK, guys. Thanks. I feel much better now."

"Not to beat this into the ground but you know Doris, the scar on your forehead is disappearing nicely." Tiger said, burping loudly.

Lars nodded in agreement. "They did a good job over at Virginia Hospital Center. Doc Galatin used two layers of stitches. One layer stitched the deep part of the cut together; the other layer of stitches took care of the visible part. And Galatin had a plastic surgeon help to close stitches using a silicon gel sheet. The Doc said the scaring would fade away in about three months.

"Which reminds me," Lars injected. "Nobody noticed but Doris was sweating and trembling before she fainted."

"Yes, and I had shortness of breath, too. All of this came on quick. The Doc said that it was an anxiety attack. If so, that was my first! No more I hope." Doris went on to acknowledge that everyone's quick action on the scene made a huge difference. "Tiger applying direct pressure, Lars getting my head above my heart which slowed the bleeding and minimized the swelling and also, Brenda calling 9-1-1... *all of you* made a big difference. So again, thank you! Great teamwork!"

At this point, you need to know a few things. Lars Neilsen formed the Alpha Team. His brother-in-law, Cory Swink, is the Arlington County Police Chief. The team has helped the Northern Virginia Police Departments with difficult cases by running clandestine, parallel investigations—helping solve five cases, where the police were absolutely clueless. All four team members are highly skilled and have risked their lives while helping the police solve these difficult cases.

Presently, the police haven't any new cases for the Alpha Team, so they decided to take a sabbatical (Lars' term) to research blunders that have occurred throughout the world.

Many months ago, they met for two days and agreed on 32 blunders. Each of them has researched these in-depth. They decided to meet once weekly to discuss the selected blunders, one at a time.

Metro 29 is their meeting place. Also, you need to know that they have added a fifth person for this effort, Olivia Smith, who wrote a book, *Mistakes That Changed History*, winning her the Pulitzer Prize. Starting with the next meeting, when the team discusses the first blunder, she will join them for each session. The team members have interfaced with her while doing the research.

Now, for a quick look at the characters... you will learn more about them as we go along:

- Lars Nielsen, formed the Alpha Team—Professor at George Washington University (GWU), part-time sleuth, West Pointer, two Vietnam tours, looks like the late Christopher Reeve (Superman);
- Brenda Little—reporter for *The Washington Post*, black belt in Tae Kwon Do, looks like Lizbeth Salander played by Rooney Mara in *The Girl With The Dragon Tattoo*;
- Nathan "Tiger" Greene—ex-sergeant US Army, served with Lars in Vietnam; helped his father in family owned funeral home business in New Orleans,

his hometown. Presently, he is the Deputy Director of Murphy Funeral Home located at Wilson Boulevard and Glebe Road. Looks like Eddie Murphy, the movie star;

- Doris Wagner—former top FBI profiler, clairvoyant, into astrology (mediumship). Looks like Veronica Lake, top femme fatale movie star in the 40s with the famous peek-a-boo hairstyle. Married Lars just this past year.

Lars closed this session. "OK gang, next Friday we begin our journey on blunders. The first one selected is that 9/11 should have been avoided."

Tiger injected, "I agree... can't wait until next Friday."

The team gives each other a traditional high-five.

"Now all of this is behind us; let's get on with our discussions on blunder number one." Lars smiled.

"Spoken well, Doc, as our team chief," declared Tiger, adding, "See you all next week for our kickoff of this incredible journey."

9/11 Montage

**Top: World Trade Center smoking on 9/11
Center: DN-SD-03-11451, United
Flight 175 hits World Trade Center south tower
Bottom: World Trade Center Fireman requests
10 more colleagues, Flight 93 Engine**

CHAPTER 3

9/11 Could Have Been Avoided

"This will be the beginning of many blunder eye-openers. With the amount of research put into this, most facts the general public probably did not know," announced Brenda, the team leader for the first blunder discussion.

The Alpha Team huddled at their favorite table, #98, anxious for Brenda to continue. She began by reading several quotes from the victims:

'Are you guys ready? Okay, Let's roll'.—Todd Beamer, United Airlines #93... crashed at Shanksville, PA.

'Something is wrong. We are in a rapid decent. We are all over the place. I see water. I see buildings. We are flying low. We are flying very, very low. We are flying way too low. Oh my God, we are way too low. Oh my God, we're...'—Madeline Amy Sweeney, Hostess, American Airlines #11... via telephone call to her supervisor before crashing into the North Tower.

'Numerous civilians in all stairwells, numerous burn

victims are coming down. We're trying to send them down first... We're still heading up'.—Captain Patrick Brown, 35th floor of the North Tower before it collapsed. Brown was one of the NY Fire Department's finest.

'We're young men. We're not ready to die'.—Kevin Cosgrove, on 105th floor of the South Tower... then it collapsed due to United #175 crashing into it.

'What do I tell the pilots to do'?—Barbara Olson, American Airlines #77, to her husband before crashing into west side of the Pentagon. Ted Olson reported that his wife said this via a telephone call that all passengers and flight personnel were herded to the back of the plane by armed hijackers, who had knives and cardboard cutters.

Brenda wiped tears away as she finished. She had spoken throughout in a choked up manner. Everyone's eyes were full of painful tears. Hearing their words had taken a toll on their emotions.

Doris was face down between her hands on the table, shoulders shaking. She lost her first husband in the World Trade Building on 9/11.

Tiger pounded his fist on the table which drew attention from other customers. "We never got total revenge! Come on... 2,996 deaths and about 6,000 injured. And look where the hijackers were from! There were 15 Saudis, two United Arab Emirates, and two from Egypt and Lebanon. We let these 19 hijackers train here on our dime and boom... they do us in!"

Lars, now choked up, added, "But we did get Osama Bin Laden, Tiger."

"Yeah Doc, he got a watery grave, but there is still one

that is empty," Tiger replied bitterly.

"Tiger is right," chimed in Brenda. "The 9/11 attack cost Al-Qaeda $500 million, but our loss was $300 billion in the event and aftermath."

Tiger jumped in and acknowledged that there were many heroes and heroines that day. "One of my favorites was Todd Beamer. He tried to reclaim control of the aircraft and led fellow passengers in the attack on the terrorists. *'Let's roll'* reminds me of us Army Rangers. We used *'Let's roll'* when it was time to attack in Vietnam."

"That's right," agreed Lars. "We used that expression a lot."

Tiger nodded and continued. "Beamer saw the pilot and co-pilot with their throats cut. Then someone said *'We're going down. We're going down'*. The aircraft was reversed to head to DC. And another passenger said, *'Let's get them'*."

Hiking up his jeans, Tiger added, "And by the way, President Bush ordered it to be shot down if it continued towards D.C. Todd Beamer was just an ordinary guy, like many of those who excelled on 9/11, yet he showed exceptional courage."

Brenda stepped in and informed everyone that of the 2,996 people who died on 9/11—265 were on the four planes, 2,606 were in the World Trade Center and surrounding area and 125 were at the Pentagon, adding, "This was the deadliest terrorist attack in world history."

Doris having regained her composure a little, piped in, "That empty grave that Tiger mentioned might be our own unless we get full justice." She swiped away another tear starting to slip down her cheek.

"Like I said," Tiger added, cuddling in to Doris, "we haven't paid them back totally... yet."

Lars squeezed Doris' hand. "True. Revenge breeds revenge. However, this deserves more of a deadly response than we have accomplished so far. An eye for an eye. We need to kick butt. After all, as Brenda said, this was the worst attack on the US ever."

Olivia saw an opening. Until now, she'd been paying close attention to what everyone was saying. "That's correct. Even worse than Pearl Harbor where 2,403 died with 1,178 wounded. And remember, over 6,000 were injured due to the 9/11 attacks. In a later session, I will talk about the Pearl Harbor Blunder."

"Now," Brenda declared, "let me explain how all of this could have been avoided. My research covered over 8,000 pages of documents, articles, opinions, journals, books, and the internet. First of all, a red flag should have gone up when a Ryder truck with 200 pounds of explosives detonated underneath the North Tower on February 26, 1993. Six people died, over 1,000 people were injured, including 88 firefighters, 35 NYPD officers and a medical service worker. The damage caused the World Trade Center to close for about one month.

"Come on everyone! This was a terrible mistake... not to pick up on this indicator that terrorists had the World Trade Center on its radar screen. At least, an indication that it was a likely future target. I'm passing out a couple of sheets with bullet points." She stopped to hand one to each member of the team. "These points are like dots that were not connected by Intel organizations. If even half had been connected, the towers might still be standing."

You may think you know all about 9/11, but now through Brenda and the Alpha Team dialog, you can discover the truth about mistakes made that could have avoided the disaster. Not hindsight or Monday-morning quarterbacking but via inexcusable, truly ignorant mistakes.

Brenda strongly stated, "Those two towers should still be a part of New York City's landscape today. All of the people killed should be still amongst us. And the 6,000 injured should never have been injured." She then began to describe her bullets:

"The bombing in 1993 was an indicator that the Towers were a target. Duh! An elementary school student can figure that out. Big failure on the part of the CIA *(Central Intelligence Agency)* and the FBI *(Federal Bureau of Investigation)*. Huge!

"The 19 terrorists received flight training from over ten US flight schools. Doesn't that send a message? The Feds knew for many years that suspected terrorists of Osama Bin Laden's group were receiving flight training in the US. The FBI was sitting on its hands, while the CIA was sleeping at the switch. Disgraceful. That's how I describe it.

"In the early 1990s, one terrorist received flight training in New York and North Carolina. His goal was to blow up twelve aircraft over the Pacific, and then crash a suicide plane into CIA Headquarters. Luckily, he was arrested before he could accomplish his goal. This was another gigantic pre-cursor that was not connected even though they arrested him. Pardon my French, but as I was going through all of this research it seemed like nobody gave a rat's ass.

"Plus, we already knew about the use of aircraft as weapons: the hijackers of an Air France flight in Algiers, 1994, planned to crash into the Eiffel Tower. FBI records show in 1991, the possibility of using planes as weapons. *Mon Dieu!* Where was everybody's' head? In the sand? Airlines, airports and the FAA had *numerous* Intel warnings, yet failed to implement better security. Not to mention, American Airlines was fined $3.4 million and United Airlines was fined $3 million for lack of security between 1998 and 2000.

"The two hijackers that flew into the towers were trained in a flight school in Florida. But my main point here is that they only wanted to learn how to steer, not take off or land. Wouldn't that tell you something if you were training these yoyos? It doesn't take a rocket scientist to figure it out!

"During the spring and summer of 2001, there was an Intel stream that something *very big* was going to happen... from the CIA Director.

"Still, *nothing* prompted urgent action. Communication was poor at the senior levels of the military, FAA *(Federal Aviation Administration),* CIA, and the FBI. Bureaucratic rivalries resulted in a lack of response. You see, if these dots had been connected, 9/11 probably would never have occurred. We were caught with our pants down. I have many more detailed events that add to the dots, also not connected, but I'll stop here."

"Man, that was an eye-opener!" exclaimed Tiger.

"I agree," said Lars. "The key mistake was the lack of sharing of information between the CIA, FBI, and the NSA

(National Security Agency). The CIA did not share pre-9/11 information on Al-Qaeda. They ran a clandestine operation. And the FAA's capabilities were weak. Two of the hijackers were on their TIPOFF Terrorist Watch List! Like Brenda said, they did not connect the dots via watch listing and sharing info in real time. The threat was real, yet imagination and common sense were missing from our leaders.

"The bottom line is that the CIA purposely withheld info from the FBI that would have prevented the 9/11 attack. An immense mistake. Inexcusable. Those two agencies have different corporate cultures. I teach this in The Business School at George Washington University. No accountability, rivalry, and liaison problems."

Doris jumped in. "You all know that I lost my first husband in the tower. He was helping a disabled woman by carrying her down from the 47th floor. He never made it." Doris' eyes teared over.

"If only they had connected some of these dots, 9/11 may not have happened," Tiger snapped, but his eyes shown compassion for Doris as Lars hugged her closely.

"Great job, Brenda," Lars stated. "We all dug into research about 9/11, but you really squeezed a lot into these points of yours, making our discussion easier. In closing, I'd like to add that in order to get answers which can lead to a strategy for any large-scale situation we need to connect the dots to see the big picture."

Olivia added her own observation. "That's absolutely right, Lars. We can draw inferences from connecting items of information. The problem here is that these Intel agencies are unable to associate one event with another, so they weren't able to find the salient feature with all the knowing... in short—the dots that connect events. Like a jigsaw puzzle. Once you start connecting the pieces together, you begin to see the big picture."

Tiger quickly injected. "How do you solve a crime without linking what is known together? We've done that in the past when we were tracking down serial killers."

"Excellent point... there is a correlation between the two," Lars surmised. "It really *is* just common sense coupled with keen imagination that allows us to see the big picture... far out there on the horizon. The Intel community is supposed to predict and prevent, but frankly they face a reactionary government—not a preventative government. We are good at reacting to events, but not very good at preventing. Realize that the FBI and CIA have dedicated people, but the lack of sharing information between them as a team effort, is what really led to this terrible disaster that could have been avoided."

Tiger stood. "OK gang, next Friday I have the lead for another blunder that should never have happened either; the *extinction of buffaloes*. I'm our animal guy so this is right up my alley."

Doris declared, "Don't forget, Tiger... we all own animals on the Alpha Team."

Traditional high-fives as everyone got up to leave.

"See you next Friday, gang. Have a good one," Lars announced, chuckling as Tiger shoveled down yet a third pancake.

Union General Phillip Sheridan

CHAPTER 4

Buffaloes Slaughtered—A Disgrace

You need to be reminded of a few things here... The Alpha Team meets every Friday at Metro 29 for breakfast. Team members have spent the last nine months researching blunders that they all agreed to after studying together for two days to select historical blunders of their choice. All agreed to the blunders, which are all-inclusive. Also, that one team member would lead a chosen blunder on a rotational basis.

They chose Metro 29, which opened in 1995, because of the quality food, prompt service, and nice atmosphere. Also, it is rather private for them... back in the far left-hand corner, table #98. Anita is usually their waitress; she knows what each member wants on the menu.

Unless one of them changes something or Anita is not working, they don't have to say a word... its automatic.

Lars—Eggs Benedict; Doris—Three-Egg Omelet with

mushrooms, feta cheese and crispy bacon; Tiger—Golden Brown Pancakes with bacon, and grits; Brenda—French Waffles with strawberries and whipped cream. Olivia—Minced Nova Scotia Lox Eggs and onions. They all get fresh squeezed orange juice... the best in the Metro area, and for drinks: Lars and Tiger—coffee; Doris and Brenda—herbal tea; Olivia—cappuccino.

All members get paid handsomely by Lars, the team leader, who uses a $500 thousand donation from a previously satisfied customer. The Alpha Team caught the murderer of her daughter.

"What I'm about to relate is the most horrific conservation story in the world's history. It is revolting and sickening." As he talked, Tiger scratched the scar on the lower right side of his cheek. A wound from Vietnam.

"Also, stomach-churning and shameful," added Doris.

Lars injected, "I know you are the lead on this one, Tiger, but of course we all do in-depth research on all blunders we have chosen... and I must admit that this huge mistake is unforgivable. Even God can't forgive this catastrophe because it involves greed, selfishness, and total disrespect of others, to include buffaloes."

Picking up on cue Tiger said, "Most of what I'm going to cover is unknown to the general public. A little *deep history* first, as we say in New Orleans. The Bison latifrons (or buffaloes) immigrated to North America during the Pleistocene Epoch, about 36 million to 11,700 years ago.

"There were times when low sea levels connected North America with Asia. Buffaloes appeared about 500,000 years ago and survived until about 20,000 to 30,000 years ago when they became extinct, which was the beginning of the *Last Glacial Maximum*. Glaciers covered huge parts of planet Earth. Up to that time, buffaloes weighing about 4,400 pounds, grazed over the Great Plains."

"Planet Earth is my favorite TV program and David Attenborough is the best narrator ever," interrupted Olivia.

In agreement, Brenda shot up two thumbs. Everyone followed.

"There's a reason I'm starting off this way," continued Tiger. "Mainly because the buffaloes were here first; 30-60 *million* roamed the American plains in the mid-19th century. A few centuries ago, 100 million American buffaloes existed here. And we screwed them over. A very sad part of our history.

"In 1840, about 60 million buffaloes roamed the Great Plains from Canada to North Texas; 20-30 million were grazing from the Appalachians to the Rockies—Gulf Coast to Alaska. The indiscriminate slaughter of the northern herd began in 1880."

"That brings sadness to my heart," shuttered Doris.

"Ready for something you didn't know?" Tiger asked and without waiting for a response, went on to state, "The US Army and professional hide hunters developed what I call *a silent conspiracy*. Big mistake. The soldiers would kill buffaloes to starve out American Indians, who depended on the buffaloes for food and clothing.

"The wheels were coming off, by the government and US Army, on how to handle the buffalo-Indian situation and we showed no sense of morality or goodness.

"One Colonel said, *'Kill every buffalo you can! Every*

buffalo dead is an Indian gone'. Major General Phillip Sheridan was charged with using whatever means necessary to force American Indians off the Great Plains and into reservations. Every buffalo hunt was the Army's business."

"You know, Tiger... this was an act of sabotage... making the primary food source of local natives scarce," declared Lars.

"You know what, Doc?" replied Tiger. "It was a Scorched Earth strategy. For those of you who don't know what that is, it means to burn everything in sight to destroy any resources; just like General Sherman used in his march to the sea in the Civil War. Destroy their stock and settle them on lands allocated to them. Poor management. Peace treaties failed and were not honored. If this was done right, things could have been squared away. President Grant refused to sign a bill passed by Congress to protect the buffalo in 1875.

"But the major culprit was the greed of the US Army and white settlers. It was a senseless and heartless destruction of the buffalo. The settlers and other professional hide hunters would take the hide and tongue, considered a delicacy, and leave the rest. So the carcasses just rotted. The Indians used the buffalo for food, plus about fifty other uses. The buffalo was sacred to them. And they only killed for what they needed—no more and there was nothing wasted."

"Tiger, that reminds me of the Vietnamese people. They don't throw away anything. They've been known to flatten Coke cans to use for roofing, for example." Lars tightened his fist. "Puts perspective into it. Now, we're spoiled. Lots of waste."

Tiger nodded in agreement and continued. "About 7.5 million buffalo were killed from 1872 to 1874. My God! That's alarming and disgraceful."

Doris breaks in. "Tiger, this is one of the biggest heartfelt blunders I know of. Absolutely inhumane. Our humanity was at stake and we messed it up."

"Reckless and deplorable," agreed Lars.

"Unspeakable atrocities. Revolting," uttered Olivia, obviously affected deeply. Her voice cracked; pinched face; throat tight.

Tiger nodded, continuing. "No checks and balances, zero control. Now, back to Sheridan again; he wanted to create a bronze medal for hunters... a dead buffalo on one side, a discouraged Indian on the flip side. I want to call a sidebar here. The bison is called the American buffalo, found in North and South America, and parts of Europe. The Cape buffalo are found in Africa and Water buffaloes in Asia. A little trivia... and irony—the Cape buffaloes kill about 200 people each year. In short, neglect, greed, and selfishness superseded proper management. Stupidity ruled those years by top leaders."

Olivia then informed everyone that regardless of the self-centeredness of all involved, the buffalo became our national mammal. It is on the nickel, started in 1938, and some sports teams use its name. Buffalo is the symbol on the Wyoming state flag and it is on Manitoba's provincial flag. So even though we slaughtered them, posthumously, the buffalo is respected and held in high regard. Native Americans still consider the buffalo to be a sacred animal and a religious symbol.

Lars wiggled in his chair, obviously disgusted. "The bottom line on this blunder is that the buffaloes were here first—back about 195,000 to 135,000 years ago. Then followed by the native Indians who arrived on the scene about 15,000 years ago. Who the hell were we to run them off? At the same time causing starvation for their women, men and children. We slaughtered the buffaloes and treated the Indians disrespectfully!"

Olivia jumped in at that point with a comment. "You've hit the main points, Tiger, which are generally missed by most people. That includes the professors and scientists who study these areas of concern. In my book, *Mistakes That Changed History*, I point out that we have a tendency to encourage our way of doing things to other people in other countries. And our way might not be suitable for them for many reasons: culture, traditions, religious beliefs... pardon my language here, but it *PISSES* me off! We are so naive, including many of our diplomats."

"You're right, Olivia," Brenda piped in, "we can't force our ways on other countries, or buffaloes and Indians for that matter. What the hell is wrong with people?"

Tiger declared, "Yeah! The Olympics does more in building relationships than anything else. Athletes mixing together in the Olympic Village really develop genuine relationships built on trust."

"This discussion has opened our eyes. We will be discussing the native Indian mistreatment in a blunder later on," Lars said.

"I'll be doing that one since I'm the only minority here," chuckled Tiger.

"Okay gang, Olivia is up next week for our discussion of Pearl Harbor," stated Lars.

"And," Olivia responded, "Let me say this. FDR *(Franklin D. Roosevelt)* should have been impeached for allowing that disaster to occur. That should raise your interest for next Friday."

"Right on," said Tiger.

Per the Alpha Team's tradition, they all put their hands in the middle, raising them up with a low cheer.

Pearl Harbor, October 30, 1941
(looking southwest)

CHAPTER 5

Pearl Harbor Miscues

Olivia opened up quickly. "FDR should have been impeached. My Lord! Just think of our losses!

"Killed—2,335 military personnel and 68 civilians; total 2,403 of which 1,177 were from the USS Arizona. Of the military deaths—2,008 were Navy, 109 were Marines, and 218 were Army. And don't forget the 1,178 wounded!

"We lost 19 Navy ships, including eight battleships—the prestige ships were either destroyed or damaged and of those, four were sunk. There were 92 Navy aircraft destroyed plus 31 more that were damaged.

"The US Army Air Corps had 77 planes destroyed and 128 damaged. Think of these statistics as I venture through some of the mistakes that caused this horrific outcome.

"It was a war crime attributed to Japan, because there was no declaration of war by Japan and it happened without warning. On the other hand, it can be considered a high crime concocted by FDR. He failed to act on a basket load of tips that war was imminent. Were all those losses I just mentioned worth not being prepared?"

"I don't think so!" Tiger butted in. "This was a huge let down."

Olivia nodded and continued. "Three days before the attack, FDR received a message from the Office of Naval Intelligence, which was a monstrous red flag and dismissed by Washington. I have a copy of that message, now declassified, which states:

'In anticipation of possible open conflict with this country, Japan is vigorously utilizing every available agency to secure military, naval, and commercial information, paying particular attention to the West Coast, the Panama Canal, and the Territory of Hawaii'.

"That means FDR and his military advisors were well aware of the *possibility* that Japan could strike the US. Even the War and Navy Departments sent out pre-war warning messages to major commands. Yet nobody paid any attention.

"The US was in a *splendid isolation* foreign policy strategy. Just like Britain in the late 19th century, when Benjamin Disraeli and Lord Salisbury wanted to avoid all alliances and entanglements. Thus, Britain remained *isolated* by choice.

"Basically, the US was sleeping at the switch, sitting on their hands... no war, keep us out of foreign intervention. A totally complacent attitude. And that left us totally unprepared. *Isolationist attitude* prevailed throughout the lands.

"Even Admirals and Generals believed that if Japan attacked Pearl Harbor, it would be by sea, which would fail, because of our protective netting. And to them... an airplane can't sink a battleship. With that mindset, the top brass were in denial."

Lars shook his head. "You know, in one day the world was changed. On that December 7th, the US changed from being an isolationist country to an internationalist country beginning on December 8th."

"That's true," agreed Olivia. "And get this, everybody— red flags were flying all over the place. They were probably waving so *obviously* hard that they smacked FDR and his top brass in their faces. I can't begin to cover all of the miscues. But there were tons of them. All mistakes that shouldn't have happened.

"The US broke the famous *Purple Code* of the Japanese. A major breakthrough. Based on an intercept, on December 6th, a US Cryptologist gave a message to her superior about the Japanese inquiring about ship movements and ship berthing positions at Pearl Harbor. Her superior said he would get back to her in a couple of days. Like the others, no sense of urgency. There are a lot of these types of occasions where duty officers were not only slow to react, but actually filed away the important messages.

"Another example, and there are several, a radar operator on Oahu saw a huge group of airplanes on his screen heading towards Pearl Harbor. His supervisor said it was probably a bunch of US B-17 bombers and not to sweat it."

"You know what, Olivia?" Doris jumped in. "We pushed Japan into a corner so they would react militarily and we could get into the war. Churchill and Roosevelt knew the European war could not be won by the Allies. They needed

the US. Many Admirals and Generals support this view...
sort of a silent, hidden conspiracy. Scary but true, I think."

"Good point, Doris!" exclaimed Olivia. "Just plain poor
leadership, incompetence, and unpreparedness at all levels."

Let's pause for a moment.

Alpha Team members are very grateful that Lars added
Olivia to the team for this blunders project. During their in-
depth research, Olivia has assisted each team member based
on her unmatched historical research. Three years ago, she
poured her wealth of knowledge into her renown book—
Mistakes That Changed History.

Born in Yorkshire, England, graduating from Oxford,
with a PhD in history from Georgetown University, Olivia is
known as a world expert in history. Her book won a Pulitzer
Prize in the history category. She advises the US State
Department on a variety of foreign matters.

Lars met her at a joint conference, Georgetown
University and George Washington University (GWU),
conducted in Washington, D.C. last year. Her depth of
knowledge is beyond reproach in researching eye-opener
mistakes that shouldn't have been made.

Olivia took a long swig of her fresh orange juice and
continued.

"We knew what was going on. Let's face it, the US
broke the Japanese *Purple Code* in 1940, as I mentioned
before, so we knew what was going on... even though they
didn't know it. By November, 1941 our intelligence
agencies had convincing intelligence (Intel) that Japan was
up to something big, including a strike on the US. As I
mentioned earlier, inexperienced Intel officers would decode

messages and then ignore their importance and just file them away. Utterly incompetent. Sometimes their superiors never even saw the messages.

"And we knew the Japanese were building a network of spies throughout their embassies and consulates," added Brenda. "Roosevelt was provided with clear signals that an attack was coming and chose to ignore the warnings."

"Exactly, Brenda!" stated Olivia. "Frankly, war warnings were flowing *all over* the place!"

Lars stroked his chin, thoughtfully. "There must have been a reason for the very top levels of our government to ignore these obvious warnings. Pitiful display of leadership. As former Army Rangers and paratroopers we would not stand for this, right Tiger?"

"Ten-4 on that, Doc," agreed Tiger.

Olivia went on, divulging some other good points.

"Several retired Admirals have stated that they feel top level officials let it happen to us, so the US could enter the European conflict. FDR provoked Japan weeks before because he didn't want to take the first action. He told Japan to get out of China and give up some geographical areas of valuable resources to them, coercing the war on purpose. Of course, Japan did not comply."

"You know, Olivia, most people have never heard of these gross mistakes. The information our research has uncovered is not readily available to the public," commented Tiger. "And the general public deserves to hear the truth!"

"Here's another sidebar for you," Doris said, jumping into the discussion. "FDR reported to Congress on December 8th, 1941 that the attack was *'A date which will live in infamy'*. Originally, it read, *'A date which will live in world history'*. Roosevelt's two speechwriters were in NYC at the time, so they had no input. FDR usually wrote his own speeches himself. I looked up the word infamy. It means: *an evil or wicked act, disgrace, shame, dishonor, notoriety.* So, whose act was wicked, theirs or our inaction based on a sort of secret plot by a top-level group? That should haunt us all!"

Brenda rolled her eyes. "What really lives in *infamy* is our intelligence and leadership failures, that led to our gross mistakes causing this horrific disaster. I feel deeply for those who died at Pearl Harbor. And we *are still paying* for that historical event that never should have happened."

"There are some necks I would have liked to ring. I 'garontee you, 'dat!" Tiger said. "Sorry. I had to toss in my favorite quote from Justin Wilson, our New Orleans favorite chef, who has passed on."

Olivia pointed out that, "The bottom line is that FDR should have been impeached. And actions taken against the cocky, complacent Admirals and Generals who were not taking an imminent attack seriously. They should have been fired."

"Downright disgusting," Lars stated, jumping in. "Reactive, not proactive, thinkers. The problem in those days was that the presidency was thought of as an untouchable office—like a king or queen. Another tidbit, for what it's worth, in the 1920s, General MacArthur told West Point cadets that the USA and Japan would go to war. He based this on Japan being overcrowded and having few natural resources. My substantive point is that we should have been well prepared. The only *good* thing was that our three aircraft carriers were out to sea. Their loss would have set us back for a year. But the fighter planes were left out in the open on the tarmac... easy targets.

"One last point—a Japanese midget sub was attacked by a Navy ship before the main attack. It was reported to an officer who not only *disregarded* the report, he took his crew out to breakfast. Again, complacency ruled the day."

Olivia nodded, affirming Lars remark. "That reminds me of Shakespeare's words, *'Out of the jaws of death',* from *Taming of the Shrew.* Sorry, had to get that in here, being from England, chaps! This entire Pearl Harbor episode is revolting, repulsive, and sickening. Again, all of these mistakes did not have to happen. Bottom line—there would have been no World War II."

"This has been an eye-opener for all of us," Lars concluded. "Next Friday, we tackle a blunder that most people have never heard of. It is absolutely surprising and shocking. It's Exercise Tiger, a preclude to the World War II invasion. I'm going to lead that one."

High fives by all. And hugs.

Tiger stayed a little longer to finish his pancakes and to flirt with Anita. When he departed, he gave her a New Orleans wink.

Charles N. Toftoy

Exercise Tiger Memorial
Utah Beach, Manche, Normandy

CHAPTER 6

Exercise Tiger—A Forgotten Disaster

All of the team members researched this horrendous blunder in great depth. It became a very emotional ride for all of them. Many times, they went to the National Archives and Records Administration in Washington, DC individually and twice as a group. When they traveled together, they met at IHOP in Ballston and rifled down pancakes, then walked to the Ballston Mall Metro station and took the Silver Line to Farragut Square, finishing by walking the two blocks to the National Archives Building at 700 Pennsylvania Avenue.

Doris liked the neoclassical architectural style of the building, dating back to 1935. As the venerable keeper of historic documents, the team members absorbed a load of documents—some secret, now declassified. They all knew the background of this D-Day invasion training exercise.

Let's summarize it here. The massive dress rehearsal took place in Lyme Bay, England, April 27-28, 1944... with landings at Slapton Sands. The beaches were similar to what they would face when invading Utah Beach, about five weeks later. This deadly farce resulted in the deaths of 749 soldiers/sailors. Some were killed by German U-boats and others by friendly fire.

This should get your attention, especially since only 197 men were killed at Utah Beach in the actual invasion. A real tragedy... forgotten and unknown by most people.

Back to the present at Metro 29...

As usual, the team were all seated at table #98. It's raining heavily outside—like the monsoons in South Vietnam.

The only switch today is that Tiger changed from pancakes to French toast, Brenda's favorite. He winked at Anita, surprised at him switching his traditional order.

"That's OK," boosted Tiger... "I'll be back to pancakes next Friday, Anita."

Anita smiled in a flirting manner. Very cute smile. A little hip action as she strutted away. Tiger sighed.

Wasting no time, Lars kicked it off. "We are trying to stay away from hindsight, 20/20, second guessing, and Monday morning quarterbacking. Rather, we need to stick with the mistakes that caused these blunders that never should have happened. But from time-to-time, I may slip up and mention points that involve a little bit of what should have been done. After all, Exercise Tiger was the biggest fiasco of WWII. A D-Day dress rehearsal that turned sour. NEVER should have happened!"

The team's research became deeper and deeper as they

uncovered erroneous reports, mischievous armchair political reports, myths, wrong estimates of casualties and other misleading information. Some reports were made by quacks, whom Lars feels are deplorable. Lars, a West Pointer, is a strong duty, honor, country guy. No lying, cheating or stealing. He continued.

"As a Ranger and paratrooper, like our own Tiger, I find it hard to understand why the exercise was allowed to go on in the first place. Potential U-boat threats were in the area and it was known that the Germans were at sea. *(In Germany it is called U-boot. A shortened version of Unterseeboot, which means undersea boat.)*

They staged just across the English Channel at Cherbourg. What's wrong with *this* picture?"

Tiger jumped in. "To have the LSTs *(Landing Ship Tanks),* moving slowly in a straight-line formation, a 2-mile flotilla (a fleet of ships or boats), opened them up for an attack. That left the rear end open. Oops, sorry to interrupt."

Lars gave Tiger the fist pump. "Yup, Tiger... that left the rear end wide open, so the last two trailing LSTs were hit. Ghastly mistake by not having destroyer escorts. Only one was available and it was far to the front. Another mistake was a massive failure of the highest degree in communications and coordination. Units were on different frequencies. This led to the *friendly* fire that killed 110 of our soldiers/sailors."

"That's inexcusable and unforgivable," exclaimed Olivia. "Those poor men!"

Tiger shot forward. "Yeah, I can tell you that they didn't sign up for this. They need to be remembered forever."

Lars moved on with more information. "When the U-boats attacked at 0203 hours, nobody woke up RADM *(Rear Admiral)* Moon, who directed this operation. How stupid can you get? That is unheard of! Moon was just ten miles away from the attacks, on his ship, the USS Bayfield.

Another big mistake was a failure to have better life vest training. This was costly. When the soldier/sailor was forced to jump into the water, the weight of the combat packs flipped them upside down. This pulled their heads underwater, drowning them. Inexcusable."

"And many didn't know how to swim, Doc," added Tiger.

Doris blurted out, "Another shortcoming."

Lars added, "There was no plan for small craft to pick up survivors. *What?* Never leave your fellow men out there to die. Also, delaying the exercise by one hour, Moon's decision, was not transmitted to all units. Doris will cover this when she discusses RADM Moon. This caused severe confusion, especially when the change was announced only five minutes before kick-off time. I'll turn this over to Doris now. She's done intensive research on RADM Don Pardee Moon. Doris..." He waved his hand towards her.

"Thanks, Lars. As you know, RADM Moon was the Director of Exercise Tiger. He received a lot of hostility from the Brits and Americans. One of General Eisenhower's aides said, *'I came away from the Exercise feeling depressed'*. General Omar Bradley called it *'a complete shambles'*. He stormed off the USS Bayfield in a rage, and that was even before the devastating U-boat attacks that left 639 men dead. Moon was chewed out by Admiral Kirk's

Chief of Staff, who asked, *'All right, Moon; tell me what happened'*. Moon just broke down."

Tiger interrupted. "But I've got to hand it to him because he pulled himself together to do brilliant planning for the complicated invasion of Utah Beach at Normandy."

Brenda added, "Not only that, but he was also chosen to direct the invasion Operation Dragoon of southern France. So the top brass had high regard for him."

Doris continued. "Let me paint a solid picture of RADM Moon: Naval Academy graduate, 4th in his Class; a gentleman, generous person; leader... true patriot... 100% loyal to the Navy, family, and friends. Unquestioned loyalty was an outstanding trait of Moon. He loved the Navy and gave his all to it."

Tiger said excitedly, "RADM Moon, to me, was a hero... not for a physical action but for high level, painstaking preparations for these invasions."

Lars popped in at that point. "And he served in both World Wars, receiving the Distinguished Service Medal, which is a military award to recognize a person who has distinguished himself by exceptionally meritorious service in a duty of great responsibility."

"I know we are not supposed to Monday Morning Quarterback this blunder and stick to mistakes," Doris went on, "But some mistakes that could be attributed to RADM Moon are: the German U-boat attacks occurred at 0200 hours. Moon was asleep in his cabin at the time about ten miles away, as mentioned by Lars. He was not awakened. Gross negligence on the part of those who should have awakened him immediately. Not Moon's fault.

WP/nsg

WAR DEPARTMENT

THE ADJUTANY GENERAL'S OFFICE

WASHINGTON 25, D. C.

IN REPLY REFER TO:

AGPC-G 201 Bolton, Louis A.
(6 May 44) 39,572,891

12 September 1944.

Mrs. P. M. Bolton,
1535 West 168th Street,
Gardena, California.

Dear Mrs. Bolton:

Your letter of 6 May 1944, addressed to an overseas instal-
lation, in which you request information concerning your son, Sergeant
Louis A. Bolton, has been forwarded to this office for reply.

It is deeply regretted that your son, who was previously reported missing in action on 28 April 1944 in the European Area, was
reported killed in action on that date, as his wife, Mrs. Welona F. Bolton,
who is designated as the person to be notified in case of an emergency,
was advised in my telegram of 10 August 1944, and confirming letter dated
13 August 1944, which states that he died in the English Channel. No
further details have been received in the War Department regarding Sergeant
Bolton's death, but you may be assured that if additional information is
received, you will be advised promptly.

I realize how futile any words of mine may be to assuage your
grief but I trust that the knowledge of your son's heroic sacrifice in
action may be a source of sustaining comfort to you in your sorrow.

You have my heartfelt sympathy in your bereavement.

Sincerely yours,

J. A. ULIO
Major General
The Adjutant General.

April 28, 1944, D-Day dress rehearsal
Body never recovered
Sgt. Louis Archer Bolton, 19 years old

RADM Don Pardee Moon, USN

"But, RADM Moon delayed the landing times by one hour. And this was not communicated to all units, which caused 110 deaths; a massive failure in communications. A Communications Officer on duty on the USS Bayfield, from 0000-0400 hours said, *'Communications failure due to different frequencies'*.

"Also, there were reports of sailors being slow in passing on Moon's orders from time to time. But as you can see... few of these failures can be attributed *directly* to RADM Moon."

Tiger snorted. "There must have been a lot of *green* sailors."

Doris nodded. "One mistake that could be Moon's was having the LSTs deployed in a straight line with only one escort. Actually, there was to be two, but one had to return to port. German U-boats could do a surface speed of 16-17 knots, so the slow moving LSTs were easy targets.

"He should have realized that the German U-boats were housed just across the Chanel at Cherbourg. But that was the mistake of someone above Moon's pay grade, I would think. And don't forget that all of this was done on Eisenhower's watch. It was his idea for live-fire and to travel far around Lyme Bay."

"Let's face it; if the hierarchy thought RADM Moon was at fault for the exercise, they would not have let him continue to direct the invasions at Utah Beach and southern France... two monstrous undertakings. By the way, Utah Beach was a tremendous success... mostly owed to Moon's articulate planning," Brenda chimed in, providing those excellent points.

Tiger exclaims, "Let's not forget this. It is important to remember that the Brits let him down. How the hell could they fire live ammunition on US Army troops who were making the landings? Someone had their head in the sand!"

Doris replied, "You may be right, but the Brits naval bombardment was to occur 50 minutes prior to the landing. They didn't get the hour delay change. It was a real screw-up.

"Let me discuss RADM Moon's suicide. What most people don't know is that he received a severe head concussion. This occurred when two German Focke-Wulf 180s flew over the USS Bayfield. The second plane circled back, having followed tracers fired by gunners on the USS Bayfield. Moon had ordered personnel not to fire on German aircraft. *That* plane dropped a bomb 50 yards off the ship's stern. It rocked the USS Bayfield and that's when Moon hit his head. It caused a severe injury. His devoted wife Sibyl read a letter written by him where he wrote that *'after the concussion he felt his mind was not as it should be'*. He was in a lot of pain. Moon, a very intense man, felt that he couldn't trust himself to make future decisions.

"After the Utah Beach invasion, the USS Bayfield sailed to the Mediterranean. RADM Moon spent hours with Admiral Hewitt on August 4th, begging him to postpone Operation Dragoon. The upcoming invasion of southern France frustrated Moon. He tried to change his superiors' minds because he felt that it would cause the death of hundreds of troops. He developed an alternative plan which would be much better and with less lives loss. The next morning RADM Moon committed suicide. His suicide prompted the *higher ups* to use Moon's alternative plan, which was very successful. The staff was ordered to regard Moon's suicide as *top secret* for the time being."

"Frankly," piped in Olivia, "Moon sacrificed himself to save lives, probably still thinking of the 749 lives lost in Exercise Tiger and the 197 lives at Utah Beach."

Tiger stated, "To clear up his actual suicide since some nutty writers have reported it incorrectly. Probably to gain fame for themselves."

Doris nodded and continued. "A steward found RADM Moon dressed in shorts and an undershirt in his stateroom on the USS Bayfield. He was sitting on a sofa with a .45 caliber pistol, wrapped in a towel, in his right hand. His eyes were open, blood trickling from his ear. The spent bullet was found in the shower. A carefully penned, articulate suicide note was found next to him. Some excerpts: *'The mind is gone... I am sick, so sick... My lovely wife and darling children... it is terrible for them. My mind is running circles with occasional nearly lucid periods and then others, the complete reverse'.*"

Doris, tears pouring down her face, breaks down. Brenda is now bawling like a baby. Olivia is shaking. Tiger and Lars wipe tears away. People in the restaurant look away.

Recomposing herself, Doris continues, her voice broken. "Many reports of Exercise Tiger and of RADM Moon himself are in error. For example, he was not insane as declared by an official *opinion paper* by RADM Lowry. Also, he was not assassinated."

All team members knew Doris as an expert in astrology and mediumship. As the nation's former top FBI profiler, she has used these techniques to catch murderers. Two years ago, she was instrumental in bringing a serial killer to justice, along with the Alpha Team, by assisting the local police. Sometimes she is successful in communicating with the dead, better known as mediumship.

"I visited RADM Moon's gravesite in Arlington Cemetery. He rests there along with his wife, Sibyl. I spent at least 30 minutes there. I felt better when I left. I hope he did too." Doris teared up again. Tiger handed her a cloth napkin.

Doris wiped her eyes and strongly suggested, "His superiors underestimated Moon's physical and mental exhaustion and the repercussions from the head blow. I feel that based on my in-depth research, his immediate superiors were at fault for not spotting his state of mind, especially after his very severe concussion."

All team members agreed by giving Doris a thumbs-up.

Lars added, "To round out the true story of Exercise Tiger, I had Brenda research survivors. Brenda, you're up."

"OK. Here goes. The survivors, those dead and missing, and their families were forgotten for 40 years. I covered more than a dozen survivors. Their stories were more like Arlington Cemetery in their mind, remembering and naming the dead, mourning deeply, and emotionally explaining all that was lost. It tore into my soul.

"I decided to summarize and paraphrase their comments and not attribute them to any particular person. These comments came from a diversity of American soldiers and sailors. Examples are: Navy—medical officer, ship fitter 3rd class, seaman 2nd class, radioman, gunners mate 2nd & 3rd class, motor machinist mate 2nd class, navigation officer, ensign, and a Navy commander; Army—sergeant: engineering brigade, sergeant: graves registration, sergeant: amphibious truck company. These are just a sample of the survivors I covered. The following comes from survivors.

"Many of the soldiers died due to poor training on the use of life jackets... they were face down in the water, legs up—drowned. Horrible sight. The captain of our LST gave his life preserver to one of the wounded. The captain died. There are so many stories it's tough to cover them all.

"Heroic actions taken by men faced with mass balls of fire, 70 feet in the air due to torpedo hits. Trucks, vehicles, tanks fully loaded with fuel. The suction of the ship's decent dragged some men under. Our LST sunk in 18 minutes. The explosion knocked me out. Our captain stayed onboard and burned to death. Water was frigid, 42°; hypothermia set in quickly. We pulled around floating dead bodies... our buddies. Some were screaming *'help me'*, *'we're gonna' die'*. Others cried, *'Mom'*.

"One ensign swam under a floating mass of burning oil to get a raft for us. Saved our lives. There was no plan to retrieve survivors... they just drowned or burned to death. Hundreds burned to death. I saw them and could do nothing. We were ordered to leave the bodies where they were, so our LST had to zigzag to keep from running over the floating bodies. That haunts me to this day. The wounded soldiers were to be treated but... no questions were to be asked and no histories taken. Anyone who talked about the casualties were to be court-martialed.

"One person I will mention by name is Captain John Doyle: *'He disobeyed orders by turning his LST around picking up 134 men from the bitterly cold water. If it wasn't for him, I wouldn't be here'*."

Lars pitches in with, "Sorry to interrupt, but I cannot fathom the idea of not trying to save those in the water after the U-boat attacks. And not informing families earlier. These are against my core values."

Doris agreed. "The leaders were so naïve to include General Eisenhower, who was responsible for Exercise Tiger. He picked the location for the landings and to have it a live-fire exercise. It was on his watch."

In closing, Brenda said, "Some of my information comes from declassified secret and top secret documents. One of the worst and most disrespectful outcomes targeted the families of men, either killed or missing. Some were hastily buried. Families did not get any information for 40 years.

"One example of many is Sergeant Louis Bolton, uncle of Laurie Bolton, who is an honorary director of Exercise Tiger Memorial, Ltd. Her father was Louis's older brother. Laurie's family did not know what happened to her uncle until 1994, 50 years later. Imagine that! Her uncle is at the bottom on the English Channel!"

Brenda smacked her dry lips. "One positive result from Exercise Tiger was learned the hard way... that vital corrections needed to be made within the next five weeks. D-Day was coming soon and right now, the troops were ill prepared. Let me summarize some of the *lessons learned*, which benefited the allied landings at Normandy.

"First, the need to have rescue craft, use the same radio frequencies, locate U-boats in darkness via illumination rockets, provide training in using the Kapok Life Preserver Jacket, loosen boot laces and backpack straps to prevent drowning, have life rafts and boats ready to be lowered... and have enough of them, carry only enough fuel to reduce combustible material, use more escort ships, pass the word on *quickly* about enemy contacts, and improve fire-fighting equipment.

"All of these recommendations are examples of flaws during Exercise Tiger. It in no way compensates for the appalling loss of lives in Tiger. But these recommendations and others were applied causing the D-Day invasion to be successful. To be frank, if it were not for Exercise Tiger, I'm not sure if the D-Day landings would have gained such a success."

Olivia remarked, "Good summary! My take is that these

749 men that died did not die in vain. They set the stage for winning World War II."

Lars explained. "Here's something most of you don't know. The term Rear Admiral came from the line of a naval squadron. In front is a Vice Admiral, and an Admiral in center, directing activities. In the rear would be an Admiral commanding the remaining ships. The rear... or Rear Admiral."

"Gee, I didn't know that, Doc!" exclaimed Tiger.

Olivia, Brenda, and Doris nodded.

In closing, Lars added, "Before you take an action you must realize the consequences. This may lead you to not take the action."

"Oh! Another gem of wisdom from the Doc," said Tiger. "That applies to Exercise Tiger I guess... too. This Exercise backfired on everyone... like a boomerang."

Olivia quipped, "I have several words for it: calamity, tragedy, debacle, snafu, a farce, shambles, and a mess. What bothers me is that those that died are unknown to most. The forgotten dead. Unremembered. The Exercise itself is forgotten, hidden and that saddens me because these families lost sons, husbands, brothers, uncles. It is important to never forget all of them. Those that died, sleep the sleep of death."

Doris uttered, "They must live forever in our hearts. They gave their lives for us and we're talking about 19 year olds... young men. They didn't know they were signing up for a grizzly disaster that could have been avoided. The simple mistakes made, as covered by Lars, could have been avoided."

Lars announced, "Well, let's have another cup of coffee.

We can talk about next week's blunder pertaining to the wrongs done to the American Indians."

Tiger ordered a side dish of crispy bacon.

From right to left: Apache leader Geronimo,
Yanozha (Geronimo's brother-in-law),
Chappo (Geronimo's son by his second wife),
and Fun (Yanozha's half brother) in 1886

CHAPTER 7

Unforgiveable Tragedy Of The Early American Indians

It was raining cats and dogs. Yet everyone made it on time to Metro 29. Lars, showing deep emotion, kicked it off.

"As our Alpha Team leader, let me start off with a few general comments, because Tiger has the lead on this unforgiveable blunder."

"Go ahead, Doc... we're all ears for gems of wisdom from our professor and fearless leader," Tiger responded.

Lars clears his throat. "The mistakes made are appalling and they form deep shadows, which are a haunting for all of us now. We live today amongst these shadows of the horrific treatment of the early American Indians. Their ghosts follow us. Unfortunately, we can't communicate with the dead. But I'm sure that if we could, they would let us know that all they wanted was recognition and respect. Recognition of the fact that they were here first and that they were true Americans. And respect of their culture and desire to maintain their land and resources."

"That is *exactly* what I wrote in my book, Lars!" said

Olivia.

"It makes me so sad," Doris added. "I feel for the thousands of men, women, and children that died." She shudders. Doris is thinking to herself about Lars's comment. *I can communicate with the dead sometimes. It radiates a warm feeling.*

"Thanks, Doc," Tiger said. "Well said. You are right; the dead never stay dead—they haunt us. Mistakes were made by all because they didn't know *jack squat*. I'm talking about the European immigrants, settlers, ranchers, farmers, miners, pioneers, and railroad men who did more harm than the fouled up US Government. But the US Government and military did their fair share of irreparable damage to the Indians.

"All of them had an antagonistic attitude towards the Indians, often calling them savages. Not being constructive or cooperative, which was a huge mistake."

Olivia nodded, agreeing. "In my book, I discovered that a hateful attitude was the biggest mistake... from day one that the Europeans set foot on American soil. They had an arrogant, disrespectful stance. And they settled on this way of thinking."

Tiger poured more maple syrup on his pancakes; stirring honey into his second cup of coffee and continued.

"There are many expert researchers and scholars who have studied the treatment of the early American Indians. Some of these consider this treatment in various terms, such as: holocaust, crimes against humanity, reign of terror, barbarism, atrocity, indiscriminate targeting, ethnic cleansing, mass murder, direct or indirect genocide, and destruction of the American Indian race. My in-depth research resulted in showing that many of these researchers and scholars compared the terrible treatment of the early American Indians to *Hitler's Final Solution.*"

"Exactly!" piped in Brenda. "Think about it! The Germans invoked direct genocide by killing Jews and others in gas chambers and via other execution methods, including horrific torture. And dying due to starvation, disease and being overworked."

"I copy that," said Lars. "In addition, the Nazis inflicted direct genocide, in some cases, by diverting food and other resources from the Jewish people."

Doris added, "And they destroyed survival essentials... seized and destroyed the land, crops, and livestock, closed their businesses, took over their homes, rounded them up into ghettos, and marched them off to concentration camps." She sighed deeply.

Brenda held her hand. She knew that Doris had a touch of Cherokee blood, of which she was proud of. She told the others, "Doris visits some of the Cherokees who are living on reservations in Oklahoma and North Carolina."

"These are extraordinary points," interrupted Olivia. "We did the same thing to American Indians—took their land, nearly exterminated the buffaloes, and relocated them to reservations. We performed partial genocide on them. Unforgiveable and very sad." Olivia took in a deep breath.

Tiger recommenced. "The agreed upon definition by the United Nations (UN), is that genocide is any of a number of acts committed with intent to destroy, in whole or in part, a national, ethnical, racial or religious group. Based on my research, I believe we committed indirect genocide. It is certainly a tragedy. After all, the American Indians went through terrible experiences—massacres (openly killing women and children), terror, torture, military occupation, sexual abuse (rape), and taking them from their ancestral lands that meant a lot to them."

"That includes sacred burial grounds, Tiger," exclaimed Lars. "Again the mistake of *attitude* looms to the forefront in that there was no respect for lands that had deep meaning to the American Indians. Very upsetting to me."

Tiger added, "And forcing children to boarding schools."

"Sorry to butt in again, Tiger, but the bottom line of this extraordinary upsetting blunder is that America committed a crime against humanity, similar to Hitler's treatment of the Jews and others. That's my take. We all researched this blunder to the nth degree *(a military term—in other words, to our utmost)*. But the reason I chose you to take the lead on this one, is because you are the only minority on our team."

"Well, you're on target, Doc. One reason why the misaligned attitude was such a mistake was there was little appreciation that the ancestors of American Indians arrived here about 14,300 years ago. They came from northeastern Asia via the Bering Straits of Alaska. So they were the first here—and we end up murdering them and relocating them into reservations... like the Nazi death camps. At least, it was like a death camp emotionally for the Indians. Having lost all that was of worth to them."

Brenda added, "This is an eye-opener for most people. I'm so downhearted about the way this was handled back then. So many mistakes were made. If this hadn't occurred, the world would be better today. It is haunting. We can't forget the American Indians that were killed. It was unfair."

"You hit the nail on the head," chimed in Tiger. "By the way, gang, Martin Luther King said, *'Our nation was born in genocide when it embraced the doctrine that the original American, the Indian, was an inferior race'*."

Doris asserted, "It seems that throughout all of those dismal years the American Indians were faced with these choices: relocation, assimilation, or a form of genocide. Most of this was caused by arrogance, greed, and selfishness on the part of the early European settlers. Later, it became the creed of the US Military to kill Indians. I'm like Brenda... sad, beyond words, about this story of betrayal and sorrow."

"I know you have all read *Trail of Tears* by John Ehle," said Olivia. "But not only were 18,000 Cherokees forced from their eastern homes, this happened to the entire American Indian population... Frankly, it's a trail of tears that covered five centuries. Disgraceful. Just totally disgraceful."

"Yes, a life of horror, betrayal, and sorrow," said Tiger. "Again, one thing that the *White Man* should have respected was that the American Indians' lands were sacred to them. Instead, they screwed over most of the tribes, including the Aztecs, Cherokees, Tainos, Choctaw, Chickasaw, Creek, Seminoles, Apache, Iroquois, Algonquian, and others. These tribes had great leaders—Sitting Bull, Crazy Horse (my favorite), Chief Joseph, Geronimo, Red Cloud, Tecumseh, Cochise, Black Hawk, and others. They should not have had to face the demeaning policies of our government. Those policies were a crushing blow and caused profound sadness amongst the tribes."

"To me," said Brenda, "the biggest mistake was not having enough sense to talk to these leaders. Actually, they were better leaders than any of ours from a genuine and practical point of view."

"Andrew Jackson's *Indian Removal Act of 1830* was an enormous mistake... just one of many. This *Act* allowed Jackson to conduct a reign of terror with the aim of ethnic cleansing," stated Tiger.

Brenda added some quotes to mark the *attitude* and set a frame of reference—"President Jefferson said, *'If ever we are constrained to lift the hatchet against any tribe, we will never lay it down till that tribe is exterminated, or driven beyond the Mississippi'*. And that *'should the Indians go to war, they will kill some of us; we shall destroy all of them'*.

Doris injected a quote from George Washington, *'the total destruction and devastation of their settlements'*. And words from John McDougal, the California Governor, *'California would make war, which of necessity be one of extermination to many of the tribes'*. I have two more, knowing that later Tiger will add more sayings which supports our theory that a preconceived notion prevailed against the American Indians. Just thinking back to that era makes me sick to my stomach."

"Mine too," said Brenda. She puts both hands on her stomach and bends over in her chair. "Makes me want to puke."

"Here are the other two," added Doris, "and the worst one ever is by General Phillip Sheridan: *The only good*

Indians I ever saw were dead'. Davy Crockett added his two cents by saying, *'We shot them like dogs'*, referring to the slaughter of 186 Red Stick Creeks at Tallushatchee. What makes me even sadder is that the dead included women and children."

"The dreadful *attitude* brought forth unfair name-calling about Indians, which was offensive and disparaging," Tiger recounted.

"Instead they were called—savages, infidels, uncivilized barbarians, injuns, heathens, beasts, wild monsters, inhumane, devilish, blood thirsty, merciless, primitive..." Tiger, shaking his head, pursues his point.

"Very few made an effort to understand the American Indian culture which was another mistake. An earnest effort in this regard would have changed history. Perhaps no Indian battles would have occurred at all. Many scholars and those who defend the US Government, back in those days, declare that the stories about atrocities against American Indians weren't as severe as covered in some of the historical works. That the *attitude* was not so *anti-Indian* as described in several books, journals, and studies."

After gorging himself on his fourth pancake, Tiger resumed. "Don't believe that for a moment. Let me provide you with a few random quotes from which I'm sure you can formulate your own view of the alarming attitudes in those ghastly years about the American Indians.

"Brenda already mentioned the worst one—General Philip Henry Sheridan in 1869 when he said *'The only good Indians I ever saw were dead'*. Lars shoots in a quick point. "As a West Point graduate myself, I know that Sheridan was in the West Point Class of 1853. He ranked 33 of 52 in that Class. In 1898 the West Point Academic Board adopted the United States Military Academy motto—Duty, Honor, Country. Sheridan certainly didn't possess those traits—he went to West Point too early! He forced his *scorched-earth* policy upon the Indians that he developed against the South in the Civil War.

"Sorry, Tiger... I know you have more but having studied Military Art, let me add this one," Lars injected.

"Hey! Go ahead, Doc," responded Tiger.

"Again, this just is another example of the inexplicable *attitude* of those who hated the American Indians without even knowing who they were or what they were all about. Narrow thinkers. I would give them an 'F' in communication skills. This one I know well. Colonel Henry Bouquet received a note from Sir Jeffrey Amherst, Commander-in-Chief of British Forces in North America that read—*'You will do well to try to inoculate the Indians (with smallpox) by means of blankets, as well as to try every other method, that can serve to extirpate this execrable race'.*"

With a hoarse voice, Lars added, "How gross is that coming from supposedly key leaders?"

"Thanks, Doc," said Tiger. "We all can see that it was a cruel *attitude* that prevailed throughout the country. What disappoints me most is that many high-level people struck out against the American Indians. There are hundreds of sayings and quotes, but I'm just providing a small sample to reinforce our view that *attitude* played a key role in the mistakes made. It's at the top of the mistakes made that caused the Indians to become hostile, which was not their choice. For example, the *Peace Policy* of President Grant—he believed that Americans had the right to take the American Indians' land and freedoms and cart them off to reservations. Indians that refused to move would be forced off their homelands by the military. The Indians knew that on the reservation they would be forced to embrace Christianity and go the Euro way... wear their clothing, learn their language, and dismiss their own culture."

Lars declared, "Here's another tidbit for you. Grant graduated from West Point in 1843. He was 21 of 39 in his Class. Like Sheridan, he missed out on the Duty, Honor, Country teachings."

"Hey! Listen to what Ben Franklin told Thomas Jefferson—*'If it be the design of Providence to extirpate these Savages in order to make room for cultivators of the Earth, it seems not improbable that rum may be the appointed means'*," Tiger snapped.

"Let me back you up with two more," volunteered Lars again. "The first one are orders of George Washington to General John Sullivan on May 31, 1779.

"He said, *'The immediate objectives are the total destruction and devastation of their settlements and the capture of as many prisoners of every age and sex as possible. It will be essential to ruin their crops in the ground and prevent their planting more'*.

"Governor William Henry Harrison of the Indiana Territory said, *'It is one of the fairest portions of the globe to remain in a state of nature, the haunt of a few wretched savages, when it seems destined by the Creator to give support to a large population and to be the seat of civilization'.*

"And there's another thing I found in Thomas Jefferson's papers, dated December 29, 1823: *'This unfortunate race, whom we have been taking so much pains to save and civilize, have by their unexpected desertion and ferocious barbarities justified extermination and now wait our decision on their fate'.*" Lars shook his head in disgust. "Both of these quotes really upset me."

"It's not necessarily the content but rather the use of words describing the American Indian as I see it," said Doris. "Look at your last two quotes, Lars... *'wretched savages'* and *'unfortunate race'*. Get my point?"

"Yup. Sure do. Try this one from Chief Justice John Marshall in 1823—*'The tribes of Indians inhabiting this country were fierce savages, whose occupations was war, and whose substance was drawn chiefly from the forest... That law which regulates, and ought to regulate in general, the relations between the conqueror and the conquered was incapable of application to a people under such circumstances... Discovery gave an exclusive right to extinguish the Indian title of occupancy, either by purchase or by conquest'.* And President Andrew Jackson, in talking about the Indians inferiority, said *'...they must necessarily yield to the force of circumstances and ere long disappear'.*"

Tiger brought forth another viewpoint. "I know that you all studied this blunder topic like I did. And I appreciate your input, especially in regards to statements made back in those early days that mark the negative attitude that was growing day by day. On the other hand, there were great

American Indian leaders who had vision and could have helped to curtail unnecessary battles. I listed some of them earlier."

"A gigantic mistake was not respecting them as counterparts," suggested Lars. "Instead, the arrogance of the US Government., military, and European immigrants prevailed showing greed and selfishness, both traits being contrary to the Indian way of life. They were humble and yet strong in their convictions."

"I'm convinced," said Olivia "that all of them should have listened to the American Indians and received their wisdom. Frankly, the *White Man* had little wisdom... only a desire to take over land and resources that did not belong to them. Disgraceful attitudes."

Doris asked, "How would you like a massive force to take over your home and push you out beyond the Mississippi? Put yourselves in their moccasins." Her eyes were full of tears. One tear dropped into her tea.

"Yes, Doris," said Lars in a supportive manner. "We are all feeling the emotional impact of this horrendous blunder. Regaining energy, he continued. "In the final analysis, the American Indians were here first, the original inhabitants of what is now the United States. And take my grandfather, on my father's side. He came over with three brothers from Norway in 1893. And here I am!"

Brenda pointed out, "We are all Native Americans because we were born here. That's why I like the term American Indian, rather than Native Americans or Indigenous People. One dumb mistake after another that could have avoided this blunder—a sad tragedy."

"I agree, Brenda," said Tiger. "I decided to use the term American Indian for our discussion this morning for several reasons:

- The original Americans were Indians;
- Crazy Horse, Red Cloud, Sitting Bull preferred to be called Indians. Very proud of it.
- Two important entities use the term American Indian:
- National Congress of American Indians and National Museum of the American Indian.
- All of us born in the US are Native Americans. So it is senseless to apply the Native American term to Indians.

Doris disclosed an important point to follow-up Brenda. "Uncalled for misunderstandings and miscalculations destined for tragedy. An uncalled for tragedy. Those European settlers felt no concern for the pain and suffering they were causing. They didn't even know anything about the American Indians. Didn't sincerely try. Big mistake right there."

Tiger exclaimed, "Unreasonable idiots!"

"We call them *dunderheads* in England," Olivia retorted.

"On the other hand, some of the American Indians were thinking differently," declared Brenda. "Some examples— *'One does not sell the land people walk on'.*—Crazy Horse; *'The ground on which we stand is sacred ground. It is the blood of our ancestors'.*—Chief Plenty Coups, Crow Tribe; *'We do not want riches. We want peace and love'.*—Red Cloud, Oglala Lakota Sioux.

"Another good one from Crazy Horse, Sioux—*'I was hostile to the White Man... We preferred hunting to a life of idleness on our reservations. At times we did not get enough to eat and we were not allowed to hunt. All we wanted was peace and to be left alone. Soldiers came... in the winter and destroyed our villages. Then Long Hair (Custer) came... They said we massacred him, but he would have done the same to us. Our first impulse was to escape... but we were so hemmed in we had to fight. After that I lived in peace, but the government would not let me alone. I was not allowed to remain quiet. I was tired of fighting... they tried to confine me... and a soldier ran his bayonet into me. I have spoken'.*"

Olivia injected, "That is the best statement I've ever heard. It explains it all. Crazy Horse was a great man and Chief."

"He was my favorite, too," added Tiger.

Doris conceded, "Chief Joseph of the Nez Perce was right when he said *'It does not require many words to speak the truth'.*"

"Yet we broke over 500 treaties with the American Indians," added Lars. "Lies, broken promises and loads of conspiracies. You can't blame the American Indians for fighting back for what was really theirs. One of the Lakota's said it best—*'Force, no matter how concealed, begets resistance'.*"

"We made some of the American Indians into savages, if you want to call them that, because they were fighting to retain their land and resources in order to live," Tiger continued. "They were respectable at the beginning; we were disrespectable to them. There's no other way to look at it."

Lars interrupted. "Again, we return to the overall *attitude* towards the American Indians. As the westward expansion grew, conflicts multiplied. A British traveler in 1784 said, *'White Americans have the most rancorous antipathy to the whole race of Indians; and nothing is more common than to hear them talk of extirpating them totally from the face of the earth; men, women, and children'*. And as we heard previously, Peter Burnett, Governor of California in 1851 said, *'A war of extermination will continue to be waged between the two races until the Indian race becomes extinct'*.

"Another example of the *attitude* was when John Chivington, former Methodist minister in 1864, said, *'Damn any man who sympathizes with Indians... I have come to kill Indians and believe it is right and honorable to use any means under God's heavens to kill Indians'*.

"The attitude of the white population of Colorado was *'Let them be exterminated—men, women, and children together'*."

"That's good information, Lars," quipped Olivia. "The stories about Indians being bloodthirsty were untrue. Think about this—The Homestead Act of 1862 promised free land to the settlers. The Land Grants were tracts of land given to railroads. This caused a push to head west, plus the gold rush in 1849. None of these westward bound people cared about the Indians. They thought of them as *flies on a horse*."

Tiger blurted out, "Hey! Why is Brenda taking such copious notes?"

"I'm just taking stubby pencil notes since we are going to make our blunders discussions into a book form," responded Brenda.

"Oh yeah, I forgot. We agreed on that early on. Pardonnez moi! We still speak French in the Big Easy. I gar-on-tee you 'dat. Justin Wilson said that a lot. The best Cajun chef in New Orleans. I loved that guy. I'm glad Lars had me take the lead on this blunder since, like he said earlier, I'm the only minority on our team."

Doris quickly points out, "My biggest problem with this unforgiveable blunder is the lack of communication. Why didn't the *White Man* leaders talk to the American Indians early on? As a result, the settlers, US Government, and military might have understood the importance of *their lands* to them. And their culture."

Brenda pondered this and explained. "That's true, Doris. That would have made it a different ball game. But the truth is, in general, Whites talk to Whites, Indians talk to Indians... and to carry this a little further... men talk to men, boys talk to boys, women talk to women, girls talk to girls, Blacks talk to Blacks, Hispanics talk to Hispanics, Jews talk to Jews, Muslims talk to Muslims, and so on... That stigma causes miss-trust, poor cooperation, and loads of misunderstandings. We trust more when dealing with others like us. So the mistakes made causing many trails of tears for the American Indians was everybody's fault... For not communicating well and respecting one another from the very start."

Olivia blurted out, "There is no excuse for the killings of American Indian women, children, and their babies so haphazardly. Blatant, random, careless, indiscriminate, and irregular attacks that ruined their livelihood. Deplorable."

Lars added, "Unfair and repulsive."

"I agree a hundred percent," said Olivia. "I don't know how to describe this tragedy. It was repugnant, loathsome, abominable, horrendous, and nauseating to me after researching this worst happening in our country's history. In the history of the world for that matter! I know we are to stick to mistakes made which if they hadn't been made might have not caused this terrible catastrophe. But let me unfold some history which supports several of our mistakes we have brought forth such as *they were here first*."

"Bring it on," whispered Tiger, gulping his coffee loudly.

Olivia continued. "Between 1500 and 1900, the American Indian population decreased from 12 million to about 270,000."

Everyone gasped, shaking their heads in disbelief.

"It's not like the Nazi holocaust... murdering six million Jews. This was an attempt at total extermination—the biggest in world history. Too bad the West wasn't large enough to fit the settlers and American Indians. But again, the Indians were here first. Frankly, from time-to-time and at various locales, genocide was committed. The Indians might have been willing to share the land and resources with the Europeans, but the newly arrived Europeans weren't about to reciprocate."

"Yup," called out Lars. "Yet again, another mistake. At least why not try to develop a strategy with common goals? Those settlers had one thing on their mind—land and resources, plus gold later on. A side-bar here... many German leaders were hung for their crimes against humanity, but nobody was ever punished for the atrocities done to the American Indians. What's wrong with that picture?"

Olivia added, "As mentioned before, over 500 treaties

were made between the US Government and the Indian tribes—*all* were broken or amended. The US Government found ways to short-change American Indian tribes and not fulfill promises."

"I have a long list of massacres; 181 to be exact, the first in 1539; last one in 1911," said Tiger. "I remember reading about one where 300 women and children were killed."

Olivia pointed out, "It could have been total genocide if collectively all the Indian haters had organized and gotten industrialized, whereas I personally call it, partial genocide. It seems that the US Government's intention was not extermination of the American Indians, however, we cannot discard an ethnic cleansing approach, like the Nazi approach."

Brenda breaks in. "Tiger, you have done a great job on this blunder... as have the rest of you in supporting Tiger. Let me close our discussion with an uplifting comment. Two American Indian women were elected to Congress in November 2018—a first."

Everyone claps and cheers.

"That is wonderful," remarked Lars. "Especially since American Indians couldn't become citizens until 1925. A beautiful way to end this incredible discussion of the worst tragedy in world history. Next week, we will discuss the sinking of the USS Indianapolis in World War II. I'll take the lead."

Everyone stood up and high-fived each other. Tiger remained to get a coffee refill and to *shoot the breeze* with Anita.

U.S. Navy Heavy Cruiser USS Indianapolis
(CA-35) underway at sea, September 27, 1939

CHAPTER 8

Sinking Of The USS Indianapolis

"I believe," **said** Lars, "that one of the reasons we chose the Indy catastrophe as a blunder was because it is the US Navy's single *worst* loss of life at sea in history. Only 316 of the ship's 1,195 sailors and marines survived. However, most important to us were the mistakes made that caused some of those deaths. Most were due to slow reaction time, poor communications, command, control and intelligence."

Doris jumped in. "Totally unacceptable. I feel deeply for those sailors, marines and their families."

"Yeah, I'm on board with that," said Tiger, scratching his chin... "the mistakes by the Navy, which if not made, would have avoided the calamity."

"Let me kick this off with some quick history," replied Lars. On July 30, 1945 the USS Indianapolis was sunk in the Philippine Sea by a Japanese submarine.

"The heavy cruiser, nicknamed the *Indy*, had a crew of 1,195. It was sent on a secret mission to deliver highly classified cargo to Tinian Island in the Northern Marianas. None of the crewmembers, including the skipper, Captain Charles McVay, knew about the contents, which consisted of two cylindrical containers and a large crate. The cargo was under armed guard 24/7. It contained the uranium core of the atomic bomb, *Little Boy*, minus the fusing, firing mechanism, and casements." Lars coughed and cleared his throat, obviously touched by this.

Tiger added, "And the crew took bets on what was contained in the crate. Ideas ranged from a new type of airplane engine, scented toilet paper for senior officers, or a gold commode for General MacArthur. You know how the troops are, Doc!"

Everyone chuckled. Lars carried on.

"One survivor said, *'Course, we didn't know what it was, but we knew it was a big deal, and we were glad to get rid of it by the time we reached Tinian'.*

"After the drop-off, the Indy proceeded to Guam following orders to sail to Leyte for training."

"That's right," added Olivia. "In my book, I covered the USS Indianapolis." *(It was her idea to include it as one of the team's blunder choices.)*

"Commander Mochitsura Hashimoto of the Japanese sub I-58 spotted the Indy at 00:15 hours as it closed the distance to about 1,500 yards. Hashimoto commanded *'Stand by'.* Then in a loud voice he yelled, *'Fire!'.*

"Two of the six Type 95 torpedoes hit the Indy in its starboard bow and amidships. Aviation fuel stores ignited... flames and explosions tore through the ship.

"Captain McVay shouted, *'Abandon ship'* four times."

She sighed, as did the others. They all took a swig of their coffee. Tiger let out a hushed burp, sort of a puff sound, and lowered his head.

"You know what?" muttered Lars. "None of them knew that a few days later, on August 6th, the Enola Gay, our American B-29 bomber, would drop a 5-ton bomb with the power of 15,000 tons of TNT on Hiroshima. Afterwards, most of the crew felt it was necessary to end the war. That's my quick summary of what happened."

"You know, Doc," Tiger suggested, "if the Japs weren't so unbearably cruel, it might not have happened. They have a terrible history to bear up their conscience... if they have any. Look at their rape of Nanjing! 20 thousand women and girls were raped, many mutilated and killed." He balls up his fist.

"Assholes! Pardon my French ladies. I should have said, *'Les connards'*." He grinned sheepishly. "Don't forget, we know French in New Orleans."

"I think we all feel the same, Tiger." Lars shook his head. "The Indy sank in twelve minutes... 300 crewmembers went down with it, while 895 were cast off into the sea. I'll be quite frank with you all, not as many crewmembers would have died if not for the incompetence of some of the Admirals, officers, and other US Navy key personnel. Gross mistakes in command, control and intelligence. That's really the bottom line. The big sorry picture."

"Spoken like a true US Army Ranger and paratrooper, Doc. I feel the same, but the Navy is good at protecting its own. Just like the Exercise Tiger cover-up." Tiger burps and farts accidently. "Sorry gang, I guess this blunder is getting to me."

"Or the refried beans you ate at El Paso last night," giggled Doris. Lars grinned and continued.

"It is unacceptable that the crew had to wait at least four days to be rescued. In their infinite wisdom, nobody knew the USS Indianapolis had sunk.

"Of the 895 crewmembers drifting in the sea, hundreds died—exhaustion, burns, exposure (temperature was 110°), shark attacks (Whitetip and Tiger sharks), drowning, and dehydration. They swam literally in gooey fuel oil."

Brenda blurted out, "Some of the mistakes I learned during my research were: failure to share sensitive intelligence, communications, scheduling procedures, escorting, and routing. Furthermore, the Indy didn't have sonar, hydrophones, or a destroyer escort!"

"What really gets me is the not having a destroyer escort," said Lars. "That is always vital. Those mistakes put the Skipper and ship in jeopardy. Now, get this... by digging deep, I found out that there was an officer responsible for tracking the Indy. This officer had received notice that the Indy had failed to arrive on schedule. He did not investigate the matter and made no report to his superiors about this fact. To me, this was the causative factor that cost hundreds of lives of sailors and marines.

"My God! Had they gotten there sooner, more may have been rescued!" Lars leaned his head back and turned his neck to loosen up. It popped. His eye were red in anger. He popped two drops of Visine in each eye.

"This is it right here, coupled with the other mistakes we've uncovered. And not by McVay. Actually, unknown to most people, three stations received distress calls. But nobody acted on them. It appears that one officer was drunk; another told his men not to disturb him; and the third thought the Japs were playing a trick... setting a trap, so he did nothing. The Navy doesn't even admit this, yet we found secret and top secret documents at the Archives in DC that confirm these gross occurrences. What's wrong with these guys? We would *never* do this to fellow Rangers. It makes me sick." Lars crunched his face in disgust.

"As a Ranger comrade of yours, Doc, I agree. We *never* let anyone down," replied Tiger. "Never!"

"It seems as if the US Navy was complacent, realizing the war was nearing an end," said Brenda. "Still... inexcusable. I'm feeling for those young men who died too early in life. They are my heroes. I agree that it is totally unacceptable. These guys were sleeping at the switch, having nice meals and coffee, while at the same time their fellow comrades were dying in the sea!

"Here's my view—if a ship is 3-5 hours overdo, then everyone should jump through their ass and report it... not wait four days!"

"Hey! I'm proud of Brenda with her tough talk. Atta' girl!" exclaimed Tiger. "I guess we are all worked up over this."

Lars leaned forward in his chair. "There are so many faults that I can't cover all of them. So, we have 300 men down with the ship... 18,000 feet under in the North Philippine Sea. God bless those that died trying to survive the elements for four days. The others are spread out in the sea."

***US Navy Captain Charles B. McVay
talks to war correspondents in Guam
about the sinking of his ship in August 1945***

Everyone paused. Complete silence. Like a morgue. All team members are shocked.

Lars mentioned something else very important. "McVay was told *'there were no escorts available and that no threat appeared in the backwaters. Things are very quiet. The Japanese are on their last legs, and there's nothing to worry about'.* This was told to the captain by the Commander of the Pacific Fleet's Advance Headquarters. Also, that McVay could steer a zigzag course if he wanted to... and it was up to his discretion... not an order. *'Little threat of enemy subs'."*

Olivia rocked in her chair, uneasy. "More of the crew would have died if it had not been for a US anti-sub patrol airplane, which by accident, spotted the Indy's thick oil spill and saw men bobbing in the water."

Tiger exclaimed, "I can hardly bear this... total disregard for the welfare of the troops. As a Sergeant E-6, I would give my life for my men. They always came first. I know Doc feels the same. Doc was my Company Commander in Nam. I saw him in action.

"Senior Navy officers knew that a Japanese sub might have been in the area but decided not to warn the Indy—for fear of disclosing that the Navy had broken the Japanese naval codes. I ask you, how poor is *that?*"

Lars stated, "Instead of facing the real errors, the top brass used McVay as a scapegoat. They were embarrassed. The higher echelons often do this to shirk their own responsibility."

"That is appalling," noted Doris.

Lars continued. "Captain McVay, a true patriot, was faced with a hung jury... guilty until proven innocent. They screwed McVay instead of penalizing those who didn't do their jobs. McVay was convicted by a US Navy Court Martial of negligence for failing to zigzag. In reality, he did zigzag the Indy during daylight, then switched to a straight-line course in the evening. The sky was obscured and there was poor visibility on the horizons. Remember, it was left up to him whether to zigzag or not. Naval intelligence let him down.

"Admiral Chester Nimitz disagreed to a Court Martial,

and issued Captain McVay a letter of reprimand. However, Admiral Ernest King, who also screwed up royally in the Battle of the Atlantic, overturned Nimitz's decision, and recommended a Court Martial."

Everyone went "Ugh!" Lars led off with a thumbs-down and the others followed suit.

"Secretary of the Navy, James Forrestal, convened it. Nimitz was the only top ranking officer with any sense in this particular matter," Lars added.

"By the way," Doris injected, "Forrestal later jumped from the 16th floor of Bethesda Medical Center in DC. A suicide by a troubled man."

Lars leaned back in his chair. "McVay was a graduate of the US Naval Academy. Earned the Silver Star by displaying courage and gallantry under fire. Additionally, he earned the Bronze Star and Navy Unit Commendation."

"He couldn't have been too shabby, Doc, since later, they promoted him to Admiral. Which proves that King had his head up his fanny. All of McVay's troops supported him."

"Good point, Tiger," said Lars. "Let me shift to live remarks by survivors. These are random and true accounts by those interviewed. Here they are... verbatim:

'We knew the ship was doomed';
'There were lots of sharks. So many. I'd see them swimming below me';
'So many friends... lost';
'I didn't have anything... not even a life jacket, so I was swimming from midnight to 5:30 in the morning';
'Men began drinking salt water; so much that they were

87

delirious. Hallucinating. In fact, a lot of them had weapons like knives, and they'd be so crazy that they'd be fighting together and killing one another';

'Some drank so much salt water that they were seeing things. They'd say the Indy is down below and they'd swim down and a shark would get them. And you could see the sharks eating your comrades';

'We had a floating cargo net with 15 sailors on it. Ten sharks hit it and all was gone. This went on and on and on';

'At any given time you could look out and see big fins swimming around and around and around. All of a sudden you heard a blood-curdling scream and you look and you see the shark had taken him under';

'Day after day went by. Skin began rotting and a lot of guys just crack, or drink the water or give up, or swim off to an imaginary island'.

"One Seaman First Class asked his friend George to get some life jackets. Returning with only one, George said, *'I think I'll go get another one'.* The Seaman told him he probably better, but never saw him again."

Lars exclaimed, "That should give you a real-life frame of reference. Here's the last one, of many I assure you. *'It was survival mode. Pulling away from the group almost meant certain death. Those who pulled away were picked off by the sharks, or drank salt water and they floated off'.*"

Lars, close to wrapping up, added, "In short, the US Navy's glaring mistakes affecting the USS Indianapolis crew of 1,195 are: 300 down with ship, 579 adrift at sea, and 316 survivors. This did not have to happen. Not Monday morning quarterbacking at all... just terrible mistakes."

Doris, hands on chin, remarks, "What upsets me is that very few people know about this blunder and the inner workings and hidden facts about all of our blunders covered so far."

"You are right," agreed Olivia. "Just like Exercise Tiger, the *American Indians* nightmare, truths about Pearl Harbor, 9/11, and so on. I'm so glad we are doing this... to wake up people of all ages."

"Ten-4 on that," snapped Tiger. "That's exactly why we are tackling these blunders—to help the general public become aware of all the mistakes in these events that shouldn't have happened. So many souls lost, that may have been saved."

Brenda blurted out, "I always remember what George Santayana, famous Philosopher said: *'Those who do not remember the past are condemned to repeat it'*. That was his most famous aphorism."

"We're about at the end here," said Lars. "This makes me sad. On November 6, 1968 Charles B. McVay, III walked out on his porch at home and a put his service revolver in his mouth and pulled the trigger. He was 70. Never lived to see his exoneration in 2001, 23 years after his suicide. He suffered mental health problems for years after the Indy Blunder."

"Understandably," agreed Doris.

"Since I'm the leader of this one, let me wrap up. First of all, as usual, I appreciate the in-depth research everyone on the team did. This was another tough one," said Lars.

"Takes a lot of digging, Doc." Tiger took a sip of his

coffee and shot a glance at Anita.

"We will always remember the Indy's crew. We should be grateful for their sacrifice, having faced horrendous conditions. They are all courageous and valorous heroes," Lars stated.

Eyes filling with tears, Doris added, "It's a matter of the soul."

Lars nodded his head. "We have to keep moving forward. Stay in motion physically and mentally. However, we can't forget those who sacrificed their lives for us."

"That's powerful wisdom, Doc," stated Tiger.

Everyone nods in agreement.

"OK. Next week we tackle the topic of slavery. It is only fitting that Brenda take the lead on this one, since her doctorate thesis was entitled: *Slavery—The Hidden Truths*, said Lars, ending today's session.

Everybody gives high-fives and bids goodbye to Anita, who winks at Tiger as he passes by.

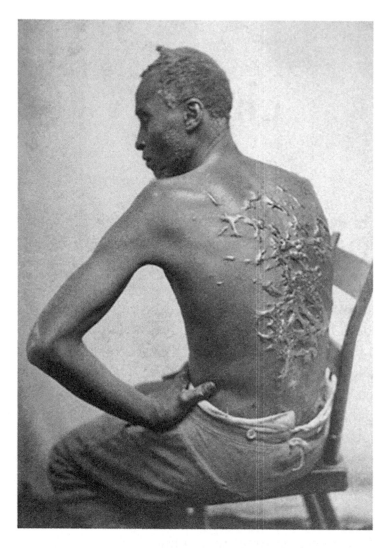

Scars of a whipped Mississippi slave
April 2, 1863, Baton Rouge, Louisiana

CHAPTER 9

Slavery: Cruel And Inhumane

Lars decided the Alpha Team was due for a break. On Tuesday they met at Sushi Zen, his and Doris's favorite Sushi restaurant, on North Harrison Street. They all had met here about two months ago and knew the healthy menu well. Lars knows what the team likes and he ordered Miso soup and salad, Edamame, and Tempura Shrimp as starters. Then Ikura (Salmon Roe), Blue Fire, Tuna Peno Roll, and Avocado Roll. Everyone had Plum wine and Mango ice cream at the end.

Tiger blurted out, "I love this place! They should patent that signature salad dressing."

Lars pointed out, "Doris and I do *carry out* often. We brought a couple of friends here two weeks ago. They had the Chicken Teriyaki, which they said was *'awesome—best ever'*."

"Have to try it sometime," chuckled Tiger. "I'm looking forward to this Friday when Brenda leads us in the Slavery Blunder."

"Me too," added Olivia. "It changed world history."

"Man, this place is packed tonight," volunteered Doris, as her eyes roamed the dining room.

Lars added, "Well, it has won many awards. See you all Friday," as they hugged the waitresses on the way out. Tiger saluted and marched out like a soldier.

Tiger is really a ham if you don't know it by now.

Fast forward to Friday at Metro 29...

Huddled together at table #98, Tiger boasted, "I like it back here in the left corner. Privacy. Yes."

Anita interrupted, "Sameo, sameo?"

"Oui, mon cheri... except today I'll switch to Doc's favorite... Eggs Benedict. Just for a change."

"Oh, Anita, I'm changing to Cappuccino, like Olivia," smirked Doris. Olivia gave her a thumbs up.

"It's great," said Anita who made notes, saying, "TGIF." Everyone grinned. Anita knows the drill.

"It's TGIF all right but I look forward to Friday because it means we are all together sharing our in-depth research," said Brenda.

"Yeah! We look forward to it," snorted Tiger. Blowing his nose loudly... not on purpose.

The Alpha Team is a close-knit team having faced death together... camaraderie at its finest. It's the closest to what Lars and Tiger experienced as Rangers and paratroopers in Vietnam. A tight bond between soldiers.

"OK. Let me kick this off," exclaimed Brenda. "First of all, slavery was flat out wrong!" Everyone nods in agreement. "If you want a work force then organize them and pay them. This was the first mistake that could have prevented slavery—despicable and unethical. It was an unfair practice orchestrated mostly by those energized by greed and selfishness. And it goes against God's wishes. We aren't supposed to *own* our fellow man; we're supposed to help them!"

Doris replied, "Sorry to butt in, and I don't mean to toss religion into the mix, but frankly those that were involved in slave trade are rotting in hell! And any of those involved in any kind of slavery now are going to hell!"

"Strong language by my petite wife, but right on target," responded Lars.

Doris is 5-foot even and looks like Veronica Lake, the 40s movie star, who stood a whopping 4 foot 11 inches tall.

Doris grinned. "May as well say it like it is, gang."

Lars scratches his left ear, continuing. "Bringing African slaves to our continent was a sad endeavor. During the 17th and 18th centuries, African people were kidnapped and sent to the American colonies. All of this was against their will. Unfair... because it deprived Africa of its most able and healthiest men and women. If this didn't happen, slavery as we know it might not have occurred. Also, here's a point that many people miss. The Civil War wasn't necessarily just about slavery—95% of the Rebel soldiers and many officers never owned a slave. More so, they had fear of Federal Government imperialism. They were fighting for states' rights—so that each individual would not be controlled by a central power... the North. One viewpoint came from a Gray lieutenant: *'I'm gonna fight till it's over. The Federal government just doesn't have the right to tell me what I can or can't do as long as I'm doing my best to live right'*. Again, many fought for the south that were against slavery—rather, they were fighting for the right of people to govern themselves." Lars was so strong about this point that he smacked the table hard with his right fist. Olivia's water glass tipped over.

"Right on, Doc," cheered Tiger. "And being black I appreciate that gem of wisdom. It seems as if important people that could have stepped up to thwart the advent of an unnecessary Blue-Gray war, seemed to be unable to walk and chew gum at the same time."

"Sorry to have carried on here, Brenda, but Doris got me going."

"That's okay, Lars. You're both in the bulls-eye," replied Brenda.

Tiger pops off with a, "Ten-4 on that!"

"Let me get some things straight that are conflicting in the writings about slavery. As Olivia can attest, some writers suffer from self-admiration and incorrectly state the facts. That's what I like about what we are doing... bringing out the unknown or little known truths," Brenda stated, sipping her cappuccino and flips back her ponytail, then continues. "Here's just one example of inaccuracy. Slavery was started in 1619. Wrong. It's true, at the time, that 20 Africans were brought to the Jamestown English colony. But it really began in 1501 when enslaved Africans arrived in Hispaniola."

Everyone looked wide-eyed. Brenda marched on.

"Listen, 12 million slaves entered the Atlantic Slave Trade... 16th-19th century period. 1.5 million died on board ships; 10.5 million arrived in the Americas. I'm providing a little history here to set up a frame of reference for us. These countries had slavery—China, Pakistan, Bangladesh, Uzbekistan, Cambodia, India, Qatar, and others. Lots of guilty parties. Feeling that it was wrong, the Brits abolished slavery in 1833, France in 1848 and the US in 1865. Here's another eye opener—between 1525 and 1866, 12.5 million slaves were shipped to the *New World.* Only 10.7 million survived the Middle Passage. They disembarked in North America, Caribbean, and South America. Slavery occurred everywhere. Just so you'll know... the following kept slaves—the Mayans, Aztecs, Sumerians, Babylonians, Egyptians, Greeks, Romans, Ottomans, Russia, and others. Thus, slavery was widespread. That's my main point here."

Olivia noted, "In my book, I covered how America should have stayed with the British Empire longer... maybe for 100 more years. A mistake. Slavery would have been abolished decades earlier. American Indians would not have faced such severe ethnic cleansing. And... America would have a parliamentary system of government. That makes policy-making easier. I'm on my high-hat because I believe the huge humanitarian gain from this dominates what gains came to the colonists from independence. We would have become a parliamentary democracy; not presidential. Of course I'm originally a Brit... still holding a dual citizenship... but in my six years of study for my book, I found that a constitutional monarchy is the best form of government. I know we need to stick to mistakes, but perhaps this was one in itself—not sticking with Britain— would have given us a better governmental system."

Brenda inserted, "When I did my thesis in grad school, I

came to that same conclusion, Olivia. Slavery was terribly inhumane."

"You are right," said Tiger. "I researched some ghastly mistakes made in regards to slaves. Here are a few—use of shackles, chains, and handcuffs in slave markets; sold at auctions... their families too; branded by irons, whippings and beatings; rubbing bird pepper, hot brine, turpentine, salt pickle and lime juice into wounds; torture using various instruments, not to mention... rape, mutilation of a body part or parts... chopped off hands with axes; hanging; burned alive, and shot at point blank range. These are some of the ways some slaves were treated."

When Doris blinked, a tear that had formed in her left eye, slid down her cheek. When it reached her lips, she smacks them together.

Tiger added, "I find it to be the cruelest and most inhumane treatment of any people in history."

"Inhumane treatment beyond belief!" gasped Olivia.

"That's a huge 10-4," replied Tiger.

Brenda sighed. "When you are a slave, you are actually a victim without rights. Let's face it, slaves are held against their will and it robs them of their humanity. Most of the slave masters felt powerful and felt that the slaves were his property... free to misuse and abuse them... because they were all his. That's easy to do if you have the mindset of many of the masters, where greed and selfishness ruled the day."

"Bastards," declared Tiger. *"Les connards."*

"I know that you all found, during your research, that some documents and information were classified," affirmed

Brenda.

For the team, the declassified material opened up a lot about the true horrors of slavery.

She continued. "Do you think back then, that they would want people to know that slaves were whipped to death, hands cut off, mothers' raped in front of their families, and so on?"

Lars butts in. "Just like today... hidden secrets—some will gross you out! I know what I'd like to do to those guys." He balls up his fists and sets his jaw.

Tiger clenches his hands and smacks them together.

"As far as being unethical, it is so unethical that it makes me sick to my stomach," Brenda said, choked up.

"Me too," adds Doris. "I've been to Africa a few times and realize that motherhood, to them, was the fulfillment of female adulthood and fertility the greatest gift in the world."

"Shame on those who interfere with this main reason to live," added Olivia.

Brenda declared, "I asked Doris to research sayings, quotes from slaves and others. Please take over now, Doris."

Doris stands up. "I went through over 600 sayings/quotes and selected those that really give us a feel for the slaves' lives. You will feel, as I did, that they are talking to us in real time. The ghosts who talk and cannot be forgotten. To make it easy, I made up a handout for you with several comments from the past. These are from diaries, letters, or snippets... on small pieces of torn paper." Doris passes them out to everyone. "You can take a few minutes to read them."

James Hopkinson's Plantation
Planting Sweet Potatoes (circa 1862/63)

Anita refreshes their drinks. Being from Africa, Anita has heard some of the remarks and her demeanor is somewhat solemn.

Sayings From Slaves:

- *'They sold my mother, sister, and brother to old man Askew, a slave speculator, and they were shipped to the Mississippi bottoms in a boxcar. I never heard from my mother any more. I never seed my brother again, but my sister came back to Charlotte';*

- *'Talkin' about something awful, you should have been dere. De slave owners was shoutin' and selling chillen to one man and de mamma and papa to another. De slaves cries and takes on somethin' awful. If a woman had lots of chillen she was sold for mo', cause it a sign she a good breeder';*

- *'Course dey cry: you think dey not cry when they was sold lak cattle? I could tell you; bout it all day, but even den you couldn't guess de awfulness of it';*

- *'I remember when they put 'em on the block to sell 'em. The ones 'tween 16 and 30 always bring the most money. The auctioneer he standoff at a distances and cry 'em off as they stand on the block. I can hear his voice as long as I live'.*

- *'I lays in the bunk two days, gitten' over dat whippin', gitten' over it in the body, but not in de heart. No suh, I has dat in de heart till dis day';*

- *'We lib in uh one room house in de slave quarter dere on de white folks plantation. My Gawd, sleep right dere on de floor... Fed us outer big bowl uv pot licker wid plenty corn bread en fried meat en dat 'bout aw we e'er eat';*

- *'Bells and horns! Bells for dis and horns for dat! All we knowed was go and come by de bells and horns';*

- *'If I had my life to live over I would die fighting rather than be a slave again. I want no man's yoke om my shoulders no more';*

- *'It was the law that if a White Man was caught trying to educate a negro slave, he was liable to prosecution entailing a fine of fifty dollars and a jail sentence...Our ignorance was the greatest hold the South had on us. We knew we could run away, but what then'?*

Doris went on to explain. "Now, those were actual writings by slaves, either from a secret diary (not allowed), or from scraps of paper or hidden letters. They treated them as top secret, like our military does today because if found they probably would have been hanged or tortured severely. Those sayings are special because they let you feel what the slaves were feeling... inside their minds. The following are more general:

General Slavery Quotes:

"This was by Frederick Douglas who wrote *My Bondage and My Freedom* in 1855: *'I didn't know I was a slave until I found out I couldn't do the things I wanted'.*

"Harriet Tubman said this: *'I think slavery is the next thing to hell'.* And also: *'I had crossed the line. I was free; but there was no one to welcome me to the land of freedom. I was a stranger in a strange land; It is retten that a man cannot Serve two masters. But it Seems that the Colored population has got two a rebel master and a union master...one wants us to make Cotton and Sugar And the siell it and Keep the money the union masters wants us to fight the battles under white officers'.*

"This is another writing by Frederick Douglas in his *Narrative Life Of Frederick Douglas: 'I have found that to make a contented slave, it is necessary to make a thoughtless one. It is necessary to darken his moral and mental vision, and, as far as possible, to annihilate the power of reason. He must be able to detect no inconsistencies in slavery; he must be made to feel that slavery is right; and he can be brought to that only when he ceased to be a man'.*

"These words were by Abraham Lincoln: *'I think slavery is wrong. morally, socially, and politically. I desire that it should be no further spread in these United States, and I should not object if it should gradually terminate in the whole Union'.*

"Lincoln also said: *'Those who deny freedom to others deserve it not for themselves'.*

"Here's a few more. Charles Sumner: *'Where Slavery is Liberty cannot be; and where Liberty is there Slavery cannot be'.*

"Edmund Burke: *'Slavery is a state so improper, so degrading, and so ruinous to the feelings and capacities of human nature, that it ought not to be suffered to exist'.*

"This one is a strong statement by Ralph Waldo Emerson: *'I think we must get rid of slavery or we must get rid of freedom'.*

"By the way, Burke also said, *'Death is natural to a man, but slavery unnatural...'*

"Patrick Henry: *'Is life so dear, or peace so sweet, as to be purchased at the price of chains and slavery? Forbid it, Almighty God'.*

"And here is the last one. Just remember all of these are

those chosen by me to paint the grim picture of slavery, in the actual words coming from real life. This was said by Kevin Bales, who calls it like it is: *'Slavery is theft—theft of a life, theft of work, theft of any property or produce, theft even of the children a slave might have borne'.*"

Doris added, "there are numerous examples of secret, hidden messages such as the one written by slave, John Washington. On a piece of wallpaper, he wrote: *'My dear mother, I take this opportunity to write you a few lines to let you know that I am well'.*

"He was the only slave to write his life story while enslaved. It was very dangerous. Union soldiers freed Washington." Doris cleared her throat.

"He wrote: *'I had began to feel like I had truly escaped from the hands of the slave master and with the help of God, I never would be a slave no more'.*"

Brenda jumped in. "It seems, Doris, that most of the slaves that wrote, expressed anxiety and concern about their families. And how many of the writings of American slaves were kept secret by them and by those that discovered any writings?"

Doris exclaimed, "I'm glad you ask. I uncovered rare diaries, letters, and other snippets on paper they wrote in unpolished English. Another example was Adam Plummer, a slave, who married Emily in 1841. He wrote in his discovered diary: *'Emily Plummer and four Childrens on November 28, 1851. Sold at public sale. Wife and children. Banished from my eyes'.*

"Much of his diary is horrifying... depicting daily events. Most slave writings are marginally literate because nobody took an interest in educating them. Their everyday lives were devastated."

Olivia nodded in agreement. "I know because I really studied this heavily for my book. Several scholars are still researching these materials and continue to be shocked. It is ongoing and they are doing a great job at getting to the truths."

Tiger wiggled in his chair. "You know, there were many types of tortures that slaves had to endure physically. I covered some specifically earlier. The bottom line is that mentally... a cruel abuse was that they were forbidden to read and write. And that's another mistake because the character of the people, not slaves, was so low."

"That's a huge, substantive point, Tiger," implored Lars. "Raise the character of the people of a nation and you abolish slavery, because it would be recognized that an organized work force is far better than one under slavery... especially for the long term."

Tiger stood up. "That's for sure, Doc!" The other guests were staring over at their table, so he sat back down.

Lars went on, dramatically. "The real standout error was having Andrew Johnson as Lincoln's Vice President. An alcoholic and racist, he undermined emancipation as soon as he succeeded Lincoln."

Doris spat out, "So our *best* president ever in history was succeeded by our *worst!"*

Lars nodded. "We have tried to stay away from political issues but really, Johnson was a disaster to the cause. He was the first president to be impeached, based on high crimes and misdemeanors. By the way, I sure appreciate the in-depth research everyone did in tackling this blunder. This has been a super discussion, revealing some facts previously unknown to most.

"Next time, Tiger and I are going to be co-captains and cover WWI together. That is, why the US should never have entered WWI. Mistakes galore."

Everyone stood up and clicked their water glasses.

Tiger snapped, "Hey," pointing to the windows. "We'd better get to our cars. That snow is really coming down!"

They all cut out quickly. En route, Tiger waved to Anita. She gave him her special wink.

WWI Montage

Clockwise from the top: The road to Bapaume in the aftermath of the Battle of the Somme, 1916 British Mark V tanks crossing the Hindenburg Line, 1918 HMS Irresistible sinking after hitting a mine in the Dardanelles, 1915 A British Vickers machine gun crew wears gas masks during the Battle of the Somme, 1916 German Albatros D.III biplane fighters near Douai, France, 1917

CHAPTER 10

WWI—The 20th Century Unnecessary Catastrophe

The Alpha Team decided long ago that Lars and Tiger, the two Ranger and paratrooper vets from the Vietnam War, should do this blunder together.

It's cold outside; snow coming down in sheets; 8-inches expected, so the team members hustled inside the warm Metro 29. Settling down at table #98, Lars wastes no time into leading off the discussion.

"Let me set a frame of reference for us. In 1914, Europe was a happy place. Countries shared their cultures, peace prevailed throughout the lands, plenty to eat, people were working, and there's no indication, whatsoever, of a pending war."

Tiger jumps. "Then Europe imploded... catching everyone unaware, including the US. A real shocker. I garontee you 'dat."

Doris confesses she is very sad about WWI. "It is a forgotten war. And some people, unfortunately, don't care."

Everyone nods in agreement.

Lars fidgeted in his seat. "Let me start this off with a jolt, which will open your eyes wide. There were many battles, with numerous mistakes, but Tiger and I have decided to concentrate only on the Battle of the Somme... the bloodiest battle in history. Get this... in one day, July 1st, 1916 the British had 57,470 casualties and 19,240 deaths. There were 20,000 casualties in the first hour—a soldier killed every 4.2 seconds. Three of four officers were casualties the first day. Half of the 143 battalions became casualties. French—1,590 casualties; Germans 10-12 thousand lost. How could this possibly happen? It's unfathomable."

"Definitely incomprehensible," agreed Brenda.

Tiger scratched his head, rolled his neck and declared, "It was due to stubbornness, ignorance, and incompetence of British and French commanders, including general officers. They had a poor grasp of tactics and strategies, Doc."

Lars jumps back in. "By the end of the Somme battles, July 1 to Nov 18, the totals were: Brits—450 thousand casualties; French—200 thousand; Germans—465 thousand. Can you imagine that? All during a brief period of only 3-1/2 months, gang! It seems that the minds of the generals were geared to believe a slaughter as an admirable or magnificent accomplishment."

"I know it sounds unbelievable, but what Lars just said is true," added Tiger. "They were lunatics. The generals hung out in the rear. Extreme time delays between observation and response. This caused soldiers on the front lines to suffer immeasurably. Land telephone lines were cut or broken up by artillery fire so they relied on runners and carrier pigeons. Too late to be of any use. Totally unacceptable."

Olivia, who had studied this battle in depth for her book, declared, "You know the results of five years of stalemate along the Western Front, a 475 mile line from the North Sea to the Swiss Border, was 5 million civilian casualties, 9 million military dead, plus destruction of quaint towns and villages. This tragic and unnecessary conflict was full of ad hoc treaties and broken promises at high levels. Policies were flawed, inept policy execution, inconsistencies, and hypocrisies reigned. Totally disgraceful." She smacked her lips angrily.

Brenda pops in. "The mistakes that could have avoided all of this completely lies in having not used prudence and just plain goodwill. That would have avoided a continental confrontation."

"Right on, Brenda," Tiger exclaimed. "You just hit a homerun. Gross mistakes were made in all of the major battles... The First Ypres, The Somme, Verdun, The Second Ypres, The Nivelle Offensive, Passchendaele, and others; All were in vain. At the Somme, Brits marched shoulder-to-shoulder right into machine gun fire; Germans firing 1,000 bullets per minute. Barbed wire stopped the Brits advances too, and there were large holes caused by ineffective artillery fire. The 50-500 yards, no-man's land... a killing field, between the Allied trenches and the Germans, was filled with corpses of both sides. The muck gummed up weapons; the wounded dragged themselves into holes and drowned; many were heard calling for *Mom*... and nobody could get out there to help them. They died in agony. Horses and mules sunk in the muck and suffocated. Rats and maggots added to the no-man's land slaughter by scavenging the decaying bodies. Germans were in concrete encased MG *(machine gun)* nests. One MG could slaughter an entire battalion.

"That's telling it like it was, Tiger," Lars exclaimed, "You know, thousands fell in enemy attacks, but then others were sent in to the same, exact slaughter right behind them. Total insanity by high commanders."

"I was just going to say that!" Brenda uttered. "And that with all the carnage, and casualties soaring, there was little change in the lines for 3-1/2 years along the Western Front. In all that time, trenches were hardened, MG emplacements were vastly improved, and more barbed wire positioned."

Lars speaks up. "Yup! Casualties mounted at an incredible rate with little gains or advantages by either side. Seems as if they were planning for the long haul. Absolutely preposterous, illogical, unreasonable, and absurd... however you might call it. But the main point is that there are so many pieces to WWI that a book could be written on each one."

Lars and Tiger had read the ten main masterpiece books about WWI, plus the Archives and other sources. They were all set for this discussion. Of course, Doris, Brenda and Olivia did their homework, too. That's the norm for the Alpha Team, as you know. They all study each blunder even though a leader is assigned to lead the discussion for each particular blunder.

Lars continues getting to the mistakes that caused the US to enter into this fiasco...

"Well, if I was a prosecutor seeking the source that caused the failure to keep the US at peace, I would nail Woodrow Wilson, without any doubt. By the way, the points we will be bringing out here would have kept us out of this unnecessary World War.

"I would charge him, as follows, but not necessarily in priority order. Tiger and I worked up these points together by combining our intensive research gathering. Why don't you lead off, Tiger!"

"Ok, Doc. Here goes:

- Letting the Brits propaganda campaign cloud his thinking. They made Germany appear to be a brute force, exaggerating to the nth degree German inhumanities. Yet the US was trading heavily with both the British and Germans. There was no initial favoritism. Wilson fell for it, being extremely naïve;
- No threat to the US. Our security was not at stake. Although he promised *'to pursue true neutrality'*, which the general public liked quite a lot. The public agreed with George Washington's belief that we should stay out of foreign affairs;
- Failure to defend the US's freedom of the seas. Inaction on his part. Terrible lack of leadership on this matter;
- Not strong enough to let Brits and France know that they depend on America's considerable economic leverage. They depended on us for nearly everything—munitions, manufactured goods, food, and loans. They could not continue their war effort

without us. So, my point is that our contributions to the war should have been all of these, but no troops. Wilson needed to have them respect our neutrality;

- He failed to reach out to the public and ask them how they felt. A severe shortcoming and grievous mistake. After all, it was our national interests that were at stake;

- President Wilson was spreading the word that America was entering the war seeking nothing for itself. Rather, *'we are fighting for ideals and lofty principles'*.

"Stupidity... no demand for payback for helping Allies. He gave away the store, so to speak."

"That's crazy as hell, Doc!" reveals Olivia. "We lose 114 thousand souls, 205,605 wounded, 4,480 prisoners, with no regard for this outcome! Wilson was a real *tosser, a sod...* as we say in England." She takes a hefty swig of her passion—herbal tea, coupled with a big frown.

Lars stands up, brushing off food crumbs from his polo shirt. "Listen, there is much more to this but Wilson is the culprit. He could have stopped us from entering this quagmire. What people don't realize is that the *Great War* result affects us even today. It is a haunting. The blunder on April 6, 1917, voted by Congress to go to war, set the stage for an agonizing century to follow. Maybe even more than a century... maybe forever."

"As I mentioned earlier, I covered WWI in my book," said Olivia. "Most of the scholars and WWI experts do not feel certain why we went to war. Many of them have written that we were not attacked and there was no national security threat. Some state there was no battleship attacked in a Cuban port—the Marne in 1898; no Pearl Harbor in1941; nothing like North Korea invading South Korea in 1950; and other provoking incidents. In 1917, American security was not at risk.

"Some reasons for entering the war, given by experts are that the German submarines had attacked ships in the War Zone. First huge mistake—the Brits skillful propaganda campaign making Germans out to be brutal people. These are weak reasons. First of all, the Germans warned us about the War Zone... don't get your ships in there. And, we were ingenuous to listen to the British when they made up alarming, false claims as to the Germans brutality. Many of our top scholars feel that our intervention was the biggest mistake in modern history."

"There's a lot of wisdom in your comments, Olivia," said Doris, nodding. "Another one to add to your list of scholars thoughts is the Zimmerman Telegram. On January 16, 1917 German Foreign Minister Arthur Zimmerman sent a dispatch to Mexico's leaders offering to support them in returning Texas and other territories to Mexico. In return, Mexico was to create disturbances on America's border to tie down military resources. What a bunch of hogwash, yet it bothered Wilson and others. We were acting like Cub Scouts... guilelessness."

Tiger said, "My take, is that WWI was a waste of our resources that could have been put to better use to strengthen our country internally. We made the mistake of not pursuing an armed neutrality policy. Instead... we were passive victims of a stupid catastrophe."

"You are exactly right," agreed Brenda. "One hang up I have is that the Lusitania was sunk in 1915, so if we were to enter the war, why not enter at that time rather than wait until two years later? 128 Americans died in that sinking. The Brits, Churchill included, let us down in that disaster by not providing an escort destroyer as required when a ship is in German sub areas."

"Exactly," echoed Olivia. "Frankly, if we had not entered the war, the Allied Powers (France, Britain, Russia, Italy, and Japan) and Central Powers (Germany, Austria-Hungary, Ottoman Empire, and Bulgaria) would have been forced by mutual exhaustion to come to the negotiating table in 1917."

Lars reinforced Brenda's comments by injecting his two major points. "First... it was a huge mistake to enter into any war when the US military had pitiful leadership, low recruitment, and a poor manufacturing base. We were forced to invest heavily into making bombs, ships, planes, a variety of vehicles, munitions, and other war-oriented materials. This investment could have been directed at improving the livelihood of all Americans. Second... stupidity and dull-headedness caused what should have been a Third Balkan War instead of a European continental war. Serbia versus Austria-Hungary. Huge mistakes that caused a more isolated, lower level battle to turn into a larger unnecessary calamity... WWI. But we're not going there! That's not our charter for this blunder discussion."

"Let me punch this out further," proposed Doris. "I feel, like many eminent scholars and WWI experts, that World War I was the catastrophe of the 20th Century. A nightmare that still haunts us because of the spill-off from it. That *Great War* spawned Hitler, Stalin, Fascism, rise of Totalitarian, etc."

"Yes, it was a pyrrhic victory for the British—too great a cost to be worthwhile," reminded Olivia.

Lars added, "And remember one war sows the seeds for future wars."

"Wow! Another gem of wisdom from our Doc," remarked Tiger, as he swerved back and forth to Patsy Cline's singing in the background. "That's my favorite—*I Fall To Pieces*. Sorry to get off track here, ya'll."

"Nobody wins as a result of war," Olivia continued. "Countries lose a generation of their youths, plus devastation."

Tiger noted, "And one thing we didn't touch on, was how this became a World War in the first place. Some say is was due to the assassination of Archduke Franz Ferdinand of Austria and his wife, Sophie, by the *Black Hand Gang* of Serbia, specifically Gavaile Princip... a *Black Hand* member. The truth is, nobody cared about Ferdinand in Austria. It took three weeks for the Austrian government to react. As we have pointed out, it should have stayed in that locale, i.e. Austria-Serbia, and not elevated to a continental level.

"At the beginning, France and Britain wanted no part of what seemingly would be another Balkan War over a minor land dispute, mainly. But it was elevated to a higher state—Germany sided with the Austria-Hungary Empire. The Germans were jealous of Britain's and France's expanded colonies. They wanted to expand and resented the other two countries' expansion. Germany wanted to be recognized as a *top global country*. They wanted to be bigger than the British naval forces. A powerful sea force.

"What I have said here is not our charter today, but just a snapshot of what caused this to be a continental war, which it should not have been in the first place!" Tiger instinctively scratched himself in the groin area. He was unaware the action did not escape everyone's eyes.

Brenda picked that moment to unload her bombshell. "I blame the statesmen of the Great Powers for being incompetent, greedy, short-sighted, and failing to act in an effective way to keep Europe peaceful—the Great Powers being those countries in the Triple Entente of 1907—France, Britain, Russia; and the Triple Alliance of 1882—Germany, Austria-Hungary, Italy."

"Yeah," said Tiger. "In short, if it had not risen to a European Continental War, there never would have been a World War! You are right, Brenda, everyone was let down by these incompetent, untrustworthy statesmen or *supposed* leaders. Can I get one more thing off my chest? Then I'm done."

All nodded, with Lars saying, "Go for it."

"As a grunt like Lars, and having been in over 30 battles in Vietnam, I can't imagine sending troops into battle, time and time again, marching into machine gun fire, shoulder to shoulder. Each one of those soldiers meant a lot to someone somewhere—mother, father, sister, brother, wife maybe or girlfriend, relatives, close friends. And look at *Pickett's Charge* at Gettysburg on July 3rd, 1863. The same thing! Marching forward toward Union reinforced bunkers in open wheat fields for 3/4 of a mile. General Pickett lost 50% of his division by following Robert E. Lee's order. Pickett never forgave Lee for giving that ridiculous order."

Tiger choked up and could not continue. Lars grabbed his shoulder tightly. It affected all of the team.

"Let me add this," said Lars. "One of the biggest of all the mistakes was poor communications between European countries, leaving messages to be easily misinterpreted.

"It was good to work closely with Tiger on this blunder. All of us have laid out mistakes that shouldn't have been made, and which caused this terrible war that put people through extreme hardships.

"Let's do something different here at the discussion's end. I'll ask each of you to give us one word to describe your feelings about the mistakes causing us to get sucked into WWI. Let's go around the table starting with Brenda:

(Brenda) "Inexcusable"; *(Doris)* "Bewildered"; *(Olivia)* "Shameful"; *(Tiger)* "Dismayed";

"And for me—Pitiful. Next time we meet, Doris is going to take the lead on a colossal blunder involving Atahualpa, Lord of the Inca Empire, and Pizarro, Spanish Conquistador, in 1532."

Doris adds, "A fascinating blunder. I wrote a paper on it while taking an Ancient History course at the University of Virginia. Yes, I'm a cavalier, as you all know."

Anita brought everyone another hot drink. It was cold outside; about four inches of snow has accumulated. The team really cares about Anita. And she always knows what they want. Tiger called her over and asked for a side of crispy bacon.

"Hey Tiger! You're going high hog, huh?" chirped

Doris.

"Yup! But it's the best bacon in the Metro area by far. I garontee you 'dat!" Tiger grinned.

High-fives and all left except the two Vietnam vets, who remained to reminisce.

They talked about the Nats baseball team and the Caps hockey team. And other *guy talk!* Lars confessed to Tiger that, "sometimes I feel that I was born too late. I would have liked to have lived back in the days of William Johnstone's western novels... the 1800s. I've read all 18 of his *Eagles Legacy series*. It was revolver versus revolver or rifle versus rifle."

"Yeah! No drones or GPS, high tech stuff, Doc. I agree."

"Doris always says that my favorite song is *Born Too Late.*"

"Hey! I know it... sung by the *Poni-Tails* back in 1958. Hey, Doc... let's hit *Sloppy Mama's* next week for barbecue."

"You're on Tiger."

***Portrait of Francisco Pizarro
by Amable-Paul Coutan, 1835***

CHAPTER 11

Decapitation Of The Inca Empire:
Pizzaro Versus Atahualpa—1532

Doris announced, "This is the most preposterous blunder of all. Pizarro, with 168 troops, defeats the Incas with 7,000 soldiers, thus overcoming an Empire. Many scholars and ancient history experts have commented that Pizarro's military victory was *'one of the most improbable in recorded history'*. The mistakes made by Atahualpa, the Inca Ruler, resulted in the end of the Inca Empire.

"We are supposed to bring out mistakes, mostly unknown by most people, which caused the unnecessary blunder. This sure is a colossal one and a big surprise to me," Brenda stated.

"That's why history is so important," added Olivia. "Again, remember what Santayana said: *'Those who cannot remember the past are condemned to repeat it'*. This certainly is another eye-opener, Doris."

"Ten-4 on that," asserted Tiger. He scratches his right ear... the top part having been ripped off by a Viet Cong sniper's AK-47, 7.62mm bullet. The punch to an AK-47 rifle is so powerful that even though it just slivered Tiger's ear, it knocked him to the ground. After that incident, he carried an AK-47 rifle for the rest of his Vietnam tour. Ditto for Lars, who was wounded twice himself.

Lars broke in. "This sure is going to be an unexpected enlightenment for most people, Doris. Most people will say, *Wow! I didn't know that!*"

"That's what we want to do," chimed Doris. "Just like Krystal Koons who always says, *'We're gonna wow ya!'* Everyone knows who Krystal Koons is, right?"

Not sure, Olivia scratches her head. Seeing this, Doris explains.

"She's the daughter of Jim Koons and the sales spokesperson for Koons Auto—Tysons Corner. She is the face of the family business. Appears in all their commercials."

"I buy all my vehicles from them and get them serviced there, too," Lars added, smiling as he looked out the window at his Grand Cherokee Jeep.

The patrons at Metro 29 noticed Tiger plowing down his pancakes noisily, as though he was starving to death. However, he did not take notice of them. He burped and then looked up. "Sorry gang, I missed supper last night."

"Sometimes, you are a *bloody bloke,*" teased Olivia.

Doris coughed and cleared her throat. "Let's get started. Atahualpa made a gargantuan mistake by his decision to meet the Spaniards at Cajamarca, a mostly empty little town, for a feast in his honor. His plan was to capture the Spaniards. Pizarro's plan was to ambush the Incas. Atahualpa arrived in a litter *(which is a kind of carriage for high-ranking people)*.It was carried by 80 noblemen and surrounded by 7,000 of his soldiers—mostly unarmed.

"A Spaniard, who was present at the battle said, *'Atahualpa himself was very richly dressed, with his crown on his head and a collar of large emeralds around his neck. He sat on a small stool with a rich saddle cushion resting on his litter. The litter was lined with parrot feathers of many colors and decorated with plates of gold and silver.*

Atahualpa was drunk. He felt that the Spaniards were no threat. And Pizarro planned an ambush. He had his cavalry and infantry occupy three long buildings and placed his artillery pieces in a stone structure in the center of the town square. The Incas were trapped in tight quarters, although they didn't realize it at the time. First, the Spaniards tipped over the litter carrying Atahualpa, killing all 80 noblemen. Cannons blasted away with pinpoint accuracy. Infantry and cavalry charged from hidden positions'.

"The cavalry, unknown to the Incas, ran down the terrified Incas as they fled the horrific scene. 2,000 Incas were slaughtered in the first hour and another 5,000 were captured and used later to add to Pizarro's forces."

Tiger declared, "Yeah! The Incas were up *Schitt's Creek* without a paddle." Everyone laughed.

Doris then mentioned that *Schitt's Creek* was one of her favorite TV series.

"Mine too," added Brenda.

"What's interesting Doris, is that no Spaniards were

killed," Olivia offered. "Only one Spanish injury... that was Pizarro himself, who had his hand cut, as he saved Atahualpa from certain death. The Spaniards were practically invulnerable from what I could gain during my research, because they wore heavy steel armor. This event was called the *Battle of Cajamarca,* Nov 16, 1532. Sorry to butt in, but I wanted to add this."

"Merci, Olivia," Doris responded. "This was Atahualpa's *grandiose* mistake. If he hadn't entered Cajamarca, he would have probably ruled the Incas until death. Once again, as a team, we are finding glaring errors that if they had not occurred, the blunder would never have happened. Other mistakes that I uncovered were:

- Atahualpa's Inca Empire was too centralized. He made all the relevant decisions. Thus, if Atahualpa can be controlled, the entire Inca Empire can be controlled. I forgot to mention earlier that Atahualpa had 80,000 soldiers under his command;
- Being too relaxed. Enjoying the hot springs just outside of Cajamarca and being drunk didn't help either;
- Curiosity. Wondering about the beasts and weapons the Spaniards had with them. But doing nothing about it;
- Nobles telling Atahualpa that the Spaniards had little capacity to fight and do any significant damage. So, based on his nobles' assessment, planned to capture the Spaniards... very complacent;
- After several battles, one of which his army defeated

the army of his half-brother in the largest battle in Inca history, a battle near Cuzco, he was slow to consolidate his rule. Pizarro arrived at the perfect time... an unstable Inca Empire;

- A failed reconnaissance of the Incas, prior to the meeting at Cajamarca. The Incas had never faced firearms or horse cavalry before. Actually, they had never seen horses before. They were quite dumbfounded. They failed to take this into account. Many of Atahualpa's soldiers were unarmed; others carried only clubs, knives, axes, and spears;
- They weren't ready to face the armaments of the Spaniards. Basically, it was the Spaniards' steel swords, helmets, and armor versus the Incas' leather armor and poor armaments. Costly mistake.

"These are some of the main mistakes that caused this blunder. Want to hear some other miscellaneous points of interest?"

All gave Doris a thumbs up.

"OK, then," grinning, she continued. "The litter carrying Atahualpa was finally turned over. Yet the nobles, whose hands or arms were severed, still tried to hold it up, being loyal attendants."

"Man, that's devotion!" exclaimed Tiger.

Doris nodded. "They were all killed. Pizarro charged on his horse yelling the Spanish battle cry, *'Santiago'* and scooped up Atahualpa who was still sitting on his litter. He saved Atahualpa's life, since he was about to be killed."

"In my research, I discovered that a kangaroo court

charged Atahualpa with treason and sentenced him to be burned at the stake," claimed Brenda.

"That's right," said Doris. "However, Pizarro offered Atahualpa an alternative, which he took—convert to Catholicism. To save his life, Atahualpa offered a ransom. He would fill a room, 22 feet long by 17 feet wide and 8 feet high, with gold, silver and emeralds; 24 *tons* of gold was brought in from all over the Inca Empire. This ransom was to gain his freedom.

"But... Pizarro felt that Atahualpa was too much of a liability to be alive and he had him executed by strangulation. An iron collar was placed around his neck on July 26, 1533 and tightened until he was strangled to death."

Olivia picked that point to note something of interest. "I found out that Pizarro was the illegitimate son of an infantry colonel and a poor woman. He was partially illiterate."

Doris continued. "Good find! And here's another piece of trivia—Atahualpa, still striving to save his life, gave Pizarro his favorite daughter, 14 years old, to take as his wife. But that didn't work just as the *Ransom Room*, full of gold, didn't work either. There's a lot more to this, but here we go again... mistakes that caused a blunder that could have been easily avoided."

"Hey! I found something too," exhorted Tiger. "I uncovered some specific information that is of special interest to us infantry *grunts*. Pizarro had 106 foot soldiers and 62 horsemen; three arquebuses *(which are portable guns mounted on a tripod),* and 2 very small light canons. Also, as our team *massacre advisor*, I must state that the massacre at Cajamarca is at the top of my list of massacres in world history."

"I might add that Tiger's list covers 287 massacres based on 516 references," said Lars.

"And... my list covers the timeframe from 88BC to 2016," boasted Tiger.

Lars ended the meeting. "It's 9:15 so let's wrap up. Next week, Olivia will lead us in the next blunder—Climate Change. I know everyone has researched this for several months, so it should be a real *grabber*."

Hands in the middle with Tiger yelling out, *"HOOAH!"* That got the attention of everyone in Metro 29.

On the way out, Lars pulled Tiger aside. "Hey comrade, did you *cut the cheese* during the session?" He squeezed his nostrils, indicating a real stinky situation.

"Yeah, Doc," Tiger grinned. "I had Louisiana Creole Smothered Cabbage last night!"

They smacked palms at the exit.

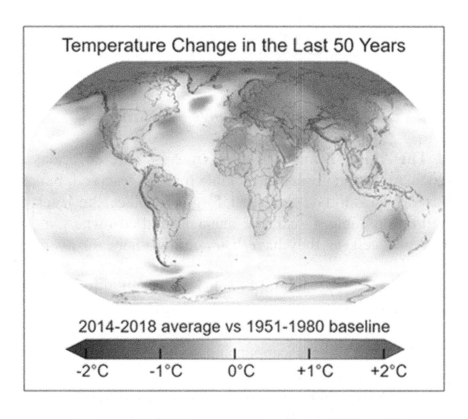

Average global temperatures from 2010-2019
compared to a baseline average from 1951-1978

CHAPTER 12

Global Climate Change—A Paradox

The Alpha Team arrived on time—8 a.m. on Friday as usual. Anita usually has their table marked reserved, but she was out sick today. And Jyll forgot to place the reserved card on the table. Oscar, the manager and co-owner, knows the team well, as they have been coming here for over one year.

"I'm so sorry," Jyll told the team. "It will only be five to ten minutes."

Oscar, walking up behind her added, "Please... go to the food bar and have a cappuccino on us. I'll let you know when your table is ready. Sorry, folks."

Tiger whispered, "Now *that's* class!" He rolled his eyes.

Lars teasingly said, "Just don't let it happen again, Oscar," smacking Oscar on the shoulder.

Everyone giggled.

"Hey! We gotta' come here for dessert sometime," Tiger exclaimed as they passed the dessert window with 24 trays of different desserts.

"Roger that, Sergeant Greene," chuckled Lars *(Tiger's former Company Commander in Vietnam)*. They sat at the 20-foot food bar—desserts staring them in the face. Henry served them all a free cappuccino. Tiger popped off a "Thanks, Henry."

A few minutes later, Oscar returned and led them past the dessert window again. Doris nearly drooled over them and Tiger smacked his lips.

"Won't happen again," Oscar apologized, stopping at their table.

"Not a problem, Oscar. Stuff happens. Thanks for the cappuccinos!" remarked Lars, as everyone sat down and got comfortable, eager to begin the discussion. Jyll set their drinks down, promising to return shortly.

First, Olivia plans to define terms, the consequences of *Global Climate Change*, and then get right into their mission—to point out the mistakes that were made which caused this to be a blunder. This one is so broad, that Olivia had previously asked Doris to assist her on certain aspects of it.

The team's analysis is based on many scientific studies and scholarly journal articles. Olivia had realized while researching this blunder, that the team should agree on definitions. During a dinner session at Bistro 29, also on Lee Highway—Highway 29 near Metro 29, they discussed this matter. And again later via telephone calls and emails. The team always communicated well. They had agreed on the five following definitions:

- Weather—can change day-by-day, rainy today, sunny

tomorrow. It's local—rain, wind, snow, hurricane, tornadoes;
- Climate—long-term pattern of weather in a particular region;
- Climate Change—change in the Earth's climate over hundreds, even thousands of years;
- Global Warming—a subset of *Global Climate Change*; an increase in the Earth's average surface temperature, mostly due to increases in greenhouse gases;
- *Global Climate Change*—includes global warming and everything else, not related only on the increase in greenhouse gases.

Olivia began. "I like the *Global Climate Change* term as it really is *the big picture*. It affects many things over time, such as agriculture, flood vulnerability of bridges, forests' production, food supply, human health, economics, ocean, coral reefs, plants and animals worldwide, biodiversity, etc.

"The big picture is that *Global Climate Change* can bring on the extinction of our planet. This will occur in about 7.5 billion years, as a result of the sun's absorption. The earth will cease to exist. Human life will be extinct in 1-4 billion years. But I'm getting off course here."

Doris adds, "Let's face it; sea levels are rising due to melting glaciers. On a visit to Alaska two years ago, Lars and I were in a small boat and saw a huge hunk of ice break off a glacier and tumble into the water about 50 meters from us. Global warming in real time. Oceans are about 40% more acidic due to warming. This causes corals to lose their vibrant colors. There are so many areas of concern that will suffer, that it would take *volumes* to cover all of them in detail. Some of the dangers are: high extinction risks for many species, rising sea levels due to breaking up of icebergs, calving (birth of an iceberg) which is what caused the *sinking of the Titanic*. Species are caught in distribution shifts, exposure to diseases like malaria, coastal flooding, etc."

Olivia nodded and continued. "Some mistakes which cause this to be a sort of blunder are:

- To use scientific models and simulations for dictating our energy policies and environmental regulations. Scientists try to measure cause and effect but it's difficult to measure climate change. We aren't really causing the climate to change in a global sense. Many scientists try to make their measurements fit their theory. They are biased quite often. Like telling the head accountant at your corporation to make the numbers fit. Despite their sound reasoning from acceptable models it leads to senseless conclusions. Climate change is too complex;
- Global warming and climate change by humans is very slow. Mother Nature rules. It is cyclic from 600BC to the present day. It goes up and down, warm to cold, cold to warm. The paradox is Mother Nature versus scientific theories. Probably 60% of the warming is natural. The best data, covering 11,000 years, comes from the Greenland Ice Cores. It shows warm, then cold, and vice versa in cycles of 172

years;

- A big shortcoming is that the majority of people don't take climate change seriously and lack knowledge about it. There are a lot of misleading statements, logical flaws, and unsubstantiated claims, as to not worrying about climate change. Most of us are ignorant about climate science;

- We have put $350 billion into climate change in the past 10 years. Is that a mistake when Mother Nature is really in charge? Possibly, but we *can* do some things to help because the global temperature changes need to be held below 2° Celsius to avoid catastrophic events. The hotter the planet gets, the more the risks of wildfires, floods, extreme droughts, and food shortages worldwide. Small changes in the Earth's temperature have huge effects. Thus, climate neutrality is vital;

- Another mistake is when we focus on the short-term, rather than the long-term. It keeps us from meaningful collective action. For example, 40% of insect species could be extinct within a few decades. That's just one, and not that I'm real fond of insects, but think of the catastrophic effect that would have worldwide;

- Lastly, and this mistake makes me boil... partisan politics divided on *Global Climate Change*. 68% of Democrats feel it is a priority—but only 18% of Republicans. *'A house divided against itself cannot stand'*, is an Abe Lincoln quote from 1858. Do I need say more? We need to get with it!"

"Mon Dieu, Olivia, that's a *wide* eye-opener," blurted Tiger.

"Most people have no clue about what we have been discussing here," Brenda added, noticing some of the other guests looking at them quizzically. "I enjoy scuba diving. I've dived the Great Barrier Reef twice. Awesome! But it has lost 50% of its coral population in the past 30 years. Due to Climate Change. A shame."

All team members shake their heads in disgust. All are certified scuba divers.

"A little trivia," piped in Tiger. "The three ingredients of beer (water, hops, barley) can be affected. Oh, heavens no!"

This brought a few chuckles from the group.

"But I found out that the US and Germany provide 2/3 of the world's hop production. Yet droughts in both countries have affected hops. Barley has been damaged in Australia by heavy rains and by droughts in England. So, as Olivia and Doris have pointed out, everyone needs to pay more attention to Climate Change." Tiger reels out his French: "Vive la biere, surtout Samuel Adams."

Lars toasted the team. "It seems as if we all can do things to help out but in the paradox, Mother Nature versus the scientists, Mother Nature (going back millions of years) wins. The reason this is a blunder is that we are guided by uncertain scientific measurements via computer modeling and simulations. Flawed models in many cases. Yes, there has been warming, but scientists need to suggest what is to be expected and what's predicted for the long term. One last point that you didn't mention as a mistake is the mistakes of the Intergovernmental Panel on Climate Change

(IPPC). Here's the problem... they functioned as a true believer instead of as a truth seeker. The best bet is to track history and be ready to meet those times, in the cycle, that will impact us.

Brenda quickly injects her thoughts, "For your information a new report from the United Nations Disaster Risk Reduction Center for Research on the Epidemiology of Disasters states: *'the planet will become an inhabitable hell for millions of people'*. In addition Al Gore, Chairman and Founder of The Climate Reality Project said, *'Solutions to the Climate Crisis are within reach, but in order to capture them, we must take urgent action today across every level of society'*.

Tiger cracks the knuckles on his right hand, adding, "I agree. That's super input, Brenda. The right thing to do is to take climate actions now, Period!"

Lars clears his throat and in a cracked voice says, "This takes global leaders to react and we have poor global leaders. Very few countries have real leaders because they are politicians. Not voted in, based on leadership background, but rather on securing campaign funds. It's all about money. And... on who you know. Gore got screwed out of being President. We would not be in this mess today, namely the Middle East quagmire, if he had been elected. I'm not necessarily a Gore fan, but let's face it. I'm a realistic optimist/enthusiast. Independent thinker; not swayed by anybody or anything. That's me in a nutshell!" Lars displays a firm jaw.

"Wow! The Doc has spoken. Darn good stuff, Sir." Tiger squirms in his chair letting out a low sounding fart. But everybody could hear it. Brenda giggled.

Lars said, "And with that folks, next week Brenda tackles a real clear cut blunder."

"Definitely. It's on the *Four Pests Campaign* of China back in 1958. A genuine horror story!" stated Brenda.

They all did the high-fives and scooted out the door. Except for Olivia, who stayed to talk to Jyll. She knows Jyll is a name of English decent and has been *itching* to chat with her for weeks.

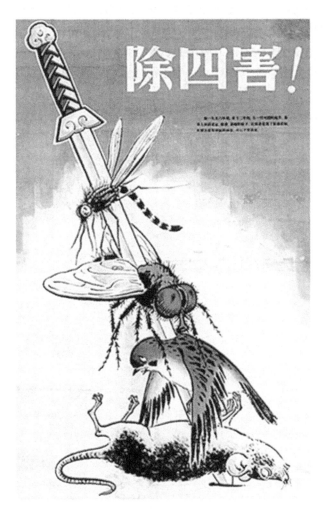

The Four Pests Campaign
Chinese Poster

CHAPTER 13

The Four Pests Campaign Debacle

Anita had already served them. Coffee and tea was steaming and much appreciated. It is extremely cold outside.

Olivia burst out with some news of her own before Brenda could get started. "Hey gang! I took Lars advice about Koons at Tysons Corners. Bought a 2016 Ford Focus Hatchback. Krystal Koons was there saying, *'When you're talkin' cars, you're talkin' Koons!'* Cool atmosphere. Sorry Brenda, let's roll!"

Brenda briefly explains the history of the *Four Pests Campaign.* That it came about because sparrows, mosquitoes, rats, and flies were spreading malaria, the plague, and typhoid all over the China heartland. Also, tuberculosis, cholera, polio, smallpox, and hookworm saturated China. 10.5 million people were infected with a liver parasite and cholera which killed tens of thousands. Infant mortality rate was 30%.

"I'm anxious to start this blunder," Brenda began.

"Scholars and research experts vary on the estimate of those that died during the *Four Pests Campaign*, 1958-1962. Here are some of the numbers I derived from my research: 20-45 million, 20-30 million, 15 million (the Chinese government's estimate...which is intentionally low), 15-36 million, 30 million, 45 million, 78 million, and 36 million.

"Of those, I believe 36 million is about right. It is based on a estimate by Yang Jisheng, a Chinese journalist, as stated in his book, *Tombstone*. Yang was published in the US, but banned in China.

"Others estimate that the *Great Leap Forward* program killed 45 million in only four years. Poor Yang suffered because China wanted to cover-up the real number of people that died due to their mistakes—most of which can be attributed to Mao Zedong, founder of the People's Republic of China."

Tiger cut in. "I discovered that the Four Pest Campaign, particularly the mass slaughtering of sparrows, caused a nationwide loss of crops. That resulted in untold millions of people who would then die of starvation."

"That's correct, Tiger. I see you've done some of your own homework," responded Brenda, winking. "The unintended consequences of Mao's program were: Numbers decimated around a billion sparrows, 1.5 billion rats, 100 million kilograms of flies, and a million kilograms of mosquitoes. Those were the big four—sparrows, rats, flies, and mosquitoes.

"Locusts then ate hundreds of thousands of pounds of grain and were able to do this because their number one predator, the tree sparrow, was being annihilated. This gave the locusts free reign and they ruled the land, causing a 70% reduction in crops production.

"In 1958, Mao Zedong started the *Four Pests Campaign* as a *hygiene* campaign. Actually, the *Four Pests Campaign* was a subset of the *Great Leap Forward* movement of the Peoples Republic of China to build a stronger and more powerful country—basically to boost the economy via industrial and agricultural changes.

"Stupidly, the entire populace was ordered to join the anti-sparrow campaign. People beat drums, fired gunshots, screamed, waved bedclothes to keep sparrows in the air. It was known that after four hours in the air the birds would fall to the ground from exhaustion. Frankly, it makes me sick."

Doris wipes away a tear. She loves all birds.

Brenda patted her on the back understandingly and continues.

"They used red flags, scarecrows, banged gongs... even set up firing lanes to shoot them down. Some of the people died falling from their rooftops when scaring away the sparrows."

Lars picked that moment to jump in. "Let me defend the sparrow. An interesting fact, though. Sparrows eat mostly insects and only some grain. In season, they only eat grubs and insects. A pair of sparrows can kill 3,400 caterpillars in one week. In India, they celebrate the sparrow."

"To me, Brenda," Tiger added, "Mao couldn't find his ass with both hands. He didn't know diddly-squat about farming."

"That's exactly right," Brenda agreed. "Remember, we

mostly blamed President Wilson for getting us into World War I... based on many huge mistakes. Well, I have to say that the blame that caused this blunder are mostly due to Mao's mistakes. Here are some of those:

- Not realizing that sparrows are an asset by eating caterpillars and other insects. This caused the famine since caterpillars went rampant throughout the country... and locusts;
- Failure to recognize that the four pests should have been rats, mosquitoes, flies, and locusts. Therefore, crops suffered;
- On another occasion, Mao replaced the sparrow with bedbugs on the list of four pests. Again, a brainless move;
- Local officials falsified the numbers of grain production to meet Mao's policies; They were all his *yes* men. Kissed Mao's fanny!
- Establishing unrealistic objectives, like catching up with Britain in seven years and the US in ten years. Completely divorced from reality;
- Not checking results of their efforts or improving policies;
- Unrealistic quotas and targets, such as China should surpass Britain in steel production in 15 years;
- Refused to accept suggestions or correct errors. Arrogant to the nth degree;
- Lack of knowledge of agriculture and industry. He knew zip about these two areas. Yet he set policies based on *seat of the pants* ideas;

"Sorry to butt in, Brenda. But I think his pants were brown most of the time," snickered Tiger and bringing laughter from the others. Brenda, still giggling, continued.

- Allowed the misuse of poisons and pesticides which developed ecological problems such as deforestation;
- Replaced the sparrows again in 1998 with cockroaches, which made no sense at all. Most people already had the habit of killing cockroaches. Trying to save face... dismally. Again, exaggerating his importance;
- Biggest of all mistakes, which is the case of most dictators—not caring about his own people. This one mistake really bothers me the most. *The Great Famine* was so severe that people started to eat other people— parents ate their children; kids ate their parents. Thousands of people were murdered—as food."

Olivia held up a finger wanting to jump into the conversation. *"And...* those are mistakes that could have been avoided. I have another three points to add to Brenda's: (1) Researchers performed autopsies on dead sparrows and found that the majority of stomach contents were made up of insects, not grains. This was a finding from China's Academy of Sciences in 1959. (2) Most deaths were unnecessary because massive grain warehouses had enough food to feed the entire country. The government's secret. Selfish communist government officials. I found this out by uncovering a classified Chinese government document... basically, top secret. And (3) Mao should have had locusts as one of the four pests. Locusts were the real devastators of crops."

Doris broke in. "I found that Frederick the Great declared a Prussian War against sparrows because they ate some of his cherries in the royal orchard in the 1870s. A price was set on every dead sparrow. They were either killed or scared away. It backfired on him. The next year he lost nearly all of the orchard fruit due to caterpillars. He countermanded his previous order on the sparrows and brought more in from far away."

"Another example," Olivia noted, "is that in the 1860s importing sparrows was in vogue (meaning fashionable). Along the eastern seaboard it was felt that sparrows would get rid of caterpillars, cankerworms, and other insects. So there *were* other examples that Mao could have learned from. But he was too arrogant to take advice from anyone. I'm not sure of Frederick the Great or Mao's IQs, but they certainly had no common sense. And neither one understood the first thing about agriculture."

"Excellent points, Brenda, and from *all* of you," Lars stated. "You know, I'm very sad about this particular discussion and so is my bride. Doris and I have a Wildlife Backyard Habitat certified by the National Wildlife Federation. We love birds. We have about 6 bird feeders and a dozen bird houses with 24/7, 365 water via a waterfall."

Everyone gave him a thumbs up.

Brenda adds, "Let me end this discussion by saying that the Four Pest Campaign ranks in the top three worst catastrophes in world history."

"Next time, Tiger takes the lead by covering the *Bay of*

Pigs disaster. Will you be ready, Tiger?" Lars asked.

"Yes sir, Doc!" Tiger salutes and clicks his heels. *"HOOAH!"*

On the way out, Olivia, a dessert freak, suggested that they each pick out a dessert and doggie bag it.

"I'll take the apple turnover," said Tiger, going first. The others followed: Napoleon—Lars, Chocolate Layer Cheesecake—Doris, Boston Cream Pie—Brenda, and Bread Pudding and a Chocolate éclair for Olivia. Anita boxed them up. After a traditional high-five outside the exit, they took off.

***Counter-attack by Cuban Revolutionary Armed
Forces supported by T-34 tanks near Playa Giron
during the Bay of Pigs invasion, April 19, 1961***

CHAPTER 14

Ill-Fated Invasion Of The Bay Of Pigs

The Alpha Team met on Monday for dinner at Anthony's off Annandale Road in Falls Church. Tiger had suggested this so as to summarize the Bay of Pigs background prior to meeting the next Friday. This would allow him, as the leader, to get right into covering the miscues that caused this horrendous blunder.

Anthony's was one of Tiger's favorite hangouts. He liked to watch the Nationals, Redskins, and Capitals in a more quiet atmosphere. He quickly ordered his usual... Buffalo Wings. Doris and Lars—Stuffed Grape Leaves; Brenda and Olivia—Mozzarella Sticks. All ordered Gyros as the entrée.

Tiger blurted out, "Iris, make sure you add crumbled feta and minced red peppers."

"Entaxei," responded Iris. She gave Tiger a wink.

She is a beauty. Her dark brown hair waved back, very large, medium-brown eyes, and thick eyelashes. Typical

Greek goddess look.

"OK. Let me get right to it," Tiger began. "The CIA poorly trained Cuban exile forces, composed of 1,300 volunteers, attacked at the Bay of Pigs against a force of 25,000 Cuban Army soldiers, 200,000 militiamen, and 9,000 armed police. Of the total Cuban force, 2,681 participated, according to the Cuban Information Archives. By the way, this was a difficult Archive to unmask.

"They were supported with twenty Soviet T-34 light tanks. The brigade was slaughtered as the combat-inexperienced exiles tried to get a beach hold. They were outnumbered by 94.8%, I figure, of those directly involved. And that doesn't include the other 209,000 available men to Castro, who actually took over command after the invasion began.

"By far, it was the worst foreign policy blunder in history. I've found that about 50% of what has been written about the Bay of Pigs is untrue and inaccurate. I uncovered confidential, secret, and top-secret documents and reports that are mind blowing—all kept from the general public. They're now declassified, but you have to dig to find them."

Lars butts in. "Sorry to interrupt, Tiger, but I bet you all don't know that there is a 4th classification above the main three; it's Crypto *(meaning Cryptographic, a category of classified information that is the highest security clearance level)*. It's above TS *(Top Secret)*.

"Tiger and I were on two Crypto missions in Vietnam. A Crypto mission means you are sworn to lifelong secrecy. You can never talk about it and it never becomes unclassified. Actually, I was involved in another one when I was with the Joint Chiefs of Staff. Please continue, Tiger."

Tiger went on. "The exile forces had little real tactical or strategic experience, or know-how. It was like the Cub Scouts planning activities for a 3-day camp—trying to earn their wolf, bear, or bobcat emblem, or teaching an illiterate person trigonometry right off the bat. The CIA's training was inadequate. And they treated the exiles *like dirt,* to quote one of them.

"I'm glad Lars let me take the lead on this one. The father of one of my best friends was selected to be on the CIA's planning team for the secret invasion of Cuba. He was an elite Ranger and paratrooper, as well as a Navy Seal. Quite a package! Within two weeks he saw how dumb and naïve the planners were, so he, and others, transferred to the State Department. The only thing I remember was that his father said, *'They got immersed in groupthink which assured a perfect failure'.*

Each team member, as usual, had researched this blunder. Tiger covered the background a little bit more, explaining that it all started with President Eisenhower's approval of the CIA's plan to oust Fidel Castro. President Kennedy, only in office for three months, inherited the risky covert operation plan after Eisenhower left office. The idea was to eliminate Castro, who supported communism and was brutal in his displays of power. Plus, he had close ties with the USSR... as their puppet."

Brenda decided to punch in a few points here. "By the way, unknown to most people, the CIA developed ridiculous plans to eliminate Castro, well before the invasion idea. A few examples that I dug out of TS documents and hidden diaries are: send scuba-diving equipment to Castro contaminated with deadly fungi—Castro loved to scuba dive; attempts were made to poison his food; the CIA planned to pack a conch (a sea mollusk), with explosives and paint it bright colors... to attract Castro while on a dive."

"Listen, as a diver, he wasn't that stupid," hinted Tiger, chuckling.

"And they used the mafia," added Doris.

After Tiger smartly covered the bottom lines, Olivia popped up. "You know, the US general public and the entire Congress, at that time, demanded that Ike do something. Therefore, Eisenhower approved a CIA proposal to take covert action against the Castro regime. This included the training of a paramilitary force to get rid of Castro."

Doris added, "And President Eisenhower allocated $13.1 million in March 1960 for the CIA to plan Castro's overthrow."

Lars injected, "Now that we are all satisfied with the general background, I can't wait for our discussions this Friday. But before we all leave, I'm treating everyone to a Baklava dessert... *the best!*" Lars wiped away some of the Gyro's Feta cheese that had crept down his chin. Meanwhile, Tiger took a large slug of his Angry Orchard beer.

All thumbs flew up high. Tiger gave the Ranger yell— not *HOOAH!* since it is conventional Army slang and Rangers are an elite force. They prefer to scream *Ranger!* with high infection, which Tiger did. Lars followed with *Ranger!* too. Everyone in the restaurant were startled, yet they cheered.

"Hold on a minute, Doc. While we are eating dessert, let me cover a few more things before we leave. That way, I can really dive into the mistakes made that caused this perfect failure when we have breakfast on Friday."

"Damn good idea, Tiger. Have at it," said Lars, as he chugs his Devil's Backbone IPA.

"This will be a snappy summary just to insure we are all on the same page. I've already stated the size of both forces facing one another. As you know, Brigade 2506 faced impossible odds... Losses: Brigade 2506—118 KIA *(killed in action)*, 360 WIA *(wounded in action)*, 1,189 captured *(75% of those ended up in Cuban prisons)*, US—4 KIA. Cuban Army—176 KIA, 500+ WIA; Militia—2,000+ KIA or WIA. The code name for the operation was *Zapata.* It was won by Castro in only 72 hours. This Friday, along with your help, I'll cover the gross mistakes that caused this unnecessary blunder to happen."

Olivia spoke out. "Let me bring forth a point, probably a little too early on, but I covered this in my book. President Kennedy should have resigned. All the needless deaths were directly on his shoulders. He let down our nation and betrayed Brigade 2506. This was the worst ever by a president, except for maybe Wilson, getting us into WWI. He should have submitted in writing... to the President Pro Tempore of the Senate and Speaker of the House, that he is unable to discharge the powers and duties of his office. Or the sleepy Congress could have pursued impeachment proceedings... for misdemeanor or high crimes. Except, let's face it... no president has ever been removed from office via an impeachment conviction. Andrew Johnson and Bill

Clinton were acquitted by the Senate. As was Trump. Lyndon Johnson should have been impeached. Sorry to have jumped ahead here, Tiger, but I wanted to nail this point down before Friday."

Taking in a deep breath, Lars exclaimed, "Obviously we are all looking forward to Friday's working breakfast. The Bay of Pigs fiasco makes me sick to my stomach. Every time the White House sticks its nose into military operations, the results are poor because they handcuff the military and they haven't any clue as to how to run anything like this."

"Hey Doc! Just like Nam! They cuffed Westmoreland something terrible. He couldn't do squat. Micro-management again. Otherwise, we would have won that war rather than leave in disgrace. Pardon me ladies, but Lyndon Johnson couldn't find his ass with both hands... in regards to fighting the Vietnam War. Il était un idiot!"

Tigers loves to use French now and then coupled with a little New Orleans dialect. He's a show-off.

On the clear, windy *(32-mph)* Friday, the team was in place, ready to hammer out the miserable, upsetting blunder. All were eating their breakfast. Brenda and Olivia switched their usual meals just for fun. Tiger took a swig of his coffee and kicked it off without delay.

"Sport fans, the rubber has met the road here. These are just some of the misjudgments that caused this shameless disaster. I've been on Pepto Bismol all week because this whole thing makes me sick to my stomach. Please join in, because I know you have researched it well, too. Especially Olivia, who covered the Bay of Pigs in her Pulitzer Prize winning book."

Turning somewhat pink, Olivia countered, "Blimey, Tiger... you are a real *berk*... idiot!"

Everyone grinned.

"Hey look, Olivia is very smart, yet humble. In the top 1% of her class at Oxford. *'Most brilliant student we ever had here',* said Professor George David Thomas, one of Oxford University's top history scholars.

"Okay, here we go... off to the races. Mistakes in no special order—can't cover all of them because there are *tons,* major and minor.

"President Kennedy—for not acting as a CINC *(Commander in Chief).* Trusting the JCS *(Joint Chiefs of Staff)* without question and his advisors who should have been fired. By advisors, I mean—Ted Sorenson, Bob Kennedy, Dean Rusk, Robert McNamara, Walt Rostow, Chester Bowles, Richard Bissell, Pierre Cabell, Tom Mann, and General Lemnitzer. They all let the rather *new* president down big time. They knew the plan was impossible and flawed, yet they let Kennedy, only 3 months on the job, go forward. Inexcusable. They are disgraceful for falling into *groupthink,* a false sense of consensus, and staying silent rather than fighting hard against the *perfect failure* plan. Unforgiveable."

Doris agreed. "Absolutely outrageous. Because of their *sitting on their hands,* men died pursuing an operation destined for failure to begin with. Sad."

Tiger continued. "In short, the blame for *Zapata's* failure was John Kennedy. Next... Allen Dulles—for wrongly expecting a general Cuban uprising on the island... against

Castro. And knowing that the invasion force was
outnumbered by at least 200 to 1. In fact, Castro had the
local populace full support. Dulles was dead wrong.

"Then there is the CIA's ignorance, incompetence, and
institutional arrogance. They were very arrogant dudes.
Their secret operations to dump Castro were ludicrous. It's
not funny, but their ideas and plans were laughable. And get
this—not *one* CIA officer spoke Spanish, they lacked Latin-
American knowledge, and had no clue as to the true culture
of the Cuban people. Also, they had no respect for the
Cubans. The CIA budget expanded from $4.4 to $46
million, which provided them the capability to create an ill-
trained, unruly invasion force within a year."

"I wonder who sapped off some of *those* funds!" Brenda
said, disgusted.

Tiger snapped off a piece of his crispy bacon. "Also...
they failed to recommend to Kennedy to cancel the
operation since success seemed dubious to all. Basically,
just to be honest with you, the CIA's operation was a
gamble based on bad intelligence, illusionary planning,
incompetent staffing, and total self-deception. The CIA is
still haunted by the death toll of some very fine men—not
recommending cancellation was a huge error on their part.

"Another mistake—if Presidential Advisor Arthur
Schlesinger had spoken up, Kennedy would have changed
his mind. Schlesinger presented serious objections to the
invasion, but suppressed his doubts at team meetings.
Critical error.

Tiger broke off another piece of bacon, grinned when he
noticed everyone waiting on his next bit of information, then

continued.

"Now here's a *really* stupid mistake. The CIA knew that there were leaks of the coming invasion. The Soviets and Cubans were aware, yet the CIA did not tell Kennedy. Actually, a TS document shows that Castro heard of the invasion and arrested those suspected of disloyalty.

"Fidel Castro had four double-agents infiltrate the Brigade 2506 training camps. They easily got information out to Castro. Extremely poor screening by the CIA of trainees.

"All of those screw-ups I have stated so far *must* turn your stomach, but this next one sealed the fate of Brigade 2506—Kennedy's monumental error in judgment of cutting back the number of B-26 aircraft from 16 to 8, to bomb the three airfields of the Cuban Air Force. It was the *paramount reason* why the invasion failed—his paranoia with not letting the outside world think that the US was involved, but rather... only disgruntled Cuban exiles. An extreme case of naivety on Kennedy's part.

"From a democratic and rule of law standpoint, this was an illegal invasion of a sovereign nation. Kennedy betrayed the brigade with the lack of the support they expected. I mean, they fully expected US air support, Navy, and US marines following them up.

"Not to mention, Kennedy changed the original invasion site. From the Escambray Mountains to the Bay of Pigs. Thus, the exiles would not have the mountains to fade into. The Bay of Pigs landing had a rocky shore and swamp. The attacking force ran out of ammunition, food and water. They were sitting ducks—with no support.

"John Kennedy's naiveté was highlighted by his comment, *'There will not be, under any conditions, an intervention in Cuba by the United States armed forces'*. A total bold-faced lie.

"Four American pilots were shot down and killed in the attacks on Cuba's airfields. Kennedy cancelled the second air strike which frankly, caused the loss. When they heard of Kennedy's internal decision, Jack Hawkins, Chief of the CIA's planning staff, screamed, *'Goddamn it, this is criminal negligence'*; Jake Easterline, CIA Project Director, screamed, *'This is the Goddamnest thing I've ever heard of'*; and the American General in charge of the second air strike threw his cap on the ground, screaming, *'There goes the whole fuckin' war'*.

"As to Olivia's earlier point about dumping Kennedy... he even said, *'If this were a parliamentary government, I would have to resign...'*. This was so grossly negligent, that Kennedy should have been offered to seek employment elsewhere.

"Ike didn't like a socialist system so close to the United States... just 90 miles away. This started the whole thing. A bit overplayed maybe by Eisenhower. As Castro said, *'We have as much right to protest the existence of an imperialist and capitalist system ninety miles from our shore as he feels he has the right to protest over the existence of a socialist system ninety miles from his shore'*. It must be noted that Ike's original plan had envisioned both US air and naval support. But Kennedy, in his infinite wisdom, changed that. When later asked why the invasion failed, Castro responded with *'They had no air support'*. Tiger cleared his throat and took a swig of his drink.

"Micro-management by the White House and a stupid CIA plan led to this stomach-churning failure. JCS gave it a 30% probability of success. That's *not* very good. Makes me wonder why the chiefs, especially Lemnizer, didn't stand up to Kennedy. They should have been willing to fall on their sword!

"Okay, that's all I have, but there are so many errors that it would take up a roll of toilet paper to list them all. I have probably left out a hundred sub-mistakes because this was a total disaster from the very beginning."

"Fantastic job, Tiger," congratulated Lars. "I feel for the Brigade 2506 commander, Pepe San Roman. He expected the US Air Force and Navy support along with US marines to follow up. Total betrayal by Kennedy, who was obviously, out of his element. Roman graduated from their Military Academy and attended the Infantry course at Ft. Benning, Georgia. I think the severe letdown and negligence by the top of the US Government led to his suicide by taking an overdose in 1989.

"Think about this—his final message was, *'We are out of ammo and fighting on the beach. Please send help'*. And again, he pleaded, *'In water. Out of ammo. Enemy closing in. Help must arrive in next hour'*. Of course, it never came. They were either slaughtered or captured."

In a choked up voice, Doris declared, "One of the things that really gets to me emotionally is the violent death of Thomas Ray—called Pete. He was shot down in his B-26. He was one of four pilots from the Alabama Air National Guard that attacked the Cuban airfields. Pete escaped to a swampy area over two miles away, but he was tracked down and shot. Castro had Ray's body frozen and placed in a Havana morgue... for all to see. Basically a *war trophy* to show US involvement. He spent thousands of dollars preserving Ray's body. Finally, his corpse was returned to Birmingham, Alabama to his family—wife, two children, and mother, who never knew of his whereabouts for four decades." Doris broke down crying. Her voice gave out. Brenda put her arm around her, in comfort.

Olivia felt it was time to jump in. "To shift direction here... many people have never known how Brigade 2506 got its name. A brigade member, Carlos Rodriguez Santana, fell off a 6,000-foot cliff while training in Guatemala. The Cuban exiles named their unit, Brigade 2506 in honor of Rodriguez, whose dog tag number was 2506. Many members of the brigade were very young. In England, we call those that planned this perfect failure various names like *wankers, arseholes*, or *tossers*."

Brenda spoke next. "This whole thing makes you lose faith in your own government. Like Exercise Tiger... lies, conspiracies, withholding truths, and cover-ups. They lack integrity and morality."

"And compassion," remarked Tiger.

Lars then pointed out, "As a former military guy, and having served in the Joint Chiefs of Staff, I am disappointed in the failure of the JSC to accept a ridiculous CIA plan. It should have been aborted early on. Absolutely a half-baked plan, which could only lead to a downright fiasco, resulting in failure.

"You know it's wonderful to be optimistic and hopeful,

but this was so screwed up from day one, that it is inconceivable to me that this invasion plan was allowed to march forward. Frankly, I have an optimistic disposition, but it's also coupled with realism. This plan was just plain unrealistic."

"Oh," spouted Olivia, "Here's something I found out when reading the few hundred pages of the CIA top secret aftermath report. It seems that during the high point of the invasion, only one main person was at the CIA headquarters."

"Talk about complacency!" exclaimed Doris. "What about Allen Dulles? Kennedy forced him to resign, saying, *'I probably made a mistake keeping Allen Dulles'*."

"Want more on Allen Dulles?" asked Olivia. "Well, he had dozens of affairs while married to the same woman. Poor Clover Todd, his wife, had to suffer through it all. As a sort of serial adulterer, his sister said, *'He had at least a hundred'*. Sometimes I think this careless and reckless character trait carries over to the work ethic, including the mishandling of the Bay of Pigs. Sort of complacency with an *attitude*."

"Wow! What a discussion this time," remarked Lars. "This one took deep research. Lots of digging into many publicly unknown facts. Let me leave you all with something that Tiger and I know well. The planning for the invasion of Cuba violated all of the Army's 9 Principles of War—Objective, Offensive, Mass, Economy of Force, Maneuver, Unity of Command, Security, Surprise, and Simplicity. Again, my startling disappointment is in the JCS, who should have shot this plan down... before it even had a chance to gain momentum. Okay then, that said, next Friday Doris takes the lead on the sinking of the Lusitania."

"I volunteered to lead this blunder because I feel so deeply for the 1,197 people who lost their lives, of which were 31 babies and 94 children. I've uncovered several declassified top secret documents and reports that open up various schools of thought—was it justified, possible cover-ups, conspiracies, foul-ups, and other relatively unknown factors leading to the sinking. And Olivia, there are plenty of *wankers* involved in this one... I assure you." Doris chuckled.

"This is going to be another eye-opener!" Lars was excited as they all gave each other high-fives.

Painting depicting the 1915 sinking of the
Lusitania by the German U-Boat U 20

CHAPTER 15

Lusitania: Avoidable Tragic Sinking—Lies, Lies, And More Lies

Time out for a moment. Remember, each member of the Alpha Team studies every blunder they have agreed to cover. Their definition of a blunder is a series of careless mistakes and decisions that develop into a blunder, which is the cumulative effect of all the mistakes. Most of the general public have never heard of many of the hidden truths unearthed by extremely deep research conducted by the team. That's just a reminder for you. The team members feel that *the general public deserves the truth.*

Now, let's see what Doris says about the fateful voyage of the Greyhound of the Sea... the Lusitania, or Lucy. A terrible calamity.

As usual, the team are seated at table #98 in the Metro 29 diner. On time... Friday 8 a.m.

Squirming in her chair, Doris utters, "Let's be honest. The Lusitania was masquerading as a passenger liner. When in fact (which I dug out from top-secret documents), it was carrying 600 tons of explosives, six million pounds of ammunition, 1,248 cases of shrapnel shells, and more. That illegal cargo, unknown to the passengers, was destined for Great Britain to help them in their war efforts.

"Lucy left Pier 54 in New York, the Hudson River, on May 1st, 1915 heading for its Liverpool destination. Having been launched in 1907, this was to be its 207th trip. Passengers felt safe because they were traveling on the fastest ship on the seas with speeds over 25 knots... a safe feeling, since submarines could only go 8-10 knots.

"Now... get this! 1,198 of 1,959 passengers died; 94 were children, 35 out of 39 babies died, as well as 128 Americans.

Doris teared up, because she realized that several mothers died with their babies tightly held in their arms... facing 52° water temperature." Doris shuttered.

Olivia announced, "I know you are going to cover the mistakes, Doris, and I don't want to skip ahead... but many British ocean liners were used to haul illegal war munitions from day one, when Great Britain entered the war. All of these ships, including Lucy, made them legitimate targets for Germany. In my book, research led me to declare that Churchill should have been tried for war crimes. He was a war criminal which cost thousands of lives when you consider all of the merchant marine ships that were sunk. Sorry to interrupt your flow, but I had to get that out there."

"Very good point!" Doris replied. Continuing and wasting no time, she followed up with a blasting comment of her own. "How could the Lusitania, the fastest ocean liner, be sunk in only 18 minutes by just one torpedo? Think of her strengths—length 785 foot, depth 34 foot, gross tonnage 30,395 tons, four boiler rooms, four propeller shafts driving steam turbines with a total power of 68,000 horsepower, and designed speed of 25 knots, yet she did attain 25.88 knots. The rudder weighed 56 tons. Everyone felt that Big Lucy, Lucy or Lusi—nicknames she was called, *(I prefer Lucy)* was unsinkable."

"To be sunk in 18 minutes with the loss of life of 1,198 passengers seems so remote," barked Tiger.

Doris wipes her eyes with her napkin before continuing. "I've uncovered more lies, than you could ever imagine— shadowy groups, silent conspiracies, cover-ups as well as extreme misrepresentations. My research included archives, top secret and classified documents, copies of interviews with survivors, along with journals, books, and other mostly unknown reports. When pieced together these tell the tale. I was able to connect the dots and it is alarming!

"First, in order to do it right by describing the screw-ups made, I have to cover it in two parts. The research has been difficult because many writers and researchers have brought forth different numbers in regards to the number of deaths and amount of contraband. I have investigated this in great detail and I believe my numbers are correct.

"However, as FDR once said, *'It is better to light one small candle in a dark room than to live forever in the dark'*. So this report on Lucy is my small *candle of truths* for you to absorb. As I go on, it will become a candle with a monstrous flame."

Lars butts in. "You know, Doris, this reminds me of what I used to tell my students at GWU. When reading a bad book there is a tendency to turn the pages quickly, or *speed-read* it. In this book, that Brenda is putting together for us, covering all the blunders, we have to turn the pages slowly, allowing for absorption of the truths. Sort of like osmosis, letting it seep into the insides of our human make-up... our whole body. And while putting all the pieces of the information together, it is easy to see that without our research, the general public probably would never know most of the facts leading to these disastrous tragedies."

"Wow! Another gem of wisdom from the professor. Super point, Doc!" exclaimed Tiger with vigor. He smashes his first into his palm. *"HOOAH!" Typical Army Ranger!*

Doris explains: "Here's what I mean by two parts. Part I covers the mistakes made that caused the sinking. Part II covers the mistakes made in regards to the unbearable loss of lives. These are two separate entities *never covered this way before.*

"You just have to separate the two. By the way, I may repeat some as I go along, so please bear with me.

"Part I—main points causing the sinking:

- Failure to provide destroyer escorts. Everyone on board, including Captain Turner, were counting on Royal Navy escorts.
- Not adhering to, or taking serious enough, the Germany Embassy warning that the Lusitania will be traveling in a war zone. The well-publicized notice, verbatim: *NOTICE! TRAVELLERS intending to embark on the Atlantic voyage are reminded that a state of war exists between Germany and her allies and Great Britain and her allies; that the zone of war*

includes the waters adjacent to the British Isles; that, in accordance with formal notice given by the Imperial German Government , vessels flying the flag of Great Britain, or any of her allies, are liable to destruction in those waters and that travelers sailing in the war zone on the ships of Great Britain or her allies do so at their own risk.

IMPERIAL GERMAN EMBASSY
Washington, D.C. 22 April 1915

- Furthermore, an earlier warning and statement of policy was issued by Admiral Hugo von Pohl, commander of the German High Seas Fleet. It was published in the Deutscher Reichsanzeiger, the Imperial German Gazette, on 4 February 1915: *(1) The waters around Great Britain and Ireland; including the whole of the English Channel, are hereby to be declared a war zone. From February 18 onwards every enemy merchant vessel encountered in this zone will be destroyed, nor will it always be possible to avert the danger thereby threatened to the crew and passengers. (2) Neutral vessels also will run a risk in the War Zone, because in view of the hazards of sea warfare and the British authorization of January 31 of the misuse of neutral flags, it may not always be possible to prevent attacks on enemy ships from harming neutral ships;*

- Not listening to Captain Daniel Dow, Lucy's regular captain, who stated that the ship should not be an armed merchant cruiser... target for German submarines. He resigned as skipper and was replaced by Bill Turner;

- Cunard Lines for shutting down one of Lucy's four boiler rooms, reducing her speed to 21 knots instead of 25.5 knots, to save money. Huge error because that actually caused the ship to be torpedoed."

Tiger butts in. "They were greedy bastards... at Cunard. Oops, sorry."

Doris grinned, continuing with her points.

- Room 40, the Brits top secret intelligence group... not informing Turner of sub activity, especially of U-20, the sub that fired the torpedo that sank the Lusitania. Room 40 was tracking U-20's every movement. Almost every two hours. Turner reduced speed to 15 knots so he could reach Liverpool at high tide. That cost him the ballgame. He was heading straight towards U-20 and those in Room 40 were sitting on their hands... doing nothing. So, failure to be at high speed and maintain a zigzag course;
- Failure to avoid War Zone by taking a northern route. No effort by Admiralty to divert Lucy's course or to provide escorts as it did for other ships. Passengers were told from the very beginning of the voyage that there would be escorts... a normal routine. Admiralty allowed all other ships to sail the north channel over Ireland, then south to Liverpool, avoiding the War Zone. Dangerous western route—not communicated to Turner. I would fire Churchill on the spot. Five destroyers in the area, but they were called back.

Found out this info from a buried, top-secret message the Brits didn't want released;

- Three attacks in last 24 hours on the Centurion, Candidate, Earl of Latham in the waters Lucy was heading into. Again, Captain Turner was not informed;

- Maybe a conspiracy. King George V met with Colonel House, Wilson's assistant, at Buckingham Palace. The King said, *'Suppose they should sink the Lusitania with American passengers aboard';*

- Failure by Turner to full-turn to dodge the torpedo, or reverse the turbine causing Lucy to slow... missing the torpedo;

- Best route not used—head along west coast of Ireland, cut in north channel to St. George's channel to Liverpool. Again, there were actually *five* destroyers available to attack U-20 and escort Lucy. Room 40 sat on their hands and did nothing. They were amateurs— university professors, naval schoolmasters, stockbrokers, bankers, clergymen, who worked in the cryptanalysis section as code breakers;

- Radio exchanges between Lucy and the Admiralty, 5th-7th of May, are still hidden... above top secret. I couldn't uncover it and nobody else has so far. There is a clue in that. A dark ugly secret and the lies run so deep that it's tough to dig them all up.

"It's all very disappointing. Admiralty, Room 40, knew exactly where U-20 was located on May 7, and that Lucy was heading straight for it. What was wrong with those guys?"

"They were duds!" shrieked Tiger. The other diners in Metro 29 turned around and stared over at their table. "In battle, you can't let anyone down. Mon Dieu!"

Lars echoed with an *Amen*. Others nodded in the affirmative.

Doris continued. "Wait, there's more! Churchill called the Lusitania *live bait*. Shows the Brit attitude. And get this—23 Brit merchant marine ships had been sunk in the preceding seven days in the War Zone area. The overall picture is this—British hunger blockade of shipments to Germany caused the Germans to establish an unrestricted campaign of submarine warfare.

"To me, the Brits were responsible for all of this. Also, they had all three of Germany's main codes: SKM—Signalbuch der Kaiserlichen, HVB—Handelsverkehrsbuch, and VB—Verkehrsbuch.

"For one, Lucy was too close to the shoreline. More blame on Churchill—he commented to Walter Runciman, President of the Board of trade, that *'it is most important to attract neutral shipping to our shores in the hope of especially of embroiling the USA with Germany'*.

"A year after the sinking the Kaiser told Ambassador Gerald in Berlin that, *'England was really responsible as the English had made the Lusitania go slowly in English waters so that the Germans could torpedo it and bring on trouble'*.

"Churchill did not pass on information from Room 40, which would have avoided this terrible tragedy. Room 40 cover-up. Lies and more lies... not acting on encoded top-secret information. The Brits might as well have aimed U-

20's torpedoes themselves. Frankly, the Admiralty took no precautions to protect Lucy.

"Turner was ordered to slow to 15 knots. Then he increased it to 18 on his own—still well below maximum speed. Of course, you want to max out going through the War Zone. Duh! This was at 10 a.m. The torpedo hit at 2:10 p.m."

Shaking her head, Olivia added, "In my study of Churchill, I discovered that he was sort of a sociopath. The callousness of his actions, or inactions, coupled with his cold and bitter pragmatism is disgusting. Let's face it—he wanted an attack on a ship with Americans on board to draw the US into the war. There was no way Britain could win without the US. In about six month, it would have been all over for them. That was the Germans belief."

Doris nodded and said, "Subs make about 8-9 knots. With four boilers running Lucy could make 25 knots. No way to catch her. Failure to use all four boilers. Cunard's big mistake. Shame on them!

"And Juno, the escort battleship, was recalled to port. A repeat, but the Germans did place newspaper ads in 50 newspapers across the US... *not* to travel on the Lusitania."

"Let me share some information that I discovered in researching for my book," said Olivia.

"Hey, let's hear it!" Tiger cheered her on.

Olivia grinned. "This is the key to the loading of contraband on Lucy. Greed. The *Secret Elite,* a group of immensely wealthy, upper class, prominent British men, formed a secret elite society. They had weapons deals with the US. They wanted the entire world to be under control of the British Empire. The society was led by Alfred Milner, a power broker. Their motto? Get this! *'End Justifies the Means'*.

"They were the framers of the illegal trade using merchant ships and passenger ships. Very powerful. All tried to cover-up this information, saying the second explosion was due to another torpedo hit. A bold-faced lie. They were evil men. Great Britain and the US pursued greater profit from human loss. Pardon my French, but they didn't give a crap! Churchill was part of this. From this he coined the phrase *live bait*."

"These guys are rotting in hell," said Brenda. "Right, Lars?"

"Yup."

"They should have been buried in a potter's field; undeserving of a traditional burial," bellowed Tiger.

Doris took a swig of her tea, adding, "This ends Part I. Now for Part II. Before we start, I must say that this research has boggled my mind because of its horrific impact on thousands of people. I mean, the poor victims dying a terrible death; survivors, families of all of those who died, survived and... about 600 of them missing." Doris groans.

"Now Part II—main points causing all the deaths:

- Bulkhead design, starboard side, was deficient, allowing Lucy to sink quicker. It sunk in 18 minutes. Torpedo hit on starboard side... a hole 20 foot long by 10 foot high. The most vulnerable spot on Lucy. By comparison, the *Titanic* sunk in 160 minutes. But that was a different ballgame;

- More than 70 portholes were left open. Many portholes burst due to air pressure. Seawater rushed in. An open porthole could omit water at 1,200 tons per minute;
- British Navy dispatched a cruiser from nearby Queenstown to rescue, but it was recalled. The worst part was those near drowning *saw* that ship leave in total disbelief. Very sad. Uncalled for and cowardly. I can never forgive the snobbish Brits for not rescuing the passengers;
- Torpedo struck; 15 seconds later a second, an even more powerful explosion occurred. Not a torpedo. This caused even more loss of lives and it also accounted for the fast sinking. Probably due to an exploding boiler coupled with some of the explosive powder and munitions stored... for Great Britain;
- They had the latest in life jackets, the Boddy, but there were no drills or exercises to have passengers to fit them on properly. Cunard Lines had no policy to have passengers try on lifejackets. Most put them on wrong being in a panic mode, which caused them to drown;
- Lucy had 48 lifeboats, could seat 2,605 passengers. Crew were inexperienced in manning lifeboats. Green sailors. Some of the crew had already died. The ship was listing, about 30°, so severely that lifeboats were not easily dropped into the sea. Some were never launched. To effectively drop lifeboats the ship needed to be stopped. However, it continued at 5 knots causing total disarray. Turner refused to have

lifeboat drills because it might cause panic or worry... spook the passengers. 26 collapsible lifeboats were piled on deck and bolted down. They were supposed to be free;

- The torpedo fired was state-of-the-art—two foot long, 350 pounds of TNT and Hexanite, an explosive called the G6. Schwieger, the U-20's captain, fired it at a depth of 3 meters. Starboard side. Perfect shot;
- Some of the passengers didn't know how to swim so without lifeboat training or lifejacket training, they didn't stand a chance;
- Absolutely no rescue attempts by other Brit ships to save passengers. They simply let everyone die;
- Many crewmen could not help passengers—trapped below decks, electric elevators failed, plus some killed outright;
- Passengers struggled for hours in the 52° water, drowning; others going down to the depths of the sea holding on tightly to their babies. There were many heroes, saving others... yet drowning themselves in the selfless display of courage... both men and women. God bless them all;
- Half of the lifeboats were unusable. The other half slung out 60 foot above the sea and 8 to 10 feet out from the hull. It scared people, so most just jumped or stayed on the decks;
- Again, no destroyer rescue. Yet the Lucifer, Legion, and Laverock, all destroyers, were idle at Milford Haven, Wales... available but never sent;
- Ship could not be steadied. Did not respond to the

wheel. Steam pressure collapsed from 195 psi to 50 psi. A drastic drop and still falling;

- Lifeboats overturned. Only 6 were launched successfully. People were spilled into the sea. Others crushed by lifeboats falling onto the decks. Some lifeboats overturned. One lifeboat, #14, sank with 11 people on board because the boat plug was not in place. Seriously?

"That ends Part II. So much could have been done to save the passengers. I feel that with just some organized concerted effort, that of the 1,198 that perished, about 1,000 could have been saved if rescued within about two hours after the sinking. That would raise the survivor level from 767 to 1,767. They could have lasted about two hours or more in the 52° seawater temperature. This is based on the fact that people become unconscious after about 15 minutes in 32° water, surviving for 45 minutes. Then hypothermia really sets in.

"Certainly, rescues could have been made within two hours *easily*, but nobody gave a damn! Don't those people have a conscience? The answer is obviously NO! Now, I asked Olivia and Brenda to research other points rather than mistakes made, which was *my* mission. Olivia, wanta' start?"

"Sure. Here are a few that are mind boggling and very upsetting; not in any order. Some may nauseate you due to the lack of concern and poor judgments made.

"It was standard British practice to sail on the basis of false, disguised manifests such as crates of weapons marked sewing machines, ammunition marked as furs, and so on. Exports of munitions from the US to Britain was blatant.

"The Tory party leaders removed Churchill from the Admiralty. But as you said, he should have been fired earlier and sent to prison for war crimes. Such as illegally transporting war munitions via passenger liners.

"Another interesting point is that Kapitanleutnant Walther Schwiegler, 30 years old, U-40's Commander with orders to *attack* transport ships, merchant ships, and warships. U-20, U-27 and U-30 were a *third U-boat half Flotilla.* U-29 was to cover approaches to Liverpool. All of Schwieger's messages were intercepted and decoded by Room 40. Room 40, as you know from Doris, had all three of Germany's main codes." She sighed.

"I'll carry on from here," said Brenda. "To add to Doris's report on the second explosion, it could have been the 250,000 pounds of tetrachloride destined for France to use to make gas bombs. Schwieger saw the second explosion— much bigger than the first. Gunpowder can explode when in contact with seawater.

"It appears to me that the Admiralty deliberately ordered the Lusitania into the direct path of U-20. This would be a way of getting the Americans into the war. As Doris said, they would have lost the war without America's help.

"And this might be interesting. It was tough to find. Lusitania's roster of passengers—949 British, 189 Americans, 71 Russians, 15 Persians, 8 French, 6 Greeks, 5 from Sweden, 3 Belgians, 3 Dutch, 2 Italians, 2 Mexicans, 2 Finns, and one from each: Denmark, Spain, Argentina, Switzerland, Norway, and India.

"All of those that worked in Room 40 should have been stalked by shadows and ghosts of their poor, inefficient doings. President Wilson was worthless. His wife died and he became distracted, or rather obsessed, with Edith Gant, who he was infatuated with to the nth degree; in deep depression over Galt's refusal to marry him. Schwieger wrote in his diary, *'that the ship was not sent through the north channel is inexplicable'.*"

Olivia jumped in. "Bodies were floating everywhere. Sea gulls were plucking the eyes out and tearing off ears of floating bodies. Fish were taking chunks out of the flesh. For a long time, bodies were washed ashore. One woman was missing both arms and legs. Infants torn apart. All mostly due to the predators of the sea.

"Just think of it—600 missing; never found, one of which was none other than Alfred Vanderbilt. Just imagine the emotional drain on their families! I'm sure the *Secret Elite* thought nothing of this, though. The photos of corpses in the morgue are horrifying. Some still dressed in their Sunday best expecting to land at Liverpool.

"Instead of declaring war in April, 1917, we should have done it in May 1915. We were two years late. Pardon my boldness here, but Wilson had no balls.

"The Brits had an incredible propaganda campaign underway, consisting of evidence that was manipulated, falsified or concealed. They did anything to cover-up the truths. But as you have heard, Doris has uncovered many of the truths.

"William Jennings Bryan, Wilson's Secretary of State, resigned, saying, *'Why should Americans travel on belligerent ships with cargoes of ammunition. Passengers and ammunition should not travel together'.* They all should have listened to Bryan's common sense message. And of course, everyone should have paid attention to the German warnings.

"Woodrow Wilson, not in his right mind, said, *'There is such a thing as a man being too proud to fight. There is such a thing as a nation being so right that it does not need to convince others by force that it is right'.* He said this in Philadelphia on May 10, 1915. The six words— *'We are too proud to fight'*—rang around the world, shocking everyone.

"And Doris covered this, but the launching of the lifeboats was total chaos. Schwieger lowered his periscope because he couldn't watch it any longer. And he didn't allow his crewmembers to view it. To him, it was frightful. Bodies were floating all over the Irish Sea. Only 289 bodies were recovered and 65 of those never identified; 885 souls were never recovered. My God! Please take over, Brenda. It's all just too upsetting."

"To continue, following Olivia's great points, Schwieger gave the order to fire the deadly torpedo. Charles Voegele, his quartermaster, refused to pass on the order to the torpedo room. He didn't want to be part of an attack on women and children. And for that he was court-martialed and put in prison at Kiel until the war ended.

"Germany was unconcerned about Wilson's earlier response to Germany. There was no US response to the sinking of a Brit passenger ship, the SS Franklin, off southern Ireland on March 25, 1915, though an American engineer was amongst the dead." She threw her hands in the air.

"Let me say a bit about the ridiculous Brit Navy policies," said Tiger. "The standard policy was to not rescue victims of a submarine attack. It would put rescue ships at risk—getting too close to a sunken ship. What a *candy ass* policy. Could you imagine us, as Army Rangers, Doc... leaving a comrade? Never happen, Bro."

"Right on, Tiger," agreed Lars. He patted Tiger's shoulder.

Brenda continued. "Evidence is clear that Churchill was responsible for the sinking of Lucy. I'm convinced. He purposely suppressed critical information. As mentioned, he was a cold pragmatist, sort of evil. Quite disturbing, even to sociopaths."

"Think about this," cut in Lars. "FDR lured the Japanese into attacking Pearl Harbor so that the US would be brought into the war. Similarly, the Lusitania appears to also be a set-up to draw the US into the war.

"Many mothers struggled in the icy water for hours holding up their infants. When lifting them into lifeboats, the children were already dead. One woman in a lifeboat said *'Let me bury my baby'*, and then let the baby float away in a burial at sea. There were so many infants floating around dead, *like lily pads on a pond.* Many bodies were damaged beyond recognition... creatures of the sea got them... fish, turtles, sharks, sea gulls... some recognizable only by pieces of fabric from their clothes; faces were eaten away, all flesh gone on many of the bodies.

"As stated earlier, why should the final two days of radio communication between Turner and the Admiralty remain classified to this day? Something smells. I tried to uncover it along with Doris, but to no avail. Obviously, it covers the wealthy criminals.

"There were many heroes, like the men who gave up their lifejackets to women and children. One great story of many is that of Elizabeth Duckworth. She saw a man in the water about to drown. She told everyone to stop rowing in order to pick him up. A sailor said *'no'*. She said, *'Yes, we can'*. They pulled the man to safety. Later, the lifeboat they were in was rescued by a fishing vessel.

"Another lifeboat passed by asking the vessel's captain to help rescue others. He refused. Duckworth said, *'You can spare me'* and jumped into the lifeboat. They saved 40 others. There were plenty of unsung heroes and heroines that we cannot forget.

"Britain imported 2/3 of its food. So Germany's submarine campaign aimed at interdicting supplies and weapons put them in a world of hurt."

"To me," said Doris, "this whole horrible disaster was caused by people who were just plain... inhumane. It was a reprehensible thing, absurd and a total macabre."

"Can I add a few words to what I feel about it?" Olivia asked.

"Sure, go ahead," Doris replied.

"A few words—frightening, unearthly, sickening, repugnant, horrific, and repulsive... Now I'm out of words. Carry on."

"Thanks Brenda and Olivia. That was real good stuff. The lies, misrepresentations, and cover-ups about Lucy's sinking have been accepted through the years as truths. But I have uncovered many *hidden facts* that bring forth the real genuine truths. I shouldn't say I, because all of us were part of this. I got a lot of help from you all," Doris said with gratitude.

Lars, choked up, jaw tight, said, "In regards to all the merchant ships and passenger liners sunk by German subs, I think of all the crewmen who were killed outright or drowned because no one attempted to rescue them. The Admiralty should love their sailors and work hard to care for and protect them. This thinking was nowhere in sight at the Admiralty and Room 40. Just remember, if nobody loves us, we cease to exist. And if we don't love our crews and our ships then we are like evil beings."

"Ladies, that was said by a true leader... our Doc." Tiger grinned with pride. "Doc, what would you have done if you had been Lucy's skipper?"

"Huh... well, to be honest, here is what I would have done. But remember I'm not a Navy puke. On the first day I would have had life jacket drills and lifeboats assigned and rigged—ready to go with emphasis on passengers being fitted correctly. Two days later I would have had a repeat exercise. You never know what can happen.

"Without a doubt, I would have taken the northern route and asked for escorts. I would request confirmation and communicated with escort destroyers' captains. That would have avoided the sinking. And if hit, passengers and crew would be ready. During the drills, it would have been found that some lifeboats were stuck in the paint. Knowledge is a valuable virtue. The crew would be more alert and capable of handling the lifeboats and the passengers, in a mannerly fashion—not chaos and total ignorance. Emergencies happen!"

"Just like basic Ranger tactics, huh!" grinned Tiger.

"10-4. OK then, this was a job well done. A tough one. Two thumbs up," said Lars as he and the others raised their thumbs.

"Next week we'll explore scientific blunders. I'll take the lead, along with Tiger. Carpe Diem!"

On the way out Doris told Olivia that she felt like she lost ten pounds during this emotional research work.

"You don't need to lose any weight!" Olivia scoffed, eyeballing the dessert table on the way out. *But I sure could.* She sighed.

Challenger Montage of several stages of the shuttle's preparation, flight, and explosion

CHAPTER 16

Failure To Stop The Challenger Launch

"Glad we could meet here at Bistro 29 for an early Monday morning lunch. Being here at 11:30 a.m. gives us a jump on the noon crowd," said Lars. "I need to get your advice on the scientific blunders we are covering this Friday. I have the lead with Tiger backing me up." Lars twists in his chair.

Everyone ordered the Cornmeal Crusted Oysters as an appetizer. They've been wanting to try them ever since Tiger said they are *'to kill for!'* Doris got the house Greek Salad. Brenda ordered the Mango Chicken with Fried Brie; Lars—Lamb; Tiger—Chicken Shawarma sandwich and Olivia—the Crab Cake sandwich. Later, they all got the homemade Cheesecake as dessert.

After a few sips of his iced tea, Lars kicked it off. "Here's my take—there were many screw ups. I'll cover these and Tiger will provide other sidebar information; sort of like what Doris did with Olivia and Brenda on the

Lusitania Blunder. Some examples I'll cover are the cause of the external tank explosion, why the Challenger exploded only 73 seconds after blast off, and human flaws which led to the decisions to launch under duress weather conditions. Sound OK?"

All agreed that it was a good approach. Tiger changes the subject to the Washington Nationals, complaining about the sorry bullpen. A little more chatter and they all left Bistro 29, heading to the National Archives together via the Ballston Mall Metro. An in-depth research quest as usual.

Forward to Friday... a nice day. All seated at table #98. Tiger is cramming down his pancakes.

Lars wastes no time. "I'll cover misjudgments, but frankly my intense research leads me back to Christina McAuliffe's father's view about the disaster. He hit the nail on the head. Ed McAuliffe wrote in his journal, *'Christa did not die for NASA or the Space Program. She died because of NASA and its egos, marginal decisions, ignorance, and irresponsibility. NASA betrayed seven fine people who deserved to live'.*

"I'll elaborate a little. A few days before the launch, Ed told his wife, Corrigan, *'You know if I could, I'd go and take her off of that'.* Just before the accident, Corrigan began to cry. Both had an unsafe feeling about the launch. Sort of a *gut feeling* or *sixth sense.*"

Lars sat up straight, rolled up his polo shirt and started out with a strong, rather upset demeanor. "Let me list some of the mistakes. Believe me gang, there are many. Talk about real eye-openers!

"This may surprise you, but NASA suffered from

groupthink. The launch had to keep on schedule, with their regular and reliable launcher *(Challenger),* regardless of the known risks. It was like a hung jury where you are guilty until proven innocent.

"It could also be that President Reagan was to deliver the State of the Union address that very evening. Of course, he would brag about the Challenger. Bottom line—financial and political concerns sort of glued NASA's thinking together to launch.

"Bob Ebeling was a Morton Thiokol contractor for NASA. Ebeling, an engineer, and four other engineers tried to stop the launch the night before. Their own managers and NASA disagreed. NASA should have listened to them. But *groupthink* had set in at NASA; rather delusional I might say.

"An engineer's language brings with it an identity. NASA's staff had a different language, instead of a shared language, which would show we are the same. Not stuck in a *groupthink* inefficient way of conducting business. A different language indicates we are different."

"That's another gem of wisdom from our Professor," uttered Tiger. He slapped his thigh.

Lars continued. "You know, here is something most people don't know. Off track a little bit here, but those in the Army branches think differently... Infantry, Artillery, Armor, Engineers—all 17 branches think and have a language all their own. Frankly, the Army, Navy, Air Force and Marines all think differently. Maybe this clears up what I'm trying to say; in reference to all the *groupthinking* remarks."

"Very true," said Tiger. "Also, not to get too far off base, I'll tell you something else that is very true. The non-commissioned officers and lower ranked Army officers know the solution to whatever they are faced with... the simple ways.

"It's the politicians and generals who drag it out and muck it up. Same thing here, gang. The engineers are in the foxholes, so to speak, and those at the higher levels just don't get it!"

"Now," Lars continued, "Back to my points about critical, unnecessary slip-ups and faults. Get this—NASA managers had known since 1977 that there was a flaw in the O-rings. They failed to report concerns to superiors."

"That is totally unacceptable. You know who does stuff like that? Idiots, morons... and clods," adds Doris.

Lars rolls on. "The O-rings had never been tested below 32°. Thiokol, NASA's contractor, recommended a minimum launch temperature of 57°. At launch time it was 28.9°. This caused the right solid rocket booster's O-ring seal to fail."

"My God, Lars... they should've delayed the launch based on that alone," injected Olivia. "In the UK we call these guys *tossers*; in plain English that means jerk-offs!"

Lars nods his head in agreement. "So a big error was the failure of Thiokol engineers to firmly convince Thiokol managers and NASA officials of the risk and delay the launch. Their presentation was not sharp and clear.

"NASA engineer Ebeling tried to stop the launch during a teleconference with NASA engineers and managers the night before. In regards to the launch, he said, *'I was absolutely sure, just as sure as death'*.

Challenger Crew, November 15, 1985

Back row: Ellison S. Onizuka, Sharon Christa McAuliffe, Greg Jarvis, Judy Resnik; Front row: Michael J. Smith, Dick Scobee, Ron McNair

"Boisjoly, an O-ring specialist engineer at Morton Thiokol, along with his group of engineers, *also* wanted to stop the launch. It was a no-brainer for them. But their NASA counterparts refused. This gets us back to the mindset differences. Closed thinking on the part of NASA. Very disappointing. Here's something that most people have never thought about... Thiokol was worried that NASA might change contractors, embarrassed by earlier postponements, and excited that Reagan would mention a successful launch during his State of the Union address.

"During that teleconferencing, Bob Lund, Thiokol's VP of Engineering, said, *'I don't want to fly until the temperature reaches 53°'.* NASA challenges them with *'quantify your claim'.*

"They did not think *for one moment* about the safety of the seven crewmembers. Thiokol battled back... *'We can't prove it will fail, but the risk is not worth a launch'.*"

"Not to interrupt your flow, Lars, but, my gracious, that alone was enough to scrub the launch! I think NASA's managers were short-sighted," cut in Brenda. "In my research, I found that at 1:30 a.m. icicles were growing—temperature was down to 29°. Icicles were two feet long on the Shuttle's upper level and on the crews' emergency escape path. The temperature kept dropping, down to 27°—and ice all over the place."

Everyone's attention was intent as Lars continues. "The O-rings failed due to faulty design. O-rings were supposed to seal a joint on the right solid rocket booster, as I mentioned before. It failed, which allowed pressurized hot gases to skirt by the O-ring, making contact with the external tank causing structural failure. By the way, the joint needed to be redesigned, but nobody did anything about it beforehand.

"Just a reminder, the O-rings are like giant washers that keep extremely hot gases from escaping. NASA had an unrealistic, overly optimistic launch schedule to adhere to. This caused their *unsafe culture* to overtake good common sense. Their motto might have been, *Launch or Lose the Budget.* I mean all launches … not just the Challenger.

"Another error to add to these I've already covered—there was no escape system for crew! NASA, in its infinite wisdom, felt that the high reliability of the Shuttle, since 1977, precluded the need.

"Faulty design of the booster joints and O-rings. NASA refused to recognize it as a problem, therefore failing to fix it. They chose to accept it as an *acceptable* flight risk."

"Mon Dieu, Doc, these guys must have been chugging margaritas." Tiger scratches his earlobe. (Remember, it was nicked by a 7.62 round from a Viet Cong's AK-47. The bottom part of lobe is missing).

Lars continues. "The Challenger sat poised with no shelter or walls surrounding it on Pad 39B. Nothing to block the Arctic wind. Nobody paid sincere attention to the National Weather Service Bulletin—*Temperatures may approach all time record lows... this could be a major freeze. All possible precautions should be taken...*"

"Good Lord, that would be enough for me, right there," said Doris. Her face was flushed red like an Ocean City sunset.

"OK team," Lars continued, "here is my last point. The launch decision is an engineering decision, not a program management decision. NASA caused this colossal blunder, thinking that they would look bad—several delays and 15 flights scheduled for the years to come. Political and financial considerations exceeded safety contemplation. That's the bottom line if you want to look at this one honestly. Their leadership was frightful. They didn't face the terrible truths. To this day, they have to be haunted by those seven crew members who trusted their own safety to NASA."

"I might add, Doc," said Tiger, "that NASA felt that the Challenger was an infallible rig. The Shuttle had completed nine missions during three years of service. That comes to

62 days, 7 hours, 56 minutes, 22 seconds in space. The 10th launch, as we know, exploded 73 seconds after launch on January 28, 1986. It had 5 delays."

Doris jumped in. "Ed McAuliffe was right. These seven people deserved to live. They were in the prime of their lives. McNair was only 36 years old, Resnik—37, McAuliffe—38, Onizuka—40, Smith—41, Jarvis—41, and Scobee—47. Christa McAuliffe was picked from 11,400 teacher applicants." She wipes tears streaming down her face as she finishes; they were so young! All eyes were filled with sadness.

Lars choked up. "We can never, ever forget these seven astronauts. They will live forever in the hearts of our American citizens." He squirms a little in his chair, taking a gulp of coffee. "Now... Tiger has some interesting, yet gruesome details which we should know about. Tiger, you're up!"

"Thanks, Doc. A lot of people want to know what happened to the crew. Here's my best take—the bodies of the astronauts were in a *semi-liquefied state that bore little resemblance to anything living.* One diver found a helmet with ears and a scalp in it. Jarvis's body floated out of the crew's compartment and was lost. Mind you, the water was murky. Sometimes rescuers could only see up to five feet. On April 15th, Navy divers found Jarvis's body, on the sea floor at 101.2 feet deep, about 0.8 miles from the crew compartment."

Doris relayed, "A report stated that there are still body parts and pieces of the Shuttle stuck in the muck of the Atlantic Ocean's floor."

"Although it was different, it is the sort of the same for the crew of the Columbia Shuttle," said Olivia. "It exploded on reentry due to a chunk of foam insulation that that fell from a bipod ramp causing a hole. This allowed hot gases inside the wing to escape. But, like the Challenger, rescue teams searched for weeks. Because the crew compartment imploded, crushing the crewmembers, body parts were scattered over farmlands, near northeastern Texas. Searchers found hands, feet, thighbones, a skull with front teeth, charred leg and torso, fragments of bodies 2 to 2-1/2 feet long. And like the Challenger, body parts are still being found today over that wide area.

Doris added, "I know we are discussing the Challenger, but also NASA's dismissive ignorance prevailed here too, since they had previous experiences with foam pieces falling apart."

Lars stated, "The terrible deaths, as detailed, even more affects our resentment of the completely preventable mistakes that caused this disaster. This was a tough mission... for us to research, in-depth, the Challenger Blunder. It's sad, but I must say that everyone did a fantastic job on this one. I'd like to close this blunder out by saying a prayer for the Challenger crew."

Lars, choked up somewhat as the team bowed their heads. *"Eternal rest grant unto them, O Lord, and let perpetual light shine upon them. May the souls of these faithful departed crewmembers, through God's mercy, rest in peace."*

All said, *"Amen."*

"By the way," Tiger murmured, "Lars and I visited the gravesite of the cremated remains of all seven astronauts buried at Arlington National Cemetery, Section 46, Grave 1129. A solemn moment for us."

"We'll exchange emails on what blunder we will cover next Friday." Lars stood and all give high-fives. On their way out, Tiger winks at Anita. This time... he gets a return wink.

Photograph of men in a boat salvaging wreckage of the collapsed Tay Bridge with other men standing on the harbor in the background

CHAPTER 17

The Tay Bridge Collapse—1879

Over the past six months, the Alpha Team researched over a hundred scientific/engineering blunders, which not only included mistakes, but also accidents. Their purpose was to agree on six for blunder discussions, running a series of scientific/engineering blunders in a row. During a team meeting that kicked off the research project, team leader Lars covered a few key points so everyone has the same frame of reference.

Some of his points were: (1) We are not looking for accidents or mistakes, but rather blunders that occurred due to underestimations, carelessness, negligence, insufficient knowledge, miscalculations, biased opinions, unit conversion mix-ups, measuring mistakes, math errors, naïve assumptions, arrogance, or *groupthink*. Also, avoidance of warning signs, oversights, and political and financial concerns; (2) The fields of science and engineering have moved forward via trial and error and have created incredible achievements in the history of the world. Big breakthroughs sometimes require big risks, which may result in big failures; and (3) Scientific trials and errors in the lab are not really harmful. But we are looking for blunders that have been harmful and caused by a multitude of errors and mistakes, of which the cumulative effect caused a blunder, as we know it. Like the Tay Bridge Collapse, which Olivia has chosen to cover for us since she is from Great Britain. The Tay Bridge is in Scotland.

Out of the 100+ researched, the team decided on the following, in the priority order of presentation at the Metro 29 breakfast sessions: Olivia—Tay Bridge Collapse; Doris—Piltdown Chicken; Lars—Mars Climate Orbiter; Tiger—Hubble Space Telescope; Brenda—Cold Fusion and Lars—Chernobyl.

Lars will bring in Alexei Semenov and Ivan Vasiliev, both born in Russia, to discuss that one. But some were actually accidents. He recognizes that other blunders could have been chosen, but some were actually mistakes. For example, the Hindenburg explosion was an accident caused by a buildup of static electricity on the airship. The spark ignited hydrogen on the outer skin. An accident.

Again, it could have been chosen, but along with about 100 others it was determined not to be a blunder, which is a series of mistakes and errors leading to and causing an avoidable disaster. However, that does not degrade the importance of the Hindenburg explosion. After all, 37 people were killed. May 6, 1937 was a frightful day.

The bottom line is the team researched over 100. Here are just a few: Mars Meltdown, MTBE *(Methyl Tertiary*

Butyl Ether), French Railway Error, Hoyle's Big Bang, Darwin's Notion of Heredity, Kelvin's Earth Age Estimate, Pauling's Triple Helix, Einstein's Cosmological Constant, Crash of NASA's Genesis Probe, N-Rays, Hindenburg Catastrophe, Collapse of the Quebec Bridge, Space Shuttle Columbia Disaster, Charles de Gaulle Airport Collapse, Bhopal Disaster, Apollo 1 and Apollo 13 Disasters, Gimli Glider, VASA Warship, Banqiao Dam Failure, Cleveland East Ohio Gas Explosion, Collapse of Tacoma Narrows Bridge, Skylab Disaster, Gretna Rail Disaster, St. Francis Dam Disaster, The Debendox Debacle, plus many others. It was a tough group decision to narrow it all down to six.

Friday morning... the team is all seated at Metro 29; breakfasts ordered, and Olivia gets right to it. "These blokes had their heads up their *arses*! I'll tell you that."

Everyone smirks and she continues.

"First, you must know that this bridge was the icon of Scotland. The longest bridge in the world. Scots were very proud of it, to include Queen Victoria, who traveled on it once. It carried the railway across the Firth of Tay between Dundee and Wormit.

"The bottom line is that rather than put the total blame on improper design, it was really shoddy workmanship as you will see. Here are the specific inaccuracies and unnecessary faults leading up to the collapse:

- Requirement was that trains were to be stopped from crossing the bridge if wind force exceeded speeds of 80 MPH. *That evening*, winds had recorded gusts of 105 MPH;

- The lugs were weak *(because the holes were not drilled out)* that were cast with the columns. Basically, the loading was underestimated and the strength overestimated;
- Metal support rods for the bridge had not been driven deeply enough into the stone foundations;
- Bad construction overall. Poor design and poor maintenance;
- Intensity of wind pressure of 10 lbs/sq foot was used in the design. This was advice provided to Thomas Bouch, the bridge designer. But American and French engineers were using 50 lbs/sq feet for wind loading;
- It was a lightweight lattice grid design, combining cast and wrought iron of low cost;
- Without going into engineering/construction detail about the iron braces, spanners, bolt heads—leave it to a witness, *'about as slovenly a piece of work as I ever saw in my life';*
- Cross bearings and fastenings were not strong enough to resist higher wind forces;
- Pressure to get the railway bridge in service quickly and minimize the cost. It was already behind schedule and over budget. This resulted in cutting corners, with the end result being a reduction of safety, similar to the Titanic situation;
- There were indications of severe winds prior to the train's departure. Winds had blown three loaded coal wagons *(30 tons)* about 400 yards uphill along a siding.

Lars butts in. "When I was with the 82nd Airborne Division, I was called on several times to be the DZ *(Drop Zone)* Safety Officer at Fort Bragg, NC. That meant I had to be at the center of the DZ and decide, using a wind direction indicator, whether it was safe for troops to jump. This reminds me of that. You have to take the wind speed very seriously. A careless mistake."

"Exactly!" agreed Olivia. "OK, moving on...

- Project Managers and Civil Engineers had subordinates not qualified to execute the work to a high standard—inability to undertake a large project, thus giving more latitude to underlings who were *green* (no experience);
- Thomas Bouch's failure to supervise properly during the construction phase. He acted like a *'daft git'*... a dummy;
- Bouch's failure to make allowance for wind loading.

"And here's something that very few people know— there was a change in the design which increased the cost and caused more delays. A telltale sign was that two high girders fell while being lifted into place... the night of February 3, 1877. A premonition of what might come later. That caused even more delays. What's wrong with this picture?

"OK. That's it. Brenda has dug up some relatively unknown facts via various research sources, including Scotland's Archive, known as the National Records of Scotland. Go, Brenda!"

"Thanks, Olivia. Here are some interesting points I found, in random order:

- Bouch was knighted in June 1879 after Queen Victoria had traveled on the bridge *(June 20, 1879)*. He died ten months after the collapse... a broken man;
- The Tay Bridge was 3,465 yards long... the length of almost 36 football fields;
- A witness said the girders in the central system were blown away, *'like matchwood'*;
- Nobody agreed on the actual death toll. Best estimate is 59—with 46 bodies recovered. Some inflated numbers were reported... 100, 80, 75; but five children under the age of 14 were victims; not 15, as often reported. Some children, rail workers, and season holders may have traveled without tickets. Sort of a quagmire;
- The train driver, David Mitchell's body, washed ashore in 1880. Others remained missing;
- Ulysses S. Grant visited the city and said *'it was a big bridge for a small city'*;
- One observer said, *'It is literally a bridge on stilts. It appears flimsy'*;
- Most people agreed that if this collapse didn't occur shortly after 7 p.m. on December 28th, 1789, it was bound to happen sometime in the future. Thank God it was on a Sunday because during the week, the train carried 300 or more passengers. Horrific as it was, it could have been even worse;

- A Court of Inquiry found these faults... badly designed, badly constructed and badly maintained;
- Unfortunately, the wind blew from the west at right angles to the line of the bridge. That put maximum wind power on the high girders.

"The passengers were just plain ordinary, good people. I reviewed the background of each passenger, ages 5-62. Here is a sample of some of their professions—weaver, table maid, seaman, railway goods guard, railway fireman, plasterer, domestic servant, mechanic, laborer, mason, ploughman, tobacco spinner, farmer, and an iron turner.

"William Topaz McGonagall, Bard of Dundee, was a poet who performed in the theaters, pubs, and public houses. He was an awful poet and is best known for his poem, The Tay Bridge Disaster, which appalled everyone. When presenting it, he was pelted with rotten eggs, vegetables and fish. It has been recognized as the worst example of poetry in English literature. There are eight stanzas. Here is the last one in that dreadful poem:

It must have been an awful sight,
To witness in the dusty moonlight,
While the Storm Fiend did laugh, and angry did bray,
Along the Railway Bridge of the Silv'ry Tay.
Oh! Ill-fated Bridge of the Silv'ry Tay,
I must now conclude my lay
By telling the world fearlessly without the least dismay,
That your central girders would not have given way,

At least many sensible men do say,
For the stronger we our houses do build,
The less chance we have of being killed.

"Can you imagine? How awful is *that?* Well, those are key points I found and now Lars wants to follow-up."

Lars nods his head, washes down a bite of bacon and begins. "If you follow the bread crumbs, they lead you back to—shoddy workmanship and an improper design. Sort of like NASA, a'la Challenger—sometimes over-thinking overtakes common sense, or worse, taking short cuts. We learned at West Point, *'Make us choose the harder right instead of the easier wrong, and never to be content with a half truth when the whole can be won'.*

"OK. This was a tough in-depth research effort by all. Good job. Next week we continue with the series of scientific blunders with Doris tackling Piltdown Chicken."

All gave the traditional high-fives and stood up to head on out to their respective places in the working world. On the way out, some glared at the dessert display. Tiger licked his lips. Brenda was thinking, *'They really need to move that thing!'*

Piltdown Chicken

Left: Archaeoraptor Model, as displayed in
The Dinosaur Museum, Blanding, Utah
Right: Fake Archaeoraptor Fossil

CHAPTER 18

Piltdown Chicken—Birds & Dinosaurs Connected?

The heavy rain outside Metro 29 didn't hold Doris back. She got right to it.

"For many years scientists were totally fooled—thinking they had found the missing link that connects birds and dinosaurs, dubbed the *Archaeoraptor Liaoningensis.*

"Now, most scientists agree that it is the biggest paleontology (hoax) blunder in world history. The curator at the Smithsonian said, *'The public is being completely bamboozled',* as soon as the scandal was announced.

"The fossil, found in Liaoning Province, China, had long arms, a small body like a bird and a long, stiff tail like a dinosaur's vertebrae. In 1999, the National Geographic Society announced the discovery of a 125 million year old fossil that solved the missing link between birds and dinosaurs. However, it was later found to be fraudulent, much to the embarrassment of National Geographic—their greatest embarrassment in its 125 year old history.

"Here's what happened... a Chinese farmer dug two fossils out of his farmland—then glued the parts together. He attached the tail of one fossil to the body of another and added legs and feet. For him, it would sell for top dollar to foreign buyers. So it was a fake... a composite. Arms of a primitive bird and tail of a dinosaur. Crazy, huh!

"And it's still going on... poor farmers dig up fossils and sell to dealers and museums. But to be authenticated, fossil digs should only be conducted by paleontologists. Many of the top scientists involved in the Piltdown Chicken Blunder said it was the worst mistake they have ever made in their life. One very famous scientist said he had made *'an idiot, bone-stupid mistake'*. Another top scientist said, *'The greatest mistake of my life'*. Yet another said, *'I was dragging in a monster'*.

"By the way, Piltdown was a name given to Piltdown Man, which was a composite of a human skull and an ape jaw discovered in 1912. Piltdown is a village near Uckfield, East Sussex, England, a small town where faked remains of early hominids were dug up in 1912. A hominid is a member of the family Hominidae, the great apes: orangutans, gorillas, chimpanzees and humans. My research into this very complicated fiasco resulted in the following errors and shortcomings. These are my bottom lines:

- Incredible human error;
- Rampant naïve assumptions;
- Lying throughout;
- Manipulation and forming of composite *(fake)* fossils;
- Secrecy prevailed causing misplaced confidence;

- Egos clashing between scientists to the nth degree;
- Wishful thinking rather than critical thinking plus *groupthink* too;
- Corruption and fraud;
- Hopelessly bad communications;
- Backbiting/backstabbing;
- Perversely unyielding;
- Failure to be patient in order to examine evidence more thoroughly.

"All of these caused this blunder which should have never happened. Actually, it seems absurd to me. And I am a lover of nature and certainly not even close to being a novice paleontologist. However, I do have common sense which needed to rule in this project. Scientists are usually extremely cautious before revealing a new discover. Wait, there's more! Here are some other specific mistakes:

- Peer reviews rejected the theory, its conclusions and evidence;
- Never printed in a scientific journal;
- National Geographic published a description of species at great risk, before scientific study, causing reputation damage—claiming the fossil was the *missing link* between the dinosaurs and birds connection;
- Mistakes were made by everyone in the project."

"Hey Doris, I read an article in Discovery magazine that

listed the Piltdown Chicken as one of the 20 greatest scientific blunders," Tiger said. "Paleontologists back then wanted to prove human evolution. Same idea as those scientists desperate to prove birds evolved from dinosaurs."

"Thanks, everyone," Lars broke in. "OK, next Friday I'll cover the Mars Climate Orbiter Blunder. Not to give away the store, but it's unfortunate that in September 1999, after ten months of travel to Mars, the Orbiter burned and broke into pieces. The cost—$327.6 million. The Orbiter was to help scientists understand water history on Mars and potential life in the past. More next time. Did I get your attention?"

"Sure have, boss!" cheered Brenda.

"Then we'll see each other next week. Glad we grabbed our umbrellas. It's pouring outside," stated Lars as everyone stood up to leave.

High-fives and out the door. Tiger broke off from the rest to use the restroom—but it was just an excuse so he could sit down at the food bar and munch out on a homemade strawberry cheesecake while having a little chat with Anita.

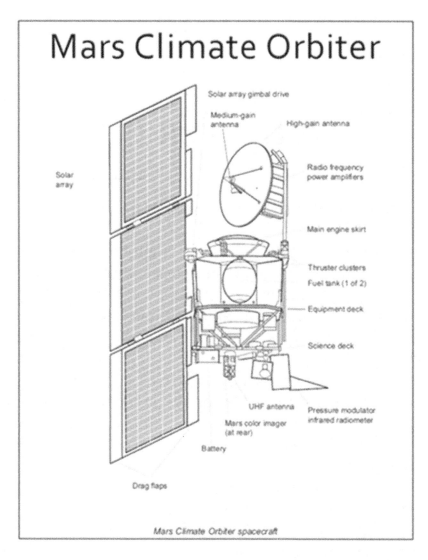

Diagram of Mars Climate Orbiter with important sections labeled

CHAPTER 19

Mars Climate Orbiter—Lost In Math Translation

Lars slightly stuttered. "This is upsetting since a high school student with a flair for science could have figured this out prior to the launch of the Mars Orbiter. It was a math problem... simply a failure to translate English units into metric units in a segment of a ground-based navigation software."

Another Friday morning has arrived and everyone is in place at their favorite table, drinks in front of them, and breakfast on the way. Another reason they so fondly referred to Anita as *Automatic Anita*. Lars has wasted no time in getting right to it.

Lars continues after taking a sip of his coffee, winking at Tiger as Anita arrives with their food. Tiger grinned as she set his crispy bacon side down in front of him.

"Its main mission was to help scientists understand Mars water history, monitor weather conditions, record changes on Mars surface due to wind, look for past climate change, etc.

"But... the miscalculations threw the spacecraft far off tract and it flew too far into Mars atmosphere, thus destroying it. Either that or it re-entered heliocentric space. Anyhow, all communications were lost.

"Digging into the bowels of the archives (pardon my reference) I discovered unbelievable and incredible errors! The cumulative effect of these mistakes made this ghastly blunder occur. Expensive too... $125 million to build it."

Seeing he now has everyone's full attention, Lars teases them by stopping to take another sip of his coffee before continuing.

"OK, gang, here are some of the key mistakes: failure to use common-units of measurements; lack of attention to detail; over-emphasis on cost cutting; mismanagement; extremely poor quality control; failure of checks and balances—double checks were not robust enough; assuming rather than checking things out end-to-end. For example, propulsion engineers at Lockheed Martin express units in pounds. But... for space missions, its converted to metric units. Nobody checked and it was not done; thus a failure to use a coherent system of units throughout. *Only the metric system should be used because it is the system science uses'*, said Lorelle Young, president of the US Metric association. *'That is so dumb'*, said John Logsdon, Director of George Washington University's space policy institute. He was referring to this fiasco.

"And, Carl Pilcher, Agency's science director said, *'It was a systematic failure to recognize and correct an error that should have been caught'*.

"Senior management leader and others were irresponsible; poor work plans—not shared up and down the line; inconsistent communications between Lockheed, the contractor, and NASA, especially between project engineering groups; PLUS! some personnel were not adequately trained for the mission.

"Tiger? Can you imagine going on a mission without training?" Lars asked, amused at the others shock on their faces.

"Uh, not for a minute, Doc!" Tiger responded, shaking his head in disgust before picking up another piece of his crispy bacon.

Lars continued. "Tom Gavin, Jet Propulsion Laboratory Administrator, said '...Something went wrong in our system processes in checks and balances that we have that should have caught this and fixed it'. He also noted, 'The problem here was not the error. It was the failure of us to look at it end-to-end and find it'.

"All I have to add is that fortunately, this wasn't the type of mission with astronauts onboard. They would have died due to a math error. OK, Brenda, what do you have?"

Brenda had been waving her hand.

"Thanks Lars; well, I found that the US is one of seven countries where SI units are not adopted. If you didn't already know, SI is the International System of Units/metric system. We are archaic. And I happen to know that the Orbiter had been gathering data for 286 days until it became unintentionally de-orbited, thus, the disaster on September 23, 1999. It weighed 1,407 pounds or should I say... 638 kilograms."

Doris added, "During my research deep into the archives, I discovered that two navigators noted the discrepancy between calculated and measured position. Their concerns, which would have solved this puzzle *before* launch, were dismissed because they did not follow the rules about filling out the form to document their concerns. And get this—a meeting of trajectory software engineers, propulsion engineers and managers was conducted to consider trajectory correction maneuvers. The attendees agreed to do it, but it was never done!"

"Listen everybody," said Tiger. "I'm really tired of all of this hogwash... where top guys don't pay attention to engineers... whom I like to think of as the guys in the trenches who *know* what's going on at the grass root level."

Everyone nodded in unison, in agreement with Tiger's statement. This was something that happened even in the business world, where the higher-ups just want more and more out of their employees, letting greed weigh in rather than what is really involved or needed to complete their requests, often leaving the ones in the *trenches* who deal with it on a daily basis, completely out of the equation.

Lars swiveled in his chair. "This was an involved process for me since I'm not a scientific chap. The bottom line is it cost $125 million and the research capabilities were lost to the US due to the incredulous, preventable errors in this blunder. I believe in *responsible prioritization,* which has been missing in most of our blunders. But... more about this concept later.

"Next week, Tiger will lead us in the Hubble Space Telescope Blunder. It'll be another short session."

Thumbs went up from everyone. Anita winked as she walked by; she had spilled the beans earlier when refilling their drinks about Tiger staying over last week to eat a dessert. Tiger took a lot of slack for that, so today, they all ordered desserts to end this week's session. It was the perfect way to top off this week's shorter session. Lars ordered the Napoleon; Tiger—Black Forest Cake; Olivia—Bread Pudding; Brenda—Cannoli; and Doris—Boston Cream Cake.

When they were finished, tradition high-fives and back out to work.

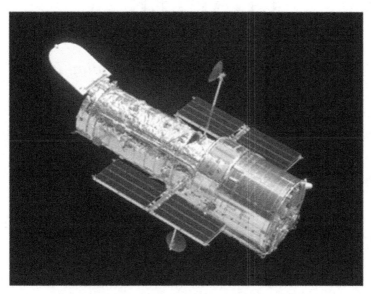

*Hubble Space Telescope as seen from the
departing Space Shuttle Atlantis,
flying STS-125, HST Servicing Mission 4*

CHAPTER 20

Hubble Space Telescope's Humiliating Failure

Anita served breakfast to the team at table #98. Automatic. No questions asked though a wink from Tiger to Anita didn't escape the others' notice.

Tiger kicked it off. "To begin with, the Hubble is named after Edwin Hubble, an astronomer. It has helped to resolve problems in astronomy. And it has made breakthroughs in astrophysics. HST *(Hubble Space Telescope)* covers many of the following and more—age and future of the universe, prevalence of black holes in nearby galaxies, discovery of distant objects... some, billions of light years away. It can discover objects in the outer reaches of our solar system. For example, a tiny fifth moon was discovered orbiting around Pluto. It can also determine the size and mass of the Milky Way.

"That said, HST has done a lot for science. It stands to reason that there is no excuse for the screw-ups made that turned this into a distressing failure. Mistakes galore, making this a terrible scientific blunder costing $4.7 billion by launch time.

"This was a tough one to research because it is extremely technical. I'm not covering the flaws in detail. Such as the primary mirror being too flat by 2,200 nanometers, or 2.2 micrometers, or 87 micro inches. This was caused by polishing to the wrong shape. Some errors were like 1/50 of a human's hair.

"But, here are some main reasons for this failure:

- The 2.4-meter primary mirror's surface was polished into the wrong shape causing a spherical aberration— preventing the Hubble from sharp focusing;
- A testing instrument error;
- No test of the complete telescope before launch;
- Ignored some tests before the launch;
- Optical test not set up correctly;
- Failure to follow the fabrication process with reasonable diligence;
- Data revealing errors were available during the fabrication process, yet ignored by Perkin-Elmer, the contractor;
- Overall leadership failure;
- Inadequate reviews during readying procedures;
- Cost overruns and schedule pressures;
- Congress cut funding, thus the scale of the HST was reduced.

Olivia butts in. "As said in Hamlet, *'In my mind's eye'*,

this strikes me with profound sadness. I feel for the scientists who try hard to make things right but, on the other hand, some acted like *wankers* on this important project. The original cost estimate was $400 million, but advanced to $4.7 billion by launch time. Wow! That blows my mind, gang! Here's something very few know. The Challenger Blunder caused a sudden halt to the US Space Program. This postponed the planned launch of the Hubble for a few years. Get this—the telescope had to be kept in a *clean room*, powered up and charged with nitrogen until a launch could be scheduled... at a handsome cost of $6 million monthly!"

"Good night!" Brenda added, jumping in. "What bothers me is the culture of NASA. Once again, we see people sleeping at the switch. Not checking and double-checking. And, like Lars has said before, *groupthink* prevails."

Doris clears her throat. "Here's a little trivia to add to Tiger's tremendous effort. Over 15,000 papers based on the Hubble's data have been published in peer-reviewed scientific journals. Thousands of scientists and engineers have counted on the Hubble's data, which is another reason why this is such an unnecessary blunder, as explained by Tiger. You know the old saying... *an ounce of prevention...*"

"Frankly, I'm floored by this blunder," cut in Lars. "Such a letdown for all of us... and I mean globally. Being a Professor in George Washington University's Business School, I am very dismayed that NASA discourages creativity or individual responsibility. This is a danger when you are dealing with highly technical instruments and parts, such as what makes up the Hubble Space Telescope."

"Hey, Doc! Isn't that what *groupthink* is all about?"

boomed Tiger.

"Yup," Lars agreed. "Well, excellent work uncovering the details for today's discussion, gang. And we're on our way for the next scientific blunder. Next week Brenda will lead us with the Cold Fusion Blunder. But I have a surprise guest after Brenda. Alexei Semenov and his co-author, Ivan Vasiliev will finish up our series on scientific/engineering blunders. They will assist us in covering the complicated Chernobyl Blunder. Then, not to get too far ahead, I'll follow them by leading us in the discussion on the failed assassinations of Adolph Hitler. See you all next week." Lars chuckled as he led Doris to the door. *That ought to keep them in suspense!*

High-fives and out the door quickly.

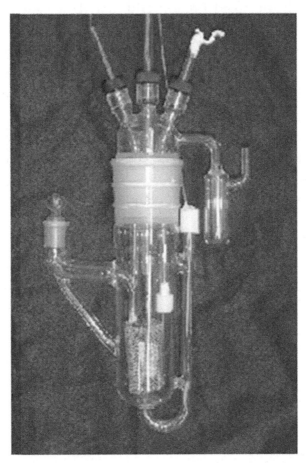

Cold Fusion apparatus at the Space and Naval Warfare Systems Center San Diego in 2005

CHAPTER 21

Cold Fusion Deceptions

"Since everybody has their breakfast, let's get it on," Brenda said, as she scratched her head under her short, tucked, layered bob.

"This is extremely complicated and different from our other blunders. It is considered one of the greatest blunders in Science and Technology. I'll try to simplify this, since it is hard for anyone to understand, except electrochemists, physicists, other scientists and researchers who study fusion related sources of energy. Actually, it is fascinating, yet difficult to grasp the concept.

"First, some definitions. The theory of Cold Fusion claims to release measurable energy from fusion reactions at or near room temperature when deuterium *(one of the isotopes of hydrogen)* is dissolved in a solid, usually palladium metal *(a chemical element that is rare and lustrous silvery-white)*. Furthermore, nuclear fusion can produce energy when the nuclei of lighter elements come together, or fuse, creating larger nuclei. Cold Fusion is an attempt to get fusion to occur under less extreme conditions, possibly as the result of chemical reactions.

"Just so you know... fusion takes place at 27,000,000° Fahrenheit. In 1989, chemists Stanley Pons and Martin Fleischmann *(P and F),* claimed they had produced fusion at room temperature. Everybody went ape! Incredible excitement in the scientific community.

"However, here are the mistakes and errors I found that elevated Cold Fusion into the blunder category:

- Did not use proper control experiments;
- Failed to address errors;
- Incorrect use of significant figures;
- P & F's claims not supported by other scientists with properly controlled experiments;
- P & F avoided a peer review. Instead, they held a press conference for fear that another researcher would get their results out first—an ego mistake;
- They made statements that violated scientific ethics and plain common sense;
- Experimental errors; inaccurate equipment.

"In the final analysis, Cold Fusion at that time was found to be a deception. It made fools of top scientists. Actually, it was a blunder for each of several scientists whose reputations became scarred. Mainly because no scientist could replicate P & F's experiment. All failed. Basically, the experiment includes palladium or nickel, in bulk, thin films or powder, deuterium, hydrogen, or both, in the form of water, gas, or plasma. P & F were attacked by scientists saying that the results were theoretically impossible.

"Lots of claims have been made. But so far, not one working device has ever been demonstrated or patented. To me, it is more like a dream than a real scientific breakthrough from all the research I gathered. Much was way over my head. And I learned that it really is impossible. Not a real phenomena, which caused a mad rush to reproduce P & F's experiments."

"Incredible coverage of a tough blunder," stated Olivia. "I found an interesting comment by Peter N. Saeta, an Assistant Professor of Physics at Harvey Mudd College: *'Some investors want to put a million if the return on investment is worth billions. But the likely return is 10 to the -40 power... meaning even investing one penny to earn possible billions would be a bad bet'*. Bottom line, I now doubt Cold Fusion is really an easy alchemical solution to the world's energy needs.

"Anyway, P & F's careers were ruined. But they continued their quest of Cold Fusion. Most scientists, later on, rated Cold Fusion as a pathological science or pseudoscience. They were always highly skeptical of it and to this day they don't talk about it. It's considered to be a disgrace. After it was found to be false, several scientists asserted, *'I knew it was nonsense'*. Others called Pons and Fleischmann incompetent and delusional."

"I know this has been our shortest blunder discussion so far, but that's because it was more cut and dry than our others. That leaves us time to chit-chat," confirmed Brenda.

Immediately everyone ordered another coffee or tea. Lars

and Tiger talked about the Nationals and Redskins. Doris, Brenda, and Olivia talked about shopping—Nordstrom's, Neiman Markus, REI, Lilly Pulitzer, Ella-Rue, Macy's and planned a girls' shopping outing soon. They also discussed running, since all three are marathoners.

"Hey, Doc any gems of wisdom before we leave?" asked Tiger.

"Yup. Just remember to laugh and smile more; it increases longevity."

As Alpha Team leader, Lars is always trying to keep the team in a high morale state, especially since they do discuss some very sad blunder results.

Suddenly, Tiger threw a strawberry in the air. It missed, landing in Olivia's tea with a definite splash.

"You're just a happy-go-lucky *wanker*."

Blushing, Tiger ordered a side order of fresh strawberries for Olivia.

Lars gave the two arms up... touchdown signal and said that Chernobyl is next. High-fives and everyone left in good spirits.

Chernobyl nuclear power plant
Pripyat, Ukrainian SSR, Soviet Union

CHAPTER 22

Chernobyl—Worst Nuclear Disaster In History

Lars invited Alexei and Ivan to lunch at the best Russian restaurant in Northern Virginia... Rus Uz, located on North Randolph Street in Arlington. He did this two weeks before they were to lead the Chernobyl Blunder discussion. That way, Lars could explain the total drill to them, including the discussion process.

They met at noon in a downpour—raining like cats and dogs. Dmitri greeted them and led them to their sparkling clean table. Alexei, Ivan, and Dmitri exchanged a few words and began laughing.

Each ordered a Baitika beer. Lars ordered a Blini appetizer... crepe stuffed with ground beef and sour cream; Alexei—Samsa... rolled dough stuffed with lamb, onions, spices and baked to a crisp; Ivan—Red Caviar Tart... pastry stuffed with cream cheese and topped with salmon caviar. They all ordered the Borsch soup... beets and cabbage, chunks of beef, with sour cream topping. These guys knew what they wanted!

Lars had met both of them at a conference in Buenos Aires three years ago. He has also coordinated several academic research projects with them and both are Russian naturalized Americans and Professors of History at Georgetown University. They grew up together in Kharkiv, about 255 miles west of Kiev, the capitol of Ukraine. They graduated together from the top university, Karazin National University, established in 1804. They earned doctorate degrees in science and technology.

Alexei told Lars about the giant Ferris wheel, in Maxim Gorky Central Park, the zoo, botanic gardens, and the great opera and ballet theater. Rich in culture and tradition—the people have lots of pride. They visited Kiev, founded in 482 A.D., many times.

Ivan covered the four major battles, around Kharkiv, between the Germans and Russians between October 1941 and August 1943. Lars got a top-notch history lesson. Finally, they both told Lars that, as he well knows, they were about to be arrested after their first scientific journal article was published. It was minutes or just hours before it would have been a disaster.

Suddenly they got asylum from the United States Embassy and were wisped away via a US Intelligence Group and flown out that night to the US.

Ivan was clear. "That was better than ending up in one of the 705 corrective colonies, serving slave labor. Very little is maintained or updated in these camps." Lars remembers the newspaper headlines back then: *'Escape from the Iron Curtain'*.

Later, they became American citizens. Long story but covered well in articles and newspaper reports. Too long to relate here. These two 58 year-old scholars are the top Chernobyl experts, as Lars well knows. During their continued research, they have had access to incredible sources: KGB Archive, Central Executive Archive of Ukraine, State Archive of the Russian Federation, Russian Archives, and Central State Archives of Ukraine.

Also, Politburo memos, diaries, notes, and minutes from some sessions. Plus many other sources, all providing them with Top Secret and even *above* Top Secret *(Crypto)* information... some of which has never been seen before. This is why Lars asked them to be the Alpha Team's guests to cover this particular blunder—it being very complicated to the outside world.

When they departed, Lars was pumped up. He couldn't wait until the team was to meet on the Chernobyl Blunder. They would learn some information—NEVER HEARD BEFORE—because it had been very well hidden and covered up.

Metro 29 two weeks later...
Lars met Alexei and Ivan thirty minutes early. It is raining buckets and very windy as Lars let them both, armed with Totes, in the entrance.

At 8 a.m. the other team members showed up... right on time. Brenda's head was soaked. Her hood wouldn't stay up. Lars raced to get her something to use as a towel. Doris kept repeating *"Brrrr"* while rubbing her hands together. Tiger wore his old Army poncho and Olivia was loosening up her

Mac. They were ready to go once they got out of the weather, dried off, and warmed up a bit.

As the wind slammed rain against the nearby window to table #98, Lars gargled with his coffee and began to cover the points that the two scientists had covered during lunch at Rus Uz two weeks earlier, adding they had both won the Nobel Prize in the '90s. The team stood and applauded. Tiger gave out a *"HOOAH"!* People in the restaurant stared bewildered. Remember—*Tiger is a happy-go-lucky guy!*

As usual, with every blunder, all team members had researched Chernobyl, but they all knew that these two guys were the real thing. And that the scientists' research would be deeper, uncovering unknowns. It was very exciting, stimulating everyone's curiosity to the max!

Both of the heroes ordered from Anita, who must've thought them to be funny, giggling lightly as they ordered rye bread with two fried eggs on toast, a slice of ham and cheese, and hot tea. The Russians call that sandwich *'butterbrots'*.

"Privyet, Anita," said Alexei, "we call our dark rye bread *chernyy khleb*."

Anita put one hand to her lips and snickered.

Since Alexei and Ivan knew the discussion procedure, as explained to them by Lars as they awaited the others arrivals, they got right to it. This was good because Lars knows how Russians are known to be like poets... *adding lots of fluff.* And his Alpha Team members have to get to their real jobs after the session.

Of course, everyone knew that the incident occurred on April 26, 1986 at the Number 4 Nuclear Reactor in the

Chernobyl Nuclear Power Plant near Pripyat, Ukraine. Alexei and Ivan decided to alternate the points about the many errors and mistakes involved in the Chernobyl disaster.

"Get ready to discover the points that have been dug up from documents having two-inches of dust on them, in the literal sense. Most... never seen before.

Ivan kicked it off. "Here starts our list of tragic mistakes:

- Inadequately trained personnel. Withdrew most control and safety rods from the core and switched off important safety systems;
- Terribly flawed reactor design;
- Culture of secrecy—the top leaders kept silent and were afraid;
- Little regard for nuclear safety;
- Cutting corners; racing to achieve prestige, like the atomic bomb;
- Ignored many early warnings;
- Fatally flawed from the beginning;
- Safety test went extremely wrong;
- Reactor building standards were sub-standard; Russians are known to fail at meeting engineering specifications even on apartment buildings—that's why it doesn't take much of a force to cause collapse;
- Weeks before the disaster, engineers pleaded to shut it down.

Lars coughed nervously, cleared his throat, and said, "Sorry to butt in on you guys but this reminds me of our previous blunders, like the Challenger, Tay Bridge, and a few others."

"You are right," Ivan replied. "We have read Brenda's notes on all of your team discussions so far."

Tiger was thinking, *These two guys are real sharp dudes'.*

Alexei spoke next. "Also, these points:

- Safety regulations were ignored by technicians and key operators—sort of a complacent attitude like displayed by NASA;
- Workers' low morale; could be the reason for shoddy work performance. Nobody has ever highlighted this, but Ivan and I believe in a high correlation between morale, work energy and efficient output;
- Shortages of construction materials;
- Poor quality control;
- Again, just poor workmanship—cannot come close to precision engineering efforts by Germany;
- Lack of organization, no teamwork whatsoever... thus low standards; many of these key mistakes are tied together;
- Plant construction completion goal shortened from three to two years. This threw everything in disarray... never to recover.

"This reminds me of the other blunders where top officials pushed for speeding up things—like the Titanic, Lusitania, Tay Bridge, Challenger, and others. Naïve, stupid leaders. Sorry to be so critical, but they do burn my ass!"

Doris squirmed nervously, as all members gave her a thumbs up. She rarely spoke so bluntly.

Alexei continued. "Moving on...

- Planners failed to understand workers' frustrations;
- Unrealistic quotas set;
- Materials sub-standard, especially reinforced concrete and steel—in short supply too;
- 170 workers suffered work-related injuries in 1978, first three quarters, by not monitoring safety equipment;
- Poorly designed test experiment—destined to be a failure from the start.

Taking a short pause, he continued. "We've been alternating these, but I will cover a *Top Secret* memo from the Soviet's Politboro sessions. It pertains to the evacuation of Pripyat. Some working copies of Politboro sessions are still secret in the Russian Presidential Archive. But let's continue. You're up, Ivan."

"Also...

- Placing nuclear power stations too close to cities—more on this later when Alexei quotes Gorbachev on a Top Secret comment he made;
- Operators lack of knowledge of nuclear reactor physics and engineering;
- Key safety switches were turned off—emergency core cooling system, local automatic control system and emergency power reduction system; they also ignored

regulations in regards to speed test completion;
- Operating reaction at low power level.

Alexei butts in. "And here is where we want to give you a verbatim print-out of the INSAG's reasons for the blunder. Some are redundant based on what we have told you, but it is good for you to see in in real print."

Olivia asks, "What is INSAG?"

"Good question! That's the *International Nuclear Safety Advisory Group*. They are a group of experts in a diversity of organizations—regulatory, technical support, researchers and academicians. All are professionals in the field of safety."

Ivan passes out the handout to everyone.

"According to the INSAG-7 Report, the chief reasons for the accident lie in the peculiarities of physics and in the construction of the reactor. There are two such reasons:

1. The reactor had a dangerously large positive void coefficient of reactivity. The void coefficient is a measurement of how a reactor responds to increased steam formation in the water coolant. Most other reactor designs have a negative coefficient; in other words, the nuclear reaction rate slows when steam bubbles form in the coolant since as the vapour phase in the reactor increases, fewer neutrons are slowed down. Faster neutrons are less likely to split uranium atoms, so the reactor produces less power *(a negative feedback)*. Chernobyl's RBMK reactor however, used solid graphite as a neutron moderator to slow down

the neutrons, and the water in it, on the contrary, acts like a harmful neutron absorber. Thus, neutrons are slowed down even if steam bubbles form in the water. Furthermore, because steam absorbs neutrons much less readily than water, increasing the intensity of vapourization means that more neutrons are able to split uranium atoms, increasing the reactor's power output. This makes the RBMK design very unstable at low power levels and prone to suddenly increasing energy production to a dangerous level. This behavior is counter-intuitive, and this property of the reactor was unknown to crew;

2. A more significant flaw was in the design of the control rods that are inserted into the reactor to slow down the reaction. In the RBMK reactor design, the lower part of each control rod was made of graphite and was 1.3 meters *(4.3 feet)* shorter than necessary, and in the space beneath the rods were hollow channels filled with water. The upper part of the rod, the truly functional part that absorbs the neutrons and thereby halts the reaction, was made of boron carbide. With this design, when the rods are inserted into the reactor from the uppermost position, the graphite parts initially displace some water *(which absorbs neutrons, as mentioned above),* effectively causing fewer neutrons to be absorbed initially. Thus, for the first few seconds of control rod activation, reactor power output is increased, rather than reduced as desired. This behavior is counter-intuitive and was not known to the reactor operators.

"Other deficiencies besides these noted in the RBMK-1000 reactor design, were its non-compliance with accepted standards and with the requirements of nuclear reactor safety. While INSAG-1 and INSAG-7 reports both identified operator error as an issue of concern, the INSAG-7 report identified that there were numerous other issues that were contributing factors leading to the incident, including:

1. The plant was not designed to safety standards in effect and incorporated unsafe features;
2. Inadequate safety analysis was performed;
3. There was insufficient attention to independent safety review;
4. Operating procedures not founded satisfactory in safety analysis;
5. Safety information inadequately and effectively communicated between operators, and between operators and designers;
6. The operators did not adequately understand safety aspects of the plant;
7. Operators did not sufficiently respect formal requirements of operational and test procedures;
8. The regulatory regime was insufficient to effectively counter pressures for production;
9. There was a general lack of safety culture in nuclear matters at the national level as well as locally.

Alexei added, "If you didn't know about RBMK, it is the unusual Soviet designed nuclear reactor that uses enriched uranium for its fuel. The real name is *Reaktor Bolshoy*

Moshchnosty Kanalny. Two reactors emerged in the 70's."

Alexei and Ivan sat down having finished relating their points of interest on the Chernobyl Blunder. The team stood up and fired high-fives at each other.

Tiger burped, grinned and then said, "This was incredible coverage by you two professors. I want to add the outcomes so you all don't think I didn't do any work." He chuckles.

The two former Russians laughed. Let out a balled fist sign. Both yelled *"Da"!*

Tiger nods and continues. "237 people suffered from radiation; 31 died within 3 months. And... get this! Areas contaminated with the offshoot from the Chernobyl disaster: Belarus... highest—14.4% of country. Then, in order, comes Ukraine, Russia, Sweden, Finland, Austria, Norway, Bulgaria, Switzerland, Greece, Slovenia, Italy, and Moldova. Covers 162 square kilometers.

"The United Nations has estimated up to 4,000 deaths and that exposed people could be up to 16,000 in Europe. Some predict 31,000. Some 40,000... while others, up to 60,000 in the long term around the globe."

Brenda tends to her ponytail and adds, "I found that the Chernobyl disaster was a more important factor in the fall of the USSR than Perestroika... the liberal reform program."

"That's true," chimed in Alexei and Ivan at the same time.

Doris proudly announced, "And I discovered that more radioactive forms of chemical elements escaped into the atmosphere than created by the atomic bombs dropped on Hiroshima and Nagasaki—that 50-185 million curies of radionuclides were scattered!"

That grabbed everyone's attention.

She added, "It is said to have been the equivalent of 500 atomic bombs like the one dropped on Nagasaki!"

"Well, I haven't said much," strained Olivia, "since I'm such in awe of Alexei and Ivan with everything they uncovered, but I do have the list of the names of the 33 known deaths due to trauma and radiation sickness. I feel for them.

"Some of the occupations were: firefighters, senior reactor control chief, inspectors, operational engineers, electricians, turbine operator, physicist, security guards... which reminds me of the Tay Bridge victims... just real good *salt of the earth* people."

Unexpectedly, Alexei and Ivan switch chairs. No explanation, except it is known that Russians do this at conferences to present a *different viewpoint.*

Alexei offers, "Ivan got into the Top Secret memos of Mikhail Gorbachev's special archive. Ivan! Carry on, comrade."

"Da. Let me read to you all a Gorbachev memo. It's from the minutes of a Politboro session conducted on June 5th, 1986. Verbatim—*'One or two accidents like this and we would get it worse than from a total nuclear war'.* He insisted on informing the West, because the West—and us in Ukraine—were using the same reactor.

"But everyone wanted to hide the truth as to the magnitude of the incident. The communist lying mantra about this was *'Nothing threatens peoples' health'.* Iron Curtain. Also, I might add that Gorbachev blasted the nuclear industry's leaders and academic scientists for making poor decisions, which included placing nuclear power stations close to cities, not approved by Party leadership or the Politboro."

"Good stuff," said Alexei. "It is my point of view that nearly all of the 49,000 inhabitants of Pripyat, 3 km away, were affected. Time will tell. This disaster will continue still, through about 2065, as a result of radiation exposure."

Ivan snaps his heels together while seated. "Before we close, I must also point out that there was no planned emergency evacuation. People didn't know what to do—I mean men, women, *and children*."

The seven of them continued on for another 45 minutes, until the rain subsided with small talk and little tidbits of facts and questions. Alexei and Ivan ranted on about their near imprisonment and other war stories. Then they began joking with each other in Russian.

"We have a closing surprise for you," said Ivan.

Everyone taps the table in excitement. "What'cha got," unloads Tiger.

"Well, you want to learn, right? So Alexei and I are going to recite a poem by the greatest Russian poet in history, Aleksandr Pushkin. This is for the women here. Pushkin had a respectful attitude toward women. Here we go:

I LOVED YOU...

I loved you: and, it may be, from my soul
The former love has never gone away,
But let it not recall to you my dole;

I wish not sadden you in any way.
I loved you silently, without hope, fully,
In diffidence, in jealousy, in pain;
I loved you so tenderly and truly,
As let you else be loved by any man.

All team members were astonished. Seeing that, Ivan told them, "Listen, as school children we learn poems by heart. You want to hear others such as: Eugene Onegin, The Captain's Daughter, Winter Morning or..."

Alexei butts in adding, "Boris Godunov, Rusian and Ludmila."

Lars responded saying, "Maybe another time but we are quite impressed. Thanks for that quick lesson. I know that Russians love poetry."

Before the team left, Lars announced that next Friday, he will be the discussion leader covering Adolph Hitler—mistakes and failed numerous assassination attempts.

Alexei and Ivan couldn't move past the dessert showpiece. Grinning, all returned to the table and had dessert, with Alexei and Ivan gobbling down Napoleon Cake.

Adolph Hitler
Official portrait, 1938

CHAPTER 23

Failure To Assassinate Adolph Hitler

As you know, the Alpha Team met over a year ago to determine the blunders that they would be discussing in the future. Compromise was in full force, kicking out some ideas, accepting others unanimously.

Lars had on his professor hat, at the blackboard, using the brainstorming method. Lining out some topics—keeping others. Keepers were checked off. They spent two full weekends doing this in a conference room at The Business School at George Washington University.

Now, when they reached Hitler as a possible target, they hit a stonewall. Like a writer stuck in *writer's block*. Or like a marathon runner *hitting the wall*. How to proceed?

This occurred because so much has been written about Hitler—what was left to cover? The team's mission was not to merely repeat what others had already written. Redundancy was something that they steered clear of.

They were aiming at bringing out true facts and

information, mostly unheard of before—hidden away in secret archives or other secret locations. Much of the information the team gathers is probably unknown by about 90% of the general public. Maybe including you!

So, they were stymied. Then, after a short coffee break, Lars suddenly slammed his fist on the mahogany table and barked out, "What about all the failures to assassinate Hitler?"

Olivia blurted out, "Brilliant!" Others raised two thumbs up. Tiger yelled out a *"HOOAH"*!

They had already worked their way through many of Hitler's mistakes in an attempt to declare one as a blunder, such as: stopping submarine warfare in the Atlantic, not wiping out Brits at Dunkirk, Operation Barbarossa... attacking Soviets on Eastern Front, Kurst salient main tank battle, Operation Sea Lion, failure to take Malta and Gibraltar, and oil fields in Libya, declaring war on the US, not using Japan better as an ally, battle of Stalingrad, using a million men in eradicating Jews... construction of camps, transporting them to camps, guarding them... a loss of needed fighting manpower, distrusting his general staff, and so on...

Of course a historian, or even yourself, can come up with other mistakes. But, again... the team realized that tons of writings have covered all of these mishaps and much more via books, journal articles, movies, documentaries, television, essays, etc.

No need to repeat what others have done in quite detail. Some of the books are masterpieces. Each team member has read all of them. Hail to those writers who have done in-depth research.

The team took a break and snagged a BLT at the GW Deli nearby. Upon returning to the conference room, they were excited about the little known background of the 40+ assassination attempts on Hitler's life. The mistakes, when put in a cluster, form the biggest blunder of WWII. The blunder is the umbrella over mistakes made in assassination attempts.

Think about it—if Hitler had been assassinated, perhaps 31.5 million Europeans would not have died, and 85 million total WWII deaths might have been avoided. But Hitler led the charge to kill Jews, gays, gypsies, those with mental and physical disabilities, trade unionists, Poles, communists, anarchists, Jehovah's Witnesses, and others. They were killed deliberately or starved to death. The word from the Fuhrer was *'make them suffer'*.

Hitler never visited a *Death Camp*. But under his mask, Hitler had the German souls in his pocket. Like he said, *'If you tell a big enough lie and tell it frequently enough, it will be believed'*. Adolph Hitler was running Germany towards ruination.

Lars stated, "The German souls are scarred forever by not fighting off Hitler and his oppressors. Some tried, God bless them, and that's why I will cover some of the forty attempts to end his life."

"Wow! I didn't know it was that many!" blurted out Tiger.

"Me either," said Doris and Brenda in unison.

"I did, because I studied all of this for my blunders book," added Olivia. "However, I didn't include the attempts on Hitler's life as one of them."

Doris noted, "What really digs me is that when a Dictator uses his/her power, as Hitler did, it saps the emotional and intellectual energy out of everyone. In this case... the German people. The core of a person is ripped out, to include snuffing out the spiritual life of a person."

Tiger wiggles in his chair. "Yeah! Just to piggyback your key comment, I think the countries that Hitler took over were under a death sentence—not your typical occupational force as Lars and I know."

OK, hang on—we are now fast-forwarding to the meeting at Metro 29 where Hitler is the topic. But first, on Wednesday, a couple of days before the meeting, Lars wanted to discuss an email he received. Lars' email to Doris, Olivia, Brenda and Tiger read: Did you get the email from Alexei and Ivan?

Tiger responded first. "Roger, but I didn't understand it, Doc."

"Me either," came the response from the other three.

"Well, I found out what *'caxap der'mo'* means. Alexi and Ivan were referring to the several hours and days after the Chernobyl incident at 1:23am on April 26th. That's when the cover-ups, deception, and betrayal began.

"The Soviet officials, as you know, were trying to downplay it... like sugar coating the embarrassing accident. So the Soviet people, not being fools, called it *'caxap der'mo'*... meaning *'pouring sugar on shit'*."

Everyone giggles simultaneously. They can hear Lars laughing and his Yorkies barking in the background.

"Okey dokey! See you all on Friday. Hitler is our target.

Out!"

The following Friday...

Everyone was on time even though there was four inches of snow already on the ground with mild flurries and a chilling 26° temperature. Anita had coffee and hot tea already set on table #98, knowing the team members would be cold.

Lars wasted no time. "Here is a handout for you all. It is a list of some assassination attempts on Hitler. Credit goes to Wikimedia Foundation, Inc. It covers the date, location, attempted by whom, and a summary. I couldn't cover these attempts more concisely.

"However, I will add more in-depth details on several failed attempts that are startling."

HITLER ASSASSINATION ATTEMPTS
(incomplete list – wikipedia.org)

Date: 1932
Location: Hotel Kaiserhof (Berlin)
Attempted By: Unknown

Summary: Hitler and several members of his staff fall ill after dining at the revered Kaiserhof hotel in Berlin. Poisoning is suspected, but no arrests are made. Hitler himself seems least affected by the alleged poisoning, possibly due to his vegetarian diet.

Date: Feb. 9, 1932

Location: Berlin
Attempted By: Ludwig Assner

Summary: Ludwig Assner, a German politician and member of the Bavarian State Parliament, sends a poisoned letter to Hitler from France. An acquaintance of Assner warns Hitler and the letter is intercepted.

Date: 1934
Location: Berlin
Attempted By: Beppo Römer

Summary: Freikorps member Beppo Römer vows to assassinate Hitler as revenge for the Night of the Long Knives but is turned over to the Gestapo before any concrete plan can be made.

Date: 1934
Location: Berlin
Attempted By: Helmut Mylius

Summary: Dr. Helmut Mylius, head of the right wing Radical Middle Class Party (Radikale Mittelstandspartei), has 160 men infiltrate the SS and begin gathering information on Hitler's movement. The conspiracy is uncovered by the Gestapo and the conspirators are arrested. Myluis escapes arrest through the aid of influential friends, including Field Marshall Erich von Manstein.

Date: 1935
Location: Berlin
Attempted By: Marwitz group
Summary: Several German officers in the Foreign office pen a letter writing that *"The oath of allegiance against Hitler has lost its meaning since he was ready to sacrifice Germany"* and that "now was the time to act" in an attempt to instigate an army coup against the Fuhrer.

Date: 1935
Location: Berlin
Attempted By: Paul Josef Stuermer

Summary: Dr. Paul Joseph Stuermer leads a resistance group composed of several officers, university professors, businessmen and government workers. The group assists several assassination attempts including Beppo Römer's attempt.

Date: Dec. 20, 1936
Location: Nuremberg
Attempted By: Helmut Hirsch

Summary: Helmut Hirsch, a German Jew and a member of the Strasserist Black Front, is tasked with planting two suitcases filled with explosives at the Nazi party headquarters in Nuremberg. The plot is revealed to the Gestapo by a double agent and Hirsch is executed by decapitation.

Date: 1937
Location: Berlin
Attempted By: Josef Thomas

Summary: On November 26 mental patient Josef Thomas is arrested by the Gestapo in Berlin after he confesses that he traveled from Elberfeld for the explicit purpose of shooting Hitler and air force commander Hermann Göring.

Date: 1937
Location: Berlin
Attempted By: Unknown man in SS uniform

Summary: An unidentified man in SS uniform reportedly tries to kill Hitler during a rally at the Berlin SportPalast.

Date: Sept. 28, 1938
Location: Berlin
Attempted By: Hans Oster, Helmuth Groscurth

Summary: A plan is formed by Generalmajor Hans Oster and other high-ranking conservatives in the Wehrmacht to overthrow Hitler in the case he declares war on Czechoslovakia. The plan involved the storming of the Reich Chancellery by forces loyal to the plot in order to take control of the government, who would either arrest or assassinate Hitler, and restore the

exiled Wilhelm II as Emperor. The plan is abandoned after British Prime Minister Neville Chamberlain concedes the Sudetenland to Hitler in the Munich Agreement, neutralizing the immediate risk of war. Many of the conspirators go on to take part in the 1944 July 20 Plot
Main article: Oster Conspiracy

Date: Nov. 9, 1938
Location: Munich
Attempted By: Maurice Bavaud

Summary: Swiss theology student Maurice Bavaud poses as a reporter and plans to shoot Hitler from the reviewing stand as he passes through the parade. His view of Hitler is blocked by the unwitting crowd and he is forced to abandon the plan. He then attempts to follow Hitler but fails. On his way back to Paris he is discovered by a train conductor and is turned over to the Gestapo. Maurice is executed by guillotine in the Berlin-Plötzensee prison on the morning of May 14, 1941.

Date: Oct. 5, 1939
Location: Warsaw
Attempted By: Michał Karaszewicz-Tokarzewski, Service for Poland's Victory

Summary: General Michał Karaszewicz-Tokarzewski and other members of the Polish Army attempt to detonate hidden explosives during Hitler's victory parade in Warsaw. 500 Kg of TNT are concealed in a ditch, ready to be detonated by Polish Sappers. However, at the last moment, the parade is diverted and the saboteurs miss their target.

Date: Nov. 8, 1939
Location: Munich
Attempted By: Johann Georg Elser

Summary: German Carpenter Georg Elser places a time bomb at the Bürgerbräukeller in Munich, where Hitler is due to give his annual speech in commemoration of the Beer Hall Putsch. Hitler leaves earlier than expected and the bomb detonates, killing eight and injuring sixty-two others. Following the attempt, Elser is held as a prisoner for over five years until he is executed at the Dachau concentration camp less than a month before the surrender of Nazi Germany.

Date: 1939
Location: Berlin
Attempted By: Erich Kordt

Summary: German diplomat and resistance fighter Erich Kordt hatches an assassination plot along with officer Hasso von Etzdorf to plant explosives, but the plan is abandoned after the security restrictions following Georg Elser's attempt to kill Hitler make the acquirement and concealment of the necessary explosives too dangerous.

Date: 1941—1943 (several)
Location: Berlin
Attempted By: Beppo Römer

Summary: Beppo Römer plots once again to assassinate Hitler along with several co-conspirators of the resistance group Solf Circle. He obtains funds from co-conspirator Nikolaus von Halem and keeps tabs on the Fuhrer's movements through a contact at the Berlin City Commandment. However, before an opportunity can present itself, the plot is unraveled by the Gestapo. Römer is sentenced to death on 16 June 1944 and executed on 25 September of that year at Brandenburg-Görden Prison in Brandenburg an der Havel.

Date: 1943
Location: Walki, Ukraine
Attempted By: Hubert Lanz, Hans Speidel, Hyazinth Graf Strachwitz

Summary: Following the war, General der Gebirgstruppe Hubert Lanz proclaims of a plan involving himself and Generals Hans Speidel, Hyacinth Graf Strachwitz & Paul Loehning to assassinate Hitler during his visit to the Army Detachment Kempf in Ukraine. According to the plan, Generalleutnant Hyacinth Graf Strachwitz was to surround Hitler and his escorts with his tanks. Lanz stated that he would have then arrested Hitler, and in the event of resistance, Strachwitz's tanks would have shot and killed the entire delegation. Hitler canceled the visit and the plan was dropped. Author Röll casts doubt on this account citing that Strachwitz's cousin, Rudolf Christoph Freiherr von Gersdorff, who attempted to assassinate Hitler in 1943, had recounted that Strachwitz had expressed the belief to him several times that killing Hitler would have constituted murder. Röll concludes that Strachwitz was too much a Prussian officer to consider assassinating Hitler.

Date: Mar. 13, 1943
Location: Flight to Smolensk
Attempted By: Henning von Tresckow, Fabian von Schlabrendorff

Summary: On the return flight from a visit to the front, Hitler visits the headquarters of the Army Group Center in Smolensk. During the visit there were several attempts to take his life:

- Under the direction of Major Georg von Boeselager, several officers were to intercept and assassinate Hitler in a grove on his way from the airport to the headquarters. Hitler is guarded by an armed SS escort; the plan is then dropped.
- During lunchtime, Tresckow, Boeselager, and others plan to get up at a sign and fire pistols at Hitler. The commander-in-chief of the Army

Group, Field Marshal Günther von Kluge, knows about the plan but decides not to intervene. However, the plan is abandoned when it becomes clear that Himmler would not be present. Kluge forbids the attack, citing his fear of a possible civil war erupting between the SS and the army.

- In a last-ditch attempt, Tresckow gives an accompanying officer a time bomb camouflaged as a packaged liqueur, which is supposed to explode on the return flight over Poland. The package containing the explosive is placed in the hold of the aircraft, where it ices up and causes the ignition mechanism to fail. Realizing the failure, Fabian von Schlabrendorff flies immediately to Germany and recovers the suitcase before it is intercepted.

Date: Mar. 21, 1943
Location: Berlin
Attempted By: Rudolf Christoph Freiherr von Gersdorff

Summary: After becoming close friends with leading Army Group Center conspirator Colonel (later Major General) Henning von Tresckow, Generalmajor Gersdorff agrees to join the conspiracy to kill Adolf Hitler in order to save Germany. After Tresckow's elaborate plan to assassinate Hitler on 13 March 1943 fails, Gersdorff declares himself ready to give his life for Germany's sake in an assassination attempt that would entail his own death.

On 21 March 1943, Hitler visits the Zeughaus Berlin, the old armory on Unter den Linden, to inspect captured Soviet weapons. A group of top Nazi and leading military officials—among them Hermann Göring, Heinrich Himmler, Field Marshal Wilhelm Keitel, and Grand Admiral Karl Dönitz—are present as well. As an expert, Gersdorff is to guide Hitler on a tour of the exhibition. Moments after Hitler enters the museum, Gersdorff sets off two ten-minute delayed fuses on explosive devices hidden in his coat pockets. His plan is to throw himself around Hitler in a death embrace that will blow them both up. A detailed plan for a coup d'état had been worked out and was ready to go; but, contrary to expectations, Hitler races through the museum in less than ten minutes. After Hitler has left the building, Gersdorff is able to defuse the devices in a public bathroom *"at the last second."* After the attempt, he is immediately transferred back to the Eastern Front where he manages to evade suspicion.

Date: Nov. 16, 1943
Location: Wolf's Lair
Attempted By: Axel Freiherr von dem Bussche-Streithorst

Summary: Encouraged by Claus Stauffenberg, Major Axel von dem Bussche agrees to carry out a suicide bombing in order to kill Hitler. Bussche, who is over two meters tall, blonde and blue-eyed, exemplifies the Nazi *"Nordic ideal"* and was thus chosen to personally model the Army's new winter uniform in front of the Fuhrer. In his pocket, Bussche equipps a land mine, which he plans to detonate while embracing the Fuhrer. However, the viewing is canceled after the railway truck containing the new uniforms is destroyed in an allied air raid on Berlin.

Date: Jan. 1944
Location: Wolf's Lair
Attempted By: Ewald-Heinrich von Kleist-Schmenzin

Summary: A similar scheme to Axel von dem Bussche is attempted by German Resistance fighter Ewald von Kleist; however, the uniform inspection is once again postponed, and eventually canceled by Hitler.

Date: Mar. 11, 1944
Location: Berghof
Attempted By: Eberhard von Breitenbuch

Summary: On March 9, 1944, Covert German resistance member Busch and his aides are summoned to brief Hitler at the Berghof in Bavaria on 11 March. Following a debate with Tresckow, Breitenbuch agrees to attempt to assassinate the Führer by shooting him in the head using a 7.65mm Browning pistol concealed in his trouser pocket, having declined a suicide attempt using a bomb. A Condor aircraft is sent to collect Busch and Breitenbuch and he is allowed into the Berghof, but is not able to carry out the plan because SS guards have been ordered - earlier that day - not to permit aides into the conference room with Hitler.

Date: Jul. 20, 1944
Location: Wolf's Lair
Attempted By: Claus von Stauffenberg

Summary: See main article: July 20 plot

After everyone had a chance to briefly review the handout, Lars continued. "Most of these assassination attempts and plots were conducted by various people—disgruntled Germans, lone-wolf gunmen, former and active military and government officials, students, resistance fighters, Nazi dissidents, and others. Most of these attempts were disorganized, careless, not properly planned and controlled, inexperienced, and lack of attention to details." Lars clears a lump in his throat, obviously agitated. "And reckless, slipshod, amateurish."

Brenda butts in. "But at least they tried, Doc. See, here we are again... faced with, as in our other blunders, mistakes that were made that shouldn't have been made. The cumulative effect of these mistakes clustered together cause a blunder in the macro sense."

"Good point, Brenda." Lars wetted his lips and made a cluck sound with his tongue. A sign that he is ready to roll... fired up. He continued. "Many of these attempts and plots fall under the radar due to the famous von Stauffenberg attempt at Wolf's Lair on July 20, 1944. Most people have no clue that the first assassination attempt was back in November, 1921.

"Attempts were made from 1921 to 1944. Actually, historians feel there were about 60, many not known by anyone. It is a gray area. I think it is higher than that because when plots were found out by the SS *(Schutzstaffel or Protection Squads)* those involved were in some cases, secretly assassinated so that the plots were never known by the German public. And there are no records of these. Hitler wanted the public to think everybody was 100% behind him—nobody ever thinking about taking the Fuhrer's life. He believed divine providence was on his side and behind his successes.

Tiger snapped, "You know Doc, some of these are really sorry assassination attempts. You and I could have taken out Hitler easily." Fired up, now standing, he hikes up his sweat pants. "Lars was an expert with every weapon and a top sniper, when called upon, with the rifle. One of the best in Vietnam."

"Merci, Tiger. I must admit that these guys were amateurs and rather sloppy.

"OK. Moving on... let me cover a few assassination attempts most people have never heard about. Some of my in-depth research comes from the *German Federal Archives* and *Adolph Hitler Archives*. Plus the usual sources we all search out in researching our blunders—books, general articles, special reports, our own *National Archives*, discussions with historians, interviews, almanacs, letters, diaries, Top Secret Nazi documents. For this one, though, in particular, I expanded the research sources, using captured dossiers, oral histories, and eyewitness reports."

"Not to get off target here," chimed in Brenda, "but whether its 40 or 60+ attempts, it's close to the CIA's attempts, under the Kennedy Administration, to kill Castro... which was more than 42 times. Fidel survived 638 attempts on his life. Just a sidebar here. Sorry to go off on a tangent, gang."

"That's all right, Brenda," replied Lars. "It just shows that a lot of Dictators are targets, and attempts often are not known to the general public. OK, here we go. And let me be clear—many attempts/plots fall under the radar because of the media hype over Operation Valkyrie. A lot of historians and writers ask themselves *'What if'* or *'Should have'*. *'What if one of these attempts were successful?'* I say, at least one should've happened. But because of mistakes that shouldn't have been made in many of these attempts, here we sit today having lost over 50 million lives as a result of failed assassinations. Plus, the extreme hardships people endured as a result of those failed attempts.

"Remember gang, we look for mistakes that could have been avoided. Because they weren't, the blunder was allowed to occur. Now I'm getting to the main part of my discussion. It's about Georg Elser. Don't forget his name. He is the number one true hero of World War II. My God! I admire him so much." Lars chokes like he just swallowed a chestnut; his eyes well up slightly. Others frown in bewilderment... not knowing what's coming. Tiger cranks his neck making a pop sound.

"But he did make mistakes that could have been avoided. Those mistakes, along with those of the many others who made attempts, led to the big picture... or in this case, the blunder—Failure to assassinate Adolph Hitler. Over 50 million lives could have been saved. Elser's mistakes, *(God bless him):*

- Lack of intelligence on Hitler;
- Acting alone... no network, thus teamwork not available to avoid pitfalls;
- Unaware of expected challenges and ability to make adjustments;
- Not reading newspapers;
- Setting timer too late;
- Not checking Hitler's departure plans *(due to fog; train rather than airplane, thus left Hall early);*
- Not realizing fog would cause Hitler to leave one hour earlier for Berlin than scheduled... that's what can happen when you act alone;
- Failure to remain at scene of explosion. Seeing Hitler leave early, he could have stopped explosion and try another time;
- Not realizing security was lax.

"Again, it is tough to criticize Elser since his meticulous planning was unmatched by other prospective assassins. Those were his mistakes, so he could have done better, yet his lone-wolf attempt was the best of all 60+ plots, to include Operation Valkyrie. That operation had about 200 participants—many of those were Generals, and others of aristocratic backgrounds.

"Elser said, *'I lived for only one purpose—preparing for the assassination'*. A solid German with a selfless goal to save his country from despair and ruination.

"He was the perfect fit to do this. A carpenter and watch maker. Worked as a laborer at the Vollmer Quarry in Konigsbronn, his hometown. He collected 105 blasting cartridges and 125 detonators. *'I knew two or three detonators were sufficient for my purposes, but I thought the surplus will increase the explosive effect'*; it sure did. He worked in the Waldenmaier armament factory in Heidenbeim where he stole explosives. For two months he stayed all night inside the Burgerbraukeller; visited there 30-35 times—a good scouting effort.

"He just *'wanted to do something' (his words)*, rather than sit by and watch his country go down the tubes. Elser felt that the workers *'would be the first to suffer and the first to fight and die'*. He was right.

"Most of those who study history miss this point. It is the *main point* and why Elser was ready to give up his life... really, for the workers. If you forget much of what I say today, please remember those words. They are the key to his extraordinary effort. He was more concerned about the needs of the workers than his own. To me, this man is the most incredible man to have ever lived.

"He knew that traditionally, Hitler gave a two-hour speech each year on November 8th to commemorate the Beer Hall Putsch of 1923 in Munich. The Putsch failed to take over the government. *'The Hall is the right place to assassinate the leadership'*, said Elser. He knew that Hitler's Berlin security was virtually impregnable. So he would have to hit him on one of his outside moves, like a visit to the front. However, it would require a shot to the head or neck since Hitler wore a bulletproof vest.

"Again, to me, Elser is the biggest hero of World War II. His planning was meticulous. Being an outstanding craftsman, he used his carpenter skills to hollow out a cavity to place his bomb. This stone pillar was behind the speaker's platform. As I've mentioned, Hitler was to speak at Munich's Burgerbraukeller Brewery. Elser's bomb had a 144-hour timer. He spent several months building the bomb and several weeks of labor to hollow out the stone. It was set to detonate at 9:20 p.m. on Wednesday, November 8, 1939.

Here's what happened. Hitler enters the beer hall at 8:10 p.m., but at 9:12 p.m. he ends his speech—about 58 minutes earlier than usual. In the past, his speeches were two hours long. The bomb goes off 8 minutes later... about 9:25 p.m. and misses Hitler by 13 minutes. Kills 8, wounds 65 including Eva Braun's father. Braun was Hitler's girlfriend and later, his wife in dying moments in the Bunker in Berlin.

"Elser was sent to Dachau Concentration Camp. The SS executed him on April 9, 1945, just three weeks before Hitler committed suicide along with Eva Braun. Hitler ordered Elser's murder. He was shot and put in a crematorium. Just a few days before his death, he told his SS guard, *'I do not regret what I did. And anyway there is no use. I believe I have done something good, but it failed, and I must suffer the consequences'.*

"I know that I have rambled on about Georg Elser, but he deserves recognition forever, although over-shadowed by the von Stauffenberg plot. If successful, he alone would have changed the entire world. Think about that, gang."

All flipped up a number one finger sign.

"As mentioned, von Stauffenberg's failed coup stole the spotlight. You all have the matrix of assassination attempts and plots, so that has made my job easier. I'll just add a little more, mostly unknown facts, like vignettes, to a few of them. Most of the conspirators did not like Hitler's brutality approach... a license to murder, loot, and rape at will. Hitler said many times over and over, *'This is a war of extermination... and we do not conduct a war in order to keep the enemy alive'*. The Generals did nothing except to protest in silence—behind closed doors—working on the silent conspiracies."

Noticeably upset, Olivia injected, "As we say in Britain, he was an *arsehole... a real wanker!* And the do-nothing Generals were all *tossers*."

All agreed and gave her the thumbs up.

Lars continued, checking his notes.

"Here are some extra points relating to a few of the attempts." Lars rolled up both sleeves of his J. Crew shirt. A short-sleeve, chambray in voyage print.

"They are not in chronological order. Rather random."

"The Berghof—Hitler's Villa—March 11, 1944. Captain Eberhard von Breitenbuch, Adjutant of Field Marshall Ernst Busch, attended a conference with a concealed Browning pistol. As he approached the conference room entrance, he was stopped by a duty sergeant. *'Sorry, no adjuntants beyond this point'.* Breitenbuch swore he would never try this again. Too nerve racking. So another plot failed. By the way, Breitenbuch was traumatized by this incident."

"What a candy-ass, Doc," blurted out Tiger. "What would the Brits call a guy like that, Olivia?"

"I'd say, a *jittery bloke,*" she responded.

"Certainly unfit for the mission," added Brenda.

"OK, moving on. Berlin—March 20, 1943—Colonel Rudolf von Gertsdorff, an Intelligence Officer, had a concealed bomb to be detonated by acid as he stood close to Hitler in an exhibit hall. He gave the *Seig Heil* salute to Hitler with his right arm, using his left hand in his pocket to ignite the chemical fuse. Hitler returned his salute. Hitler left before the acid could act. Gertsdorff raced to the restroom and flushed the fuse down the toilet. Another lucky escape by Hitler... by about ten minutes.

"February, 1944—Infantry Captain Axel von dem Bussche planned to blow up Hitler and himself. Bussche was to model a new Army winter overcoat. The Brits conducted an air raid which destroyed the uniforms. Another overcoat attempt was made in March, 1944, but again the RAF *(Royal Air Force)* conducted an air raid which forced the cancellation of the demonstration.

"The Berghoff—July 11, 1944—Lt. Colonel Count Claus Schenk von Stauffenberg attempted to kill Hitler, as you know. He had a bomb hidden in his black briefcase. It was aborted because Goering nor Himmler were present. The coup leaders wanted to wipe out the entire leadership. Not just Hitler.

"And there was Rastenburg—July 15, 1944—Same

attempt but Himmler was absent. Aborted. Frustration is at a high level amongst the some 200 participants involved in this coup to take over the country. Maurice Bavaud, a Swiss, tried multiple times to kill Hitler. Each time Hitler was not where he was supposed to be. On one attempt, at a rally, spectators blocked his view by raising their hands giving the Nazi salute. Police picked up Bavaud at a train station. Found his gun, a forged letter of introduction, and another document addressed to Hitler. Gestapo tortured him until he admitted his plans. He was sent to the guillotine in 1941. Here's just another example of unknown attempts. More careless attempts by Bavaud.

"July 7, 1944—General Helmuth Stieff, member of German Army Headquarters planned to kill Hitler, but didn't have the guts to do it. It was all set up at a display of uniforms near Salzburg. Hitler hated Stieff, a dwarf of a man, calling him a *'poisonous little dwarf'*.

"Let me say this now. Hitler had tight security. His bodyguards were *quick shooters*. He wore a bulletproof vest and would change scheduled times for visits; even postpone or cancel them. He knew he was a target, but would not admit it because the *'Divine Providence has given him this calling'*. He felt impenetrable."

Lars stopped to sip his drink and clear his throat before continuing. But he was fired up and began again, without hesitation. He had everyone's full attention.

"Berlin—September 28, 1938—Lt. Colonel Helmut Groscurth, Counterintelligence. He was horrified at what Hitler and his regime was doing especially with the massacres of Jews, noblemen, and intellectuals. He kept trying to push his superiors for a coup d'état. General Walther von Brauchitsch, a commander-in-chief, told Gruscorth, *'I simply cannot do it'*, referring to the plot which he thought was exposed.

"1939 Berlin—Erich Kordt—He had a high honorary rank in the SS *(Schutzstaffel)*. Closet anti-Nazi. Conspiracy planner. He planned to blow up Hitler himself at a daily briefing. The coup failed. Kordt said, *'Never since 1933, was there such a good chance to free Germany and the world'*. Kordt was still ready to go forward with the assassination plan, but Elser's attempt caused Hitler's security teams to be on high alert. Lt. General Hans Spedel, General Rommel's Chief of Staff, led conspirators in the west to get the conspiracy to continue even though Hitler was alive.

"Josef *'Beppo'* Romer, a war veteran and journalist, and a team of communists developed plots to kill Hitler. These plots never went any further than the table... like many others nobody has ever heard of.

"1938—Helmut Hirsch, a Jew, joined the *Black Front*, a Czech anti-Nazi group. A member of the group gave Hirsch instructions to pick up some bombs to kill Hitler. The member was a Nazi spy. Poor Hirsch was beheaded in 1939.

"March 13, 1943—General Helmuth Stieff gave a Hitler aide two bottles of Cointreau triple sec. They were dummies, filled with explosives using a Brit Intel 30-minute timer. Upon landing in Berlin, a fellow conspirator raced out to trade off the dummy bottles with real ones. The bombs were both duds. Hitler would have definitely died if the bombs went off.

"March 20, 1943—At an Exhibit of war trophies in Berlin, a German Colonel stood next to Hitler with a bomb in his right pocket. Had a 10-minute timer. When he found out Hitler was only staying 8 minutes, he disarmed the bomb. *'Divine intervention'?*

"Operation Foxley—1944—A British plan by SOE *(Special Operations Executive).* Detailed preparations made but no attempts made to act on any plans. Ideas: Shoot him on his daily morning walk—he took leisurely walks to a teahouse in Berchtesgaden. This would be easy because, as stated in a dossier, *'he cannot bear to feel himself watched'.* He was a real addict... always drank tea with milk. Brits were going to poison his tea but they thought the drug would muck up the color. But milk would have covered that up. Unfortunately, the Brits didn't know about Hitler's habits. A severe shortcoming on their part."

Olivia jumped in. "We call them *tools*, or stupid non-performers, lacking mental capacity, or a fool."

Lars chuckled. "Well another idea of the SOE tool was to execute an aerial bombardment and paratrooper assault of Hitler's Berchtesgaden Alpine Retreat and blowing up his personal train, the Fuhrezug or Fuhrersonderzug, as it went through a tunnel. And another of the variety of ideas that flowed at SOE was to impregnate his clothes with anthrax.

"Also, full of ideas, the Brits considered poisoning his food. But then they found out that his food was specially prepared and tasted.

"July 20, 1944—Operation Valkyrie—This one we know about. Von Stauffenberg planted a briefcase under the oak table in Hitler's situation room. A few next to him died. The briefcase was kicked to the other side of a thick wooden table which, by accident, shielded Hitler.

"Let me be more specific about this. At 12:37 p.m. von Stauffenberg places his black briefcase containing 2,000 grams of Plastik-In explosives, a standard British bomb, under the map table. He excuses himself. At 12:42 p.m. the bomb explodes. Colonel Brandt, who took von Stauffenberg's seat, had kicked the briefcase away to give himself more room. This saved Hitler's life. Using von Stauffenberg was ridiculous.

"Nobody has ever written about the point I'm about to make. Having a man, with no right hand, only 3 fingers on his left hand, and blind in one eye trying to put together a 2.2 pound block of plastic explosive... to put the bomb together, using pliers to crush the end of a detonator. And... under rush conditions. This Colonel had to dress himself using his teeth and one arm with two fingers missing."

Olivia piped in. "Just for your info, von Stauffenberg's wife and four children were imprisoned. At the time of her arrest, she was pregnant. She gave birth to her fifth child while in prison and one of her brothers was executed."

"And von Stauffenberg was the most handsome man in the entire German Army," cited Doris.

"Yeah! Better than Tom Cruise who played him in the movie, *Valkyrie*, in 2008," said Tiger. "Von Stauffenberg was a stud. Cruise... on the other hand, is more of a wimp. Good looking but sort of a fake stud look." Tiger wiggled in his seat as he said, "You gotta' be kidding!"

Lars continued. "Adolph Hitler ordered those found guilty in this attempted coup to be *'hanged like cattle'*.

"General Henning von Tresckow, who was the main German resistance organizer, ate a grenade the day after the failed plot. Just before his suicide he said, *'The whole world will vilify us now, but I am still totally convinced that we did the right thing. Hitler is the archenemy not only of Germany but of the world. When, in a few hours' time, I go before God to account for what I have done and left undone, I know I will be able to justify what I did in the struggle against Hitler. None of us can bewail his own death; those who consented to join our circle put on the robe of Nessus. A human being's moral integrity begins when he is prepared to sacrifice his life for his convictions'.*"

Lars swallowed hard. "I think this was directed at the 200+ participants in the coup d'etat attempt. Many committed suicide. Most assassination attempts and plots are relatively unknown to us and to even the German general public. One reason is because they were kept in the dark, obscured, due to the popular von Stauffenberg's July 20, 1944 failed attempt. Yes, as I mentioned earlier, the Operation Valkyrie has taken precedence over most of them, unfortunately.

"Think about this. Most assassination leaders really were supporting Nazism up until it looked like the ballgame was over. For example, von Stauffenberg fought in the invasion of Poland, Battle of France, Operation Barbarossa, and the Tunsia Campaign. He won the Iron Cross, 1st Class, German Cross *(Gold)*, and Wound Badge *(Gold)*. Others had similar awards, so you see... these plotters were heavy duty into the Nazi scheme. Frankly, not genuine assassins like Elser. That's why I have put heavy emphasis on Georg

Elser. Now, don't get me wrong... these resistance leaders deserve a lot of credit but they were part of the problem themselves until they woke up."

"Hey! I know what you're saying, Doc," remarked Tiger, rubbing his hands together and cracking his knuckles, much to the dismay of the ladies present. "It's like—let's kick the Jews butts and everyone else, but as soon as the tide turns, we change with the tide."

Olivia adds her two cents. "The German people are guilty forever. That's it in a nutshell. Germany started World War I and II. The world views the Nazi era as the historical responsibility of the German people. Von Stauffenberg and his clan felt the need to revolt because their conscience was affecting them to the nth degree."

Tiger roars excitedly, "You know what this entire Nazi reign was? A circus. A puppet show. Hitler was the puppeteer and the German people, including his staff, were his puppets. He just pulled their strings and they did whatever he demanded. They couldn't even respond; they were made of wood."

"What a *super* analogy, Tiger," pipes in Lars.

Tiger, Brenda, Doris, and Olivia had agreed earlier to research other matters in regards to Adolph Hitler.

Doris starts off with her information. "Adolphus Schicklgruber was Hitler's real name. Born on April 20, 1889 in Braunauam Inn, a small town in Austria-Hungary. His father, Alois Schicklgruber, changed his name to Hitler on January 7, 1887.

"Man! I didn't know that," chimed in Tiger, cracking his knuckles again.

Olivia added, "When I did my blunders book, I got into Hitler's secret medical history. He was a sickly man. Digestive problems, stomach pains, facial twitches, clumsiness, erratic movements. And... he suffered from Hypochondriasis: the fear of future serious illnesses. Constant complaining *(I mean everyday)* to Dr. Morell of diarrhea, constipation, and headaches. He had Parkinson's and Huntington's disease... hand tremors, and a shuffling gait."

"My God. I wonder if he took all of this out on his way of ruling Germany?" said Brenda.

"Could be," exclaimed Lars. "Nobody has ever written about that. An excellent point. Some historians and Hitler scholars feel that he had schizophrenia symptoms, too.

"I checked into his medical records along with Olivia. She didn't want to tell you this, but he had monarchism... one testicle, and the tiniest penis the doctors had ever seen. Fit for the Guinness World Records. Except the book was published too late... 1955. Ho Ho! It was a joke to the Brits who sang a version of Colonel Bogey's March. It was sung throughout pubs in England. It went like this:

'Hitler has only one ball, Hitler his pecker is quite small, Hitler da, da, da, Hitler, da,da,da,da,da, da, da, da, da, da; Oh yes Hitler has only one ball, Hitler his pecker is quite small, Hitler, da, da, da, Hitler, da,da...'

"You have to Google *Colonel Bogey's March* to get the melody. You should get the original tune played by the band of HM Royal Marines, Plymouth Division, conducted by

Major FJ Ricketts. Then, you can sing along with the words. Hitler *hated* that version and any German caught singing it was executed immediately. To pardon the expression, *it pissed him off!*"

Everyone laughed and gave Tiger a loud cheer. Brenda laughed so hard that she started choking. Doris slapped her on the back.

"Thank you for that, Lars," said Olivia, her cheeks a little blushed. "To continue with the Hitler medical information, Hitler used many drugs: Cocaine, opiates, morphine, methamphetamines, and vitamins in high doses intravenously. I think, at his end, his blood veins must have been totally ruined."

"In Mein Kamp, his autobiography, he stated that he wanted to be a professional artist. However, he failed the entrance exam twice *(1907 and 1908)* of the Academy of Fine arts in Vienna. He worked mostly in watercolor. His artistic lack of talent is summed up well by John Gunther, an art critic. *'They are prosaic, utterly void of rhythm, color, feeling, or spiritual imagination. The architect's sketches; painful and precise draftsmanship: nothing more. No wonder the Vienna professors told him to go to an architectural school and give up pure art as hopeless'.*"

"Thanks, Olivia! That was real good. It's too bad he wasn't accepted because if accepted, he would never have been the Fuhrer," stated Lars.

"Really puts a different aspect on his leadership," maintained Doris.

Tiger gave a thumbs up.

Brenda said, "He lived in a homeless shelter while trying

to sell his art pieces. You probably don't know this, but Hitler painted hundreds of works and sold his paintings and postcards to earn a living from 1908 to 1913. It was a simple case of survival."

Tiger blurted out, "Well, he sure didn't like the Hitler version of Colonel Bogey's March. *HOOAH!* I'd like to have sung that to his face before I drilled him with my trusty .45. A head shot for sure. By the way, talk about things you don't know, did you know he liked to whistle *When You Wish Upon A Star,* especially for dinner guests? Can you imagine guests having to put up with that? But, everyone just sucked up to Adolph."

"Gee, I'm taken back by that because *Pinocchio* is one of my favorite movies, even though it goes back to 1940. That song was the movie's theme song sung by Cliff Edwards in the character of Jimmy Cricket." After that comment, Doris took a swig of her herbal tea.

Olivia added, "Since Pinocchio's nose grew longer and longer as he told lies, it reminds me of something Hitler said many times: *'If you tell a big enough lie and tell it frequently enough, it will be believed'.* This was mentioned earlier."

Tiger bellows out loud, "Yo! If that's the case, Hitler's nose must've been about a hundred meters long!"

Everyone chuckles at that.

"What a frigging liar," Tiger stated. "Let's face it; the entire Hitler era was dominated by lies. Lies, lies, and more lies. And the German people, who are known to be easily led, fell for the charade, consisting of an absurd grand strategy."

Brenda pipes up. "Let me add a little tidbit. German soldiers poured 180 liters of petroleum over Hitler and Eva Braun's bodies in the Chancellery Garden."

"Let me piggyback Brenda's remark," said Doris. "Hitler's bones have been moved several times. Actually more like burned bones to ashes. A KGB Officer, Vladimir Gumenyuk, posed as a fisherman, drove into the mountains and standing on a cliff over a small stream, tossed the ashes into the wind. The brown dust disappeared over the stream. Gumenyuk refused to give the location. A secret he took to his grave; fear of it becoming a pilgrimage site. *'Twenty seconds and the job was done'*. It was the last flight of the Fuhrer. This was hard to track down. So many writers and historians have different views on the whereabouts of Hitler's remains. But this is the most accurate, I think."

"We are near to closing out this marvelous discussion, gang. And I hate to close it out with a dreadful thought but here it is. Although dead, Hitler has us marching towards an open grave... we just don't realize it." Lars scratches his chin. "He still emanates a silent power beyond death. Hitler will never be gone... the damage he has caused is permanent. The winds have taken his ugly dust everywhere— worldwide. The German souls are scarred forever by not fighting off Hitler and his lunatic leadership group.

"Hitler's ashes will follow all of us wherever we go. It's like a mobile grave following you around... in the shadows. Hitler raced Germany to ruination and as a result, we walk and run over his literal grave forever and ever. It's been over 70 years and we are *still* affected by him. By causing this unfortunate blunder, not assassinating Hitler, the Germany people are guilty and the entire world will never forget... forever."

"I'm going to add a little scripture here," said Doris. "Deuteronomy 19:21—*'Thus you shall show no pity: life for life, eye for eye, tooth for tooth, hand for hand, foot for foot'*. I think Adolph Hitler miss-read this if he read it at all. Although he was a voracious reader. However, don't forget... he was also, a school drop-out."

Wrapping it up, Lars said, "In chasing down each of our chosen blunders, we attempt to dig deep for hidden facts, unknown to most of our country's population. That is our quest... to explore and render the truths."

Doris added, "If they had only known at the time. I've got the lead for next Friday's discussion on John F. Kennedy's assassination. See you all then."

All stand and smack hands together.

Tiger, with bulging eyes, said, "Hey look! The snow has doubled since we started... must be eight inches out there now! Let's scram!"

John F. Kennedy (JFK)

CHAPTER 24

JFK Assassination: So Many Questions Left Unanswered

All were seated. Anxious. Ready to hear Doris' comments about the mistakes made that caused the Kennedy assassination. But first, Lars wanted to make a point that was not mentioned during the Hitler Blunder last week. He stated that even after World War II ended, many Germans... the majority of the 70.7 million population, felt that German resistance members were blatant traitors. Von Stauffenberg and his coup d'état group were widely regarded as German betrayers. As was Georg Elser. They were all objects of revulsion to most Germans. At this point, Tiger couldn't take it any longer.

"Those Krauts looked the other way! Did nothing. They lacked moral courage. Sorry, but I have a case of the *ass* with them." Tiger pounded his fist on the table. Being black, his face looked like a red-hot tomato.

"But today, those *traitors* of the 1940's are perceived to be heroes by the public," said Olivia.

Lars remarked, "Olivia is right. And by the way, we've been a little hard on the Germans. I have a lot of German friends. Most Americans respect them for their perfectionism and precision in all fields of endeavor. They are very efficient and disciplined. Well organized. Sorry to delay you, Doris, it's all yours. Carry on."

"I'm going to make this rather brief because I am only going to cover the miscues that caused this blunder. The rest of his assassination has been covered by books, movies, articles, documentaries... heavily; but simple things that could have been done to prevent the incident has had very poor visibility. These things were done due to carelessness, poor insight or... lack of coordination. These points have escaped most of us, to include writers and historians, as well as journalists. Here are *uncalled for* mistakes:

- Cancel the trip to Dallas in the first place. It was a mistake to go. Red flags had gone up before the trip. Not paying attention to warnings. Multiple people had warned him in advance, which included four separate confidants;
- Travelling in an open limousine. Should have been a closed, bulletproof limo. Kennedy insisted on riding without a protective bubble saying, *'All the better to see and be seen'*. He should have been overruled by a Secret Service bodyguard. Not professional when again, lots of red flags were flying before this Dallas visit;
- The FBI and the CIA screwed up this one... badly. Failure of them to track Oswald better. They needed

to act on intelligence *in their own files!* More aggressive surveillance of Oswald. Come on, everybody... he had just visited the USSR and Cuban embassies in Mexico... meeting with spies *and* a KGB assassinations' expert;

- Secret Service man riding on left side of limo. Nobody on right side. A gross shortcoming;
- Parade route and times *widely publicized* in newspapers and radio networks;
- Also, the FBI and CIA needed to pay more attention to the Mafia and Castro. Both hated JFK *(John F. Kennedy)*. Threats from both were *under the table;*
- Failure of security to cover all buildings. Should have spotted Oswald on the 6th floor of the Texas School Book Depository, and shot him dead. Frankly, this is basic coverage for a presidential motorcade!

"That's it. I couldn't find much, even in the archives, about this—that includes TS documents, now declassified. But a lot of this is just common sense."

Lars cut in. "You couldn't find much because it was a cover-up, Doris. We have all read the Warren Commission Report, which was filled with cover-ups and vague information. I counted nineteen; then used the Air Force speed reading method to get through the rest."

"Same here, Doc," blurted out Tiger. "I had to drink several *5-Hour Energy* drinks to stay with it. A real bureaucratic piece of crap—888 pages. Yipes! Missed the point that it might have been a cover-up involving LBJ and others. Johnson looked too smug for me."

"Jolly good," said Olivia. "Simply a *blue ribbon* cover-up. The American people are so ignorant... it shocks me. Not in intelligence; I mean... just *not getting it*."

Tiger scratched his left ear; the one partially shot off in an ambush in Vietnam. "You know... Lars was an expert with the rifle. As an Army Lieutenant, he represented the USA in the Leclerc Rifle Championships in Europe... which is kind of like the Olympics. I don't think even *you* could have shot Kennedy from that 6th story window. Huh, Doc?"

"Let me say this—that Italian Carcano rifle was a piece of crap... just to be quite honest, gang. Awkward and unpredictable. It was a cheap, old weapon with bolt and trigger pull problems. It was an inexpensive, surplus Italian carbine using a 6.5 x 52mm cartridge. Model 91/38. Sort of like the Japanese Arisaka weapon... rough working. Not good. I must admit, as good a shot as I am, I could not have fired 3 shots in succession within 5.6 seconds. This had to be a *frame-up* operation. On top of all of this, Oswald, as a Marine, was a terrible shot. He scored 191 on a 190 to 250 scale, as a Marksman. The scale is Marksman *(lowest)* to Sharpshooter to Expert *(highest)*. One Marine said they all used to laugh at Oswald when he was at the rifle qualification firing range. He would consistently get *Maggie's drawers*. That means a red flag is waved from the range pits indicating a clear miss."

"Also, Doc... the rifle was a cheap model Oswald bought for $19.99 from Kleins Sporting Goods via mail order. Rifle cost without scope was $12.79," added Tiger.

"And... the telescopic scope was unreliable and inaccurate. A cheap Japanese scope," stated Lars.

"Here's something else," announced Brenda. "He used that same weapon about seven months prior to the Dallas shooting, to try to assassinate retired Major General Edwin A. Walker in Dallas. Missed him—the bullet deflected hitting a nearby window frame. Where were you *then*, CIA and FBI?"

Doris jumped back in. "We are only trying to determine the mistakes made that caused this terrible assassination of a US President. Not to pin the assassination on anybody. That said, there are many unanswered questions about his assassination. It definitely should've been prevented and someone knows the truth, but it was so well covered up, the truth may never be known. Personally, I don't think Oswald acted alone. I think he was the proverbial *fall guy*."

"That's correct," agreed Olivia. "Out of interest, Kennedy seemed to see the writing on the wall. On the plane that morning, he told Jackie, *'We're heading into nut country today'*. Then he added, *'If someone wants to shoot me from a window with a rifle, nobody can stop it, so why worry about it?'*

"His last words, *before* being shot, were *'No, certainly can't'*, replying to Nellie Connally's comment to him, *'You certainly can't say that the people of Dallas haven't given you a nice welcome'*. Milliseconds later he was shot dead. Jackie's immediate words were, *'They shot him... Oh, Jack! What have they done'?*"

"Now, in closing," Doris said, "If JFK were alive today he would be 100 years old. Probably sailing from Hyannis Harbor to Nantucket Sound."

All balled their hands into a fist and punched them

together. Lars announced that for the next discussion on Friday, Tiger would take the discussion lead, covering Hurricane Katrina.

On their way out, each team member picked out a carryout desert as ordered earlier via Anita.

View of flooded New Orleans in the
aftermath of Hurricane Katrina

CHAPTER 25

Hurricane Katrina: Failures, Failures—And More Failures

Friday, 8:02 a.m. All seated at table #98. Clear day, yet somewhat chilly.

There was a warm mist in Tiger's eyes as he was ready to start the discussion as today's leader. Then he suddenly broke down... crying like a baby. Choking. Snorting. Tiger is such a tough guy; it took the team by surprise.

But then everyone remembered that Tiger's Aunt Kiara drowned in her attic during the hurricane. Sixteen others drowned in their attics during Katrina. They endured a suffocating death trap. Most tried to leave a note. Kiara left a note scribbled on a piece of shingle that was stored inside: *'I love you, I'm gonna' die'.* He was very close to her.

Doris got up and ran over to him. They hugged tightly for about two minutes. Everyone was silent. You couldn't hear a pin drop. Sometimes, a hug without words is better than any words that could be said. It speaks for itself. Silent words.

Lars walked to the men's room with his arm around Tiger. Two war heroes having fought together in Vietnam. Side-by-side. Both wounded twice in close combat. Lars, the captain; Tiger his reconnaissance sergeant.

You may have forgotten—Doris is married to Lars. She was the FBI's top profiler and is big into astrology. Very sensitive... strong feelings for all people. While the two men were gone, she philosophized with Brenda and Olivia.

"Inside all of us, lies a mystery. When we solve it, we find out who we really are. Just like planting a seed. It germinates, grows and grows, until the mystery is released. Out bursts a cotton boll, or a flower, or maybe even you... whatever. Lars and Tiger know who they are. They radiate self-confidence coupled with kindness," said Doris.

The women talked about this. Doris concluded saying, "All men should try to achieve that. Well, enough of this *women's talk;* here they come."

Upon their return, Tiger apologized softly. "OK gang, I'm totally composed now. Never cried over this until now, oddly enough. Been 15 years. Holding it inside. Not only did I lose my very best friend, Aunt Kiara, but also her sister, Alyssac. She is one of the 705 persons still missing. My wife Briana lost her uncle Ethan, who drowned trying to save people. All of us were close. A tight family trying to run a funeral service company in the *Big Easy*. OK, I'm ready to roll." Tiger seemed to be completely composed by this point.

Everyone gave him a thumbs up and reached over to pat him on the back, which obviously encouraged Tiger to march on.

"Just think—1,836 people died during Katrina; 705 still missing and 30 bodies unidentified.

"A real fiasco blunder because the death toll should have been much lower. By the way, about half of the Louisiana victims were over 74 years old. Many inexcusable mistakes were made that allowed tens of billions, of gallons of water to spill into the New Orleans area. It flooded 80% of my city." Tiger groans. Eyes damp. "Some places had over 20 feet of water! That said, here are some of the errors that should not have happened:

- Unreliable flood control system. That's the overall huge mistake;
- Levees were not high enough and not resistant to face category 3-5 level hurricanes; keep in mind, New Orleans is already eight feet below sea level;
- Flood walls inefficient for a region where disastrous flooding is to be expected. Not installed according to original design to save money. I'm not going to get into it now, but the government is at fault here... by cutting funding to the Corps of Engineers, which caused them to take short cuts to stay at reduced budget levels imposed upon them. Total disregard for residents' safety. Poor decision-making at the highest levels of government."

Tiger pauses to regain his composure.

"Again, we have a load of *tossers* and *wankers*," injected Olivia.

"Before I continue, we want to know what wankers means. We understand tossers... meaning show-offs, but wankers?" asked Tiger.

"It is a Brit term for having distain for somebody; some Brits call a person a tosser if he or she masturbates excessively. And a person that you have a low opinion of. Looks like we have a pot full of wankers and tossers who were involved in this one, Tiger."

Everyone chuckles. Again, Tiger regains his composure. "OK, a few more points...

- Emergency pumps and canal closures were not installed *or* were ineffective;
- The Corps of Engineers had no external review board to double-check floodwall designs. The levee boards needed to check this also, since it was part of their responsibility... maintenance;
- A big construction mistake—engineering reliability reduced due to driving sheet piles to depths of only 17 feet, rather than between 31 and 46 feet. This was due to the Corps misinterpreting results from a sheet pile load test;
- This is the bottom line—levees and floodwalls failed. Inadequate design and construction by the US Army Corps of Engineers, mostly due to the cuts in funds. Plus, negligent maintenance and upkeep by the New Orleans Levee Board, who were sitting on their hands, I guess. Sand existed in 10% of locations instead of thick clay. Engineers overestimated the strength of the soil. What I mean is, the design calculations exceeded

what actually existed under and near certain levees. The soil below the levees was weaker than that of the I-wall design. I got all of this info from an interview with a sharp Engineer officer. Possibility of water-filled gaps was ignored. A huge mistake! My God!

- Layers of peat had poor shear strength and a high water content *(peat layers start at about 30 feet below the surface)*. Thus, most major breaches were the result of overtopping and erosion. Eyewitnesses, to include a jazz lover friend of mine observed this—levees and floodwalls topped by floodwaters first, then breached due to erosion. Several levees and floodwalls probably failed at weak-link junctions where different levee or wall sections were joined together. This is a key point, but if you research this hurricane, you won't typically *find* this covered-up point. I had to dig deep to find it. Gosh! I'm shocked at the negligence all the way around the horn!

"An extra point. Just so you know, originally the levees were constructed to prevent damage to seasonal flooding. It goes back to the years 1717 to 1727, when the French built the first levees. The levees only measured three feet and hardly withstood the Mississippi River overflow.

"Over the years, the levee construction was increased to withstand a category 3 hurricane. Katrina started out as a category 5; at landfall a category 3. Over 50 failures of levees and floodwalls were reported. Frankly, I found that rather than the wind velocity being the villain as most people believe, it was the tremendous storm surge that was the monster in the case of Katrina. When you talk to eyewitnesses, they'll tell you that the storm surge was the culprit.

"By the way, Uncle Ethan is a hero in the Crescent City. He saved three people before going under water—never to be seen again." Tiger's eyes became misty.

By this time, Doris's eyes were running over with tears streaming down her face. She had to excuse herself. Olivia joined her. Brenda wiped a tear away with her napkin. Lars patted Tiger on the back saying, "They'll be right back, Tiger."

"I know, Doc. This is tough stuff. But I feel good letting out the real truths today. Lots of these facts have been hidden... kept in the shadows."

Brenda said, "I lived in New Orleans too, Tiger. I got my undergraduate degree at Tulane. Residents there always talked about money being taken away from flood protection; put into Mardi Gras support instead. Most feared a future hurricane disaster; they knew they were walking on eggs. The Mississippi river is 30 feet above sea level. And New Orleans is sinking 2 inches each year. They are now living amongst these shadows of past failures."

"I agree 100%," said Olivia, having returned. "The Corps and Levee Board are a bunch of *sods*. These gross errors, noted eloquently by Tiger, form shadows for the future, Brenda. They are a haunting for the Corps of Engineers... for design and construction, and the Levee Board for maintenance. They knew that the *Big Easy* was vulnerable for many years."

"Hey, Olivia... *sod?* Definition please," asked Tiger.

"Unpleasant or disapproval of a stupid *arsehole*." Olivia explained.

Lars butted in. "Here's my take. Like NASA, there was a lack of concern for the safety of New Orleans residents. Isn't that it in a nutshell? I mean, poor emergency planning. Experts state that New Orleans will be underwater in the year 2100. This is according to a 2016 NASA study. Some parts of New Orleans are 15 feet below sea level! To me, the Katrina catastrophe culprit equals human errors. Sloppy all the way around, gang. Really upsets me. Hey! It can happen again."

Tiger explains, "Just remember, my research was aimed at only the causes for the disastrous flooding—not aftermath errors. Most of my research was based on Archives, the Smithsonian, eyewitnesses' accounts, and various Katrina reports online. But I do know that the Disaster Plan ignored the *three days prep* before the storm made landfall."

"In researching, we always dig deep," said Lars. Tiger pops his chest up with pride. "To get the truths, often hidden, and make our information as accurate as possible."

"For example, Doc—the number of Katrina deaths vary by writers. Some state 1,118; 1,838; over 1,400; 1,833; and many say over 1,800. But the true number is 1,836, as follows: LA—1,577; MS—238; FL—14; AL, GA, OH—2 each; KY—1. That equals 1,836 souls," Tiger hung his head.

Lars pulled Doris' chair out for her when she returned, having regained her composure. Her mediumship causes her to experience death with an emotional connection, more so than the average person. "This is what I mean by stupendous research that you all conduct for all of our blunder discussions." Lars said proudly.

"Again, here's my take on these inexcusable failures, one after another. The Corps is responsible for the design and construction of the levee system. Inferior, shoddy workmanship and inadequate design. The local levee boards *(or NO Levee Board)* are responsible for maintenance of flood protection structures. Poor maintenance, oversight, and extreme negligence on random checks, plus poor judgment on the necessary funding requirements needed by the Corps to do the job right."

Doris tosses in her bottom line, "They all needed the will to prepare properly, thinking about the safety of the people first—blacks and whites, with no favoritism."

Tiger agrees. "Yes! August 29, 2005 was a sad day with many sad days to follow. And I feel very bad for the families of those still missing wives, husbands, daughters, sons, babies, or other relatives. It crushes your heart."

"Here's something I found," offered Olivia. "Ray Seed, a geotechnical engineer at the University of California in Berkley, backs up our findings. He said, *'People didn't die here because the storm was bigger than the system could handle. People died because mistakes were made and because safety was exchanged for efficiency and reduced costs'*. Seed was the head of an Independent Levee Investigation Team."

Doris remarked, "OK Tiger, I know you covered the inexcusable mistakes that caused the flooding. You stayed clear of the political aspects or quagmire. But let me mention a few things here. Let's be very candid and honest. These people should have been fired or removed immediately: President Bush; LA Governor Kathleen Blanco; Ray Nagin, New Orleans Mayor; FEMA Director Michael D. Brown and Vice President Dick Cheney. All of them were guilty of criminal negligence. I know you can't actually *fire* Bush, but you could try for impeachment. He was aloof.

"These are despicable people—disregarding the fine people of New Orleans, especially in the case of Bush. Why? Bush delayed response directly causing chaos for at least five days. Later, he took a fly-by and had his usual dumb, blank look... like, *what do I do?* Blanco—late in getting Federal Guard troops to subdue growing civil unrest. Reluctant to give mandatory evacuation order. Nagin—failed to execute New Orleans' Disaster Plan, and Brown—had no clue as to what was going on. A real tosser, right Olivia?"

"Yeah, Doris, I know about him. A real *tosser* is right! This is real good. Most folks don't know about this. And I don't think they know about some of Tiger's key facts that he unearthed."

Tiger jumped back in. "Like Cheney—for ordering Southern Pines Electric Power Association's manager to divert power crews to electrical power stations in Collins, MS? He gets an award for being a dumb, uninformed asshole.

"So who saved the day? Ordinary people, black and white residents who became superheroes and super-heroines during those treacherous days of gloom. God bless them. Some lost their lives trying to save others. The bottom line on the government response is lack of leadership, mismanagement, and incompetence in relief efforts. I covered the inexcusable elements that caused 80% of the city to be flooded. But the government failures added to the numbers of deaths and those missing. Totally disgraceful."

Olivia put in her two bits. "They are all *arseholes*; thinking only of themselves and job security. Useless *wankers!*" Her statement came out a little bit louder than anticipated. Some of the other guests at Metro 29 turned to stare at their table.

"Unacceptable, unforgiveable! Damn those stupid government people that the *Big Easy* put their trust in," Tiger barked.

"Great job, Tiger! You more than covered the mission today," Lars said.

Everybody cheered. People in the packed restaurant were probably wondering if they were sports coaches or something.

"Next time, we tackle the human, economic, and environmental disaster caused by the explosion of the Deepwater Horizon drilling rig. Better known as Deep Water—the Gulf Oil Disaster. Brenda studied this as a journalist with the Times-Picayune newspaper in New Orleans. See you all on Wednesday, as my latest email told you, for a surprise dinner. More later."

All put their hands in the middle of table #98 and to their surprise... Anita put her hand in there too. "Hip Hip Hooray!"

Then, out the exit.

Gulf Oil Spill

CHAPTER 26

Gulf Oil Spill—The Nightmare Well From Hell

After the Katrina discussion, Lars decided to treat the Alpha Team to dinner at Coastal Flats in Tysons Corner. Most team members were obviously sad after researching Hurricane Katrina. When they all left Metro 29 last Friday, Lars saw their pinched faces and the stress in their eyes. Plus, near the end of the discussion, everyone was talking as if their throats had tightened up. The in-depth Katrina discussion had upset everyone. Yet, it was a fantastic discussion... straight to the point. Lars was proud of his team. He wanted to buck up the team's morale.

They met on Wednesday evening, two days prior to the next discussion meeting... targeting the Gulf Oil Spill. Lars ordered the awesome Blue Crab and Shrimp Fritters as a starter... for everybody. All ordered a glass of Merlot... Boderan Bordeaux. Tiger got the Drunken Ribeye, marinated in CF Great American Ale. Olivia and Doris ordered the Jumbo Lump Crab Cake. Brenda got the Pecan

Crusted Trout. All wrapped it up at the end with Key Lime Pie, except Doris. Daring to be different, she got the Warm White Chocolate Bread Pudding, her favorite. Lars twisted in his chair... feeling good. Morale soared back to the usual 100%. He knew that the next discussion would be another heartbreaker.

Friday morning...
The gang was digging in as if they have never eaten before! Anita had already served them breakfast. Brenda decided to start... as a working breakfast. She reminded them that this was the worst accidental offshore oil spill in world history.

Aside from it being an acute and environmental calamity, it resulted in the deaths of 11 crewmembers with 17 injured, and 98 with genuine post-traumatic stress disorder. They were all rig brothers. They had a close bond. Nearly 210 million gallons of uncontrolled oil spilled into the gulf with devastating results.

After providing this background, Brenda declared, "after I give you some of the mistakes, Doris will follow me to give the findings of the President's Commission Report, which might duplicate some of my points... not in any particular order. Here goes...

- In the blowout preventer—dead batteries, bad solenoid valves, leaking hydraulic lines; all ignored;
- Cement did not seal. Oil and gas leaked out. Cement was not adequately tested;
- Two mechanical valves failed, thus oil and gas flowed

freely;

- Pressure tests results misinterpreted—the well was not under control;
- Did not detect increases in pressure in well. Increase should have been spotted 50 minutes before rig exploded;
- Failure to divert mud and gas away from rig;
- Onboard gas detection system failed;
- Blowout preventer failed to work properly—eight minutes prior to explosion, crew tried to close valve. Flat battery and a defective switch made it impossible to close safety valves in blowout preventer;
- Missed warning signs;
- No action taken when mud started spewing from the rig floor;
- Failure to contain hydrocarbon pressures in the well. This could have been contained by the cement in the bottom of the well, the mud in the well, the riser, and the blowout preventer. Nobody appreciated the risk associated with this;
- BP's failure in cementing decisions and procedures, which involved six major decisions and risk factors. Cement was defective;
- Rig crew not properly trained to meet emergency situations. Failure to train for worst-case scenario *(Well from Hell)*. Note: there was a ton of bravery and courage amongst the crew to try to save their brothers;
- Poor decision-making process between BP and other companies. Also, extremely poor communications

within BP and with its contractors. Failure to share information. All had a lack of appreciation of risks;

- Flawed design for cement used to seal the bottom of the well. The seal underwent a test. It was judged a success, when in fact... it was incorrect. Problems prevailed;
- Inadequate safety system;
- Failure to put into place an O-ring seal to prevent a burst of gas from shooting up the pipe;
- Transocean document from 2001 identified 260 design errors. BP cut corners, *especially* in well design;
- Inadequate contingency planning;
- Lack of reliable diagnostic tools. Example—blowout preventer had a pressure gauge accurate to 400+ pounds per square inch. Thus, not accurate readings;
- Finally, here's a specific mistake, of many—BP had only six centralizers, whereas 15 additional centralizers probably would have prevented the blowout. It seems that they were caught up in *groupthink*. My God, I was floored by all the mistakes and the disregard for crew safety. This crew of 126 brothers are guys we can be proud of;
- A backlog of 390 items with overdue maintenance.

"There are more details to all of this, but I tried to give just bottom lines. I asked Doris to look at the National Commission's Reports. That will add depth to my research of unnecessary errors. Some of her points may be repetitive to mine, but that's fine. Take it away, Doris."

Everybody applauds Brenda. Tiger comes over and gives her the fist shake. Doris decided to stand up to present her findings. She scratched her chin, straightened up her blue denim, peplum long-sleeved blouse and cleared her throat. *(Remember... Doris is very sensitive.)* Brenda grinned because she knew that Doris had her back *big time* with super facts. Doris handed out a copy for everyone and began.

"Most of this comes from Figure 3, page 14 of the *Recommendations* booklet by the National Commission on the BP Deepwater Horizon Oil Spill and Offshore Drilling. It is 63 pages. The full report is like a book, 7" x 10", 1-1/4" thick, 380 pages, paperback. Got to give them credit for lots of examples of decisions that increased risk at the 18,000 foot Macondo well.

"For most decisions there was a less risky alternative available. And most decisions were made to save time and money. When are we ever going to learn—safety first! Lastly, except for one, the decision-maker was BP. I've listed them as written in the document verbatim:

- Not Waiting for More Centralizers of Preferred Design;
- Not Waiting for Foam Stability Test Results and/or Redesigning Slurry;
- Not Running Cement Evaluation Log;
- Using Spacer Made from Combined Lost Circulation Materials to Avoid Disposal Issues;
- Displacing Mud from Riser Before Setting Surface Cement Plug;

- Setting Surface Cement Plug 3,000 Feet Below Mud Line in Seawater;
- Not Installing Additional Physical Barriers During Temporary Abandonment Procedure;
- Not performing Further Well Integrity Diagnostics in Light of Troubling and Unexplained Negative Pressure Test Results;
- Bypassing Pits and Conducting Other Simultaneous Operations During Displacement;
- Smoking onboard was common.

"Let me close by pointing out that this Commission *(Bob Graham, William K. Reilly, Frances Beinecke, Donald F. Boesch, Terry D. Garcia, Cherry A. Murray, and Fran Ulmer)* did an outstanding job. Their research and exemplary leadership was beyond reproach. And their recommendations will help industry and our government to improve the safety of offshore drilling operations in the future."

"This is a humiliating *pratfall*," declared Olivia.

"Pratfall?" questioned Tiger.

"That is Brit for blunder. Also, these managements were *gormless*, another Brit term, for lacking intelligence, dull, complacent, lackadaisical—all owed to the managements of BP, the well owner, Transocean, the rig owner, Halliburton, and Cameron. Not sharing information or coordinating together. They professed an air of smugness in my opinion.

"And so, with that culture they missed warning signs. I think the entire industry has a culture of complacency and revenue maximization, and safety is not a primary concern.

Money, shortcuts, and speed seems to be their goals, unfortunately."

Doris sat down and Brenda continued the discussion. "Let me carry on from here. The Gulf of Mexico accounts for about 96% of our total offshore oil production. Thus, there should be better oversight. Frankly, the government and industry could have prevented this from happening. They are at fault and better buck up or there could be a repeat of this type of disaster."

"Very true," Tiger chimed in. "Think about the damage to shellfish, corals, turtles, birds, aquatic vegetation—all ecosystems, wetlands, fish *(tuna, amberjack),* dolphins, etc. Totally disgraceful. Makes me mad and sad at the same time." He clinched his teeth.

Doris interrupts. "I'm a huge turtle fan. Most of my past scuba diving was in locations loaded with turtles. This accident caused losses of endangered sea turtles—Kemp's Ridley, Loggerheads, Green Sea Turtles, and the critically endangered Hawksbills. They shouldn't have had to die in this cruel manner."

Tiger blurts out, "I know we are all chipping in with various points, but here's something that *brule mon cul...* burns my ass. Now sit back and get *this*, gang.

"In July, 2015, BP agreed to pay $18.7 billion in fines... the largest settlement by a Corporation in US history. If they have money like that, why cost cut to begin with? Frankly, shortcuts don't work, long-cuts do. Selfish. Do it right; these guys lives are at stake out there!"

Olivia adds, "You know, Steve O'Rourke, a Justice Department attorney offered a common sense penalty to impose: *'... has to be high enough that companies of this size won't let a spill like this ever happen again. But again, not so high as to be ruinous to their operation'.* All give her a thumbs up.

"As we learned as cadets at West Point," Lars stated, *Make us to choose the harder right instead of the easier wrong, and never be content with a half truth when the whole can be won.* In other words, do it right the first time, as Tiger says."

Doris cut in next. "I studied about all the crew members that died. They left a total of 21 children. You don't read about this anywhere. Whatever they paid the families, it is merely an olive branch gesture compared to the loss of these fine young men, ages 27 to 56."

The team could tell Doris was upset. They could even hear her swallowing lumps back in her throat. Lars quickly moved in and put his arms around her. Her tension subsided, so Lars continued for her.

"These were honorable, hard working men who loved their families and country. Although they are still missing, it can be considered an honorable burial at sea. They don't need an empty grave. This doesn't give closure to loved ones, but I think they will never be forgotten. Thus, they live on forever in our hearts. God bless them." All team members crossed their hearts.

"You are right, Lars", said Doris. "Arleen Weiss, 59 year-old hairdresser, mother of a 24 year-old son said, *'I knew all along that BP was the devil in that accident. It doesn't matter how much money anyone pays, It doesn't nearly amount to what we've lost'.*

"Billy Anderson, who lost his son, said, *'the BP settlement doesn't bring my boy back, but it does show everybody that they're guilty and everybody knows it'*.

"Another family member, Naomi Beckham, aunt of crane operator Dale Burkeen, said, *'It's hard for us. We ain't got no closure. We don't have a body for him'*. According to Dale's mother, *'BP never offered an explanation or apology. Zero compassion'*.

"Let me add a few other points," said Brenda. "Based on interview information from 21 crew members and written statements, they said that crew members were buried under smoking wreckage; that shrapnel pieces cut them down; swallowed by fireballs with firestorms 100 feet high. Andre Fleytas, bridge officer, heard lots of screaming... *'we're going to die'*. Mike Williams had no choice but to jump from the burning oil rig... 60 feet into the sea. But Mike, like many others, felt suicidal—*'I had a death wish for a long time; I just wanted to be with them. It felt like I had cheated death'*. He was the last man to leave the rig. Most of the 98 who survived without any injury suffered *survivor guilt*.

"Plus, I found that BP used cheap fixes to save money and time. I found this statement from Attorney Tony Buzbee very interesting.

"He said, *'In the case of the Deepwater Horizon, workers had finished pumping cement to fill the space between the pipe and the sides of the hole and had begun temporarily plugging the well with cement; the cement job was finished, and pressure testing occurred. Despite there being problems with the pressure testing, Transocean and BP chose to continue displacing the mud, as if the cement job had been* *successful. This was a grave error. For cementing to be effective, the right mix must be used, and the cement must have time to harden. Naturally, the decision to displace the cement is ultimately made by the company—in this case, BP. Because BP was paying $500,000 daily to lease the rig, naturally there is incentive to rush the job. If the cement mix was inadequate, or if insufficient time was given for it to harden, Halliburton (the company that performed the cementing) and BP (the company for whom Transocean was working) will have major liability'.*

"On top of this, BP passed over crucial tests of the well cement lining. This was a gross error on their part. I disagree with Buzbee a little bit on the *'...naturally there is incentive to rush the job'.* Sure I get it, but not to rush with safety as a low priority. They were six weeks behind and $58 million over the budget. These guys need to learn their lessons better, especially since they had already learned (or should have) from their previous accidents at Texas City and in Alaska. I'm angry."

"In my book," said Olivia, "I quoted Confucius, who wrote, *'Learning without thought is labor lost; thought without learning is perilous'.* He was born in 551 BC. Seems as if we haven't learned much. Wisdom prevails. Not many wise management people on *this* project. Sorry to interrupt. Please continue, Brenda."

"Mike Mason, oil rig worker, said that he observed cheating on blowout preventer tests at least 100 times. BP employees were present, as subcontractors faked the test results.

"And here's my last key point which is a summary of the

Senate findings from New Orleans—50 minutes before the well blew, flow indicators revealed that more fluid was coming out of the well than was being pumped in. Then, 41 minutes before the explosion while the pump was shut down for a *sheen test,* the well continued to flow when it should not have and drill pressure rose, another troubling result, according to the document.

"Also, according to the committee memo, 18 minutes before the explosion, abnormal pressures and mud returns were observed and the pump was abruptly shut down. The data suggests that the crew may have attempted mechanical interventions at that point to control the pressure but soon after, the flow out and pressure increased dramatically and the explosion took place. Stephen Davis said, *'It was the biggest explosion I ever heard in my life. It's like we walked straight into hell'.*"

"Great work," said Lars. "Some of the aftermath reminded me of Exercise Tiger; that is, not letting those affected to be able to talk freely. BP acted like the Gestapo. The crew survivors were kept in isolation for 50 hours, which was deliberate by Transocean. Wearing down the men who were extremely tired to begin with... not having slept for those 50 hours. They did this so the men would sign statements denying that they had been hurt, or had witnessed the explosion that destroyed the rig.

"Who are they kidding? This isn't a communist country! Remember, 11 workers died, 17 were injured, and 98 were left with severe PTSD.

"Anthony Buzbee, the Houston lawyer said, *'These men were told they have to sign these statements or they can't go home'*. That's why I say it reminds me of Exercise Tiger... *'None of you guys say anything or you'll be court martialed'*. Remember?"

"The US District Judge, Carl Barber, assigned the percentages of the total fault as follows: BP—67%. Transocean—30%, Halliburton—3%. I would have upped the percentage on Halliburton because I think, as a novice offshore oil person, that the cement was the start of the problem. Barber let them off too easy—in my humble opinion," Doris added.

Olivia, tapping her spoon on her tea saucer, adds quite emotionally, "Here are some more random findings I uncovered. More mistakes and discrediting actions:

- Pockets of corruptions at the Mineral Management Service(MMS);
- Erosion of professional culture;
- No handbook for inspectors. Frankly, this is unheard of, and extremely disappointing;
- More emphasis on quantity of inspections rather than quality of inspections;
- Some MMS employees accepting gifts from oil and gas companies;
- A lack of resources, dwindling as time went by, called a starvation diet;
- The US Coast Guard's last revision to the applicable marine safety rules was in 1982. That's 28 years, since the rig exploded on April 20, 2010. Good Lord, this is unacceptable.

"Anyhow, that's my input. So see, I did my research too!"

"Let me say this, since we are about wrapped up here. The oil and gas industry is remarkable for their technological innovations through the years. As the board that investigated the Columbia Space Shuttle Disaster stated, *'Complex systems almost always fail in complex ways'*.

"But... like NASA, there is no excuse for a complacent culture, especially in regards to safety. Safety always comes first. I hope that a lot of management people were fired over this well explosion. Need fresh blood in these companies."

After these remarks, Lars smacked his fists together. His fellow US Army Ranger, Tiger followed his lead.

Lars added, "Great work! This was an incredible discussion. Extremely well researched. Gracious, Brenda."

Everyone applauded.

Doris chimed in. "I know we are about to close down, but I want you all to hear an "I AM" prayer for the Gulf Oil Crisis." It's a prayer written by Frederick and Mary Ann Brussat. I'll just read the first three stanzas of 17 stanzas:

WE ARE ONE

I am the ocean, mighty, wild, and free
and I am being poisoned with oil
From a hole humans drilled into the earth's skin
flows a stream I cannot stop, threatening all I shelter.
Breath to breath, body to body, we are One.
So be it.

I am a worker who died when the BP oil rig exploded.
I was trying to support my family
and supply a needed resource to my country.
Now I will never see my family and friends again.
Breath to breath, body to body, we are One.
So be it.

I am a worker injured in the Deep Horizon explosion
and I worry about the safety of the oil industry.
I want to know why the regulations and procedures
that were supposed to protect us failed.
Breath to breath, body to body, we are One.
So be it.

All bowed their heads with Lars leading with an *Amen*.

"Next time our discussion centers around the Turks attack against Constantinople in 1453," added Lars. "Led to the fall of Rome. I'll lead this one. Cheers everyone. I'm proud of you all so, as a surprise, I have a dessert for each of you to take with you."

Anita brings in the desserts to a loud *"HOOAH!"* by Tiger, who winks at her. The wink is reciprocated.

Charles N. Toftoy

Constantinople

CHAPTER 27

Fall Of Constantinople In 1453—Caused New European Regional Order

All are settled in at Metro 29. On time as usual... 0800 hours.

Lars announces, "Before I start, Doris took a survey of you all this week in regards to your favorite TV shows."

Doris likes to break things up for the team now and then. She gave the results. "Here's how it shook out, gang, not in priority order: All went for the following: Game of Thrones, Fargo, Deadwood, Dexter, Sopranos, and Breaking Bad.

"Then... The West Wing—Lars and myself. Orange is the New Black—Brenda and I, ER—Olivia, NYPD—Brenda, The Wire—Tiger, Sherlock—me."

"Thanks Doris," said Lars. "Oh! By the way my top favorite was Game of Thrones. OK, here we go with Constantinople." Lars cleared his throat, wiggled in his chair and took a swig of coffee. The others giggled. Lars always wiggles in his chair during their blunder discussions.

"This could be the biggest blunder in the history of the world, except for the fact that few people even know about it. Basically, the Fall of Constantinople was a turning point—the end of the Middle Ages and the beginning of the Renaissance. So... 1453 was the turning point in world history. It ended the Byzantine Empire... better known as the Eastern Roman Empire.

"The Roman Empire dated to 27 BC and lasted 1,500 years. I took the lead on this one because I studied this in our Military Arts and Science Course at West Point. I still have my old research materials, but of course I updated myself. Read most of the masterpiece books on Fall of Constantinople, plus journal articles and archive documents. I'll try to keep it simple, short and sweet because it is complicated.

"Constantinople was a gem... the largest and richest urban center in the eastern Mediterranean Sea. Finally, the Byzantine Empire fell, having fought off the Ottomans for 100 years. And the Byzantine Empire had endured for about 1,000 years. The Fall of Constantinople ended an era for Europe. Frankly, that's the bottom line, gang. A catastrophe for Venice and Genoa. And the end of the *old* Roman Empire.

"That's a lot for you, all in a nutshell, but sets the stage for mistakes made that caused this to occur. I've listed some points, which are lack of tactical and strategic abilities, poor leadership—when the Genoese commander Giovanni Giustiniani was wounded, the Byzantines became disorganized; the Kerkoporta Gate was accidently left open at the height of battle and the Ottoman soldiers rushed in and raised their banner on top of the Inner Wall. Chaos ensued... followed by panic and retreat.

"They were outnumbered 10-1; 80,000 Turks versus 8,000 Byzantines who were inside the walls—no reinforcements from indifferent western kings who did not respond to Constantine XII's urgent pleas—the assumption being that the gigantic walls would withstand the attacks by Mehmed II's Turk troops. These walls had withstood 23 sieges since the first siege by the Goths in the year 378 AD. The walls had been impregnable. But... the Theodosian Walls failed the city... known as *lieu de memoire*.

"Failure to accept Mehmed II's offer to let Constantine and his people leave unharmed if he surrendered the city. But Constantine responded with *'It is not for me or anyone else here to surrender the city. We are committed willingly to die and not try to save our lives'*. This is the most famous answer in history, known as one of the most majestic responses. A sidebar—the emperor fought side-by-side with his troops, defending the Romanos Gate, to his death.

"Moving on, there was the failure to take advantage of the high walls—couldn't counter heavy canon bombardments. The walls tumbled after 53 days of heavy canon fire. Guns expended 55,000 pounds of gunpowder; 5,000 shots for 47 days.

"Lack of citizens support; turned down Orban's offer of his making large bronze guns due to shortage of funds. Orban was a Hungarian canon founder who made the offer in 1452. This, possibly, would have saved Constantinople.

"Those are the primary mistakes that doomed

Constantinople. Orban, turned down by Constantine, then offered his skills to Mehmed II. Mehmed knew the city had been besieged 23 times... all failures due to the powerful walls. Positive that no army could bust through the walls, Orban told Mehmed, *'I can cast a canon of bronze with the capacity of the stone you want. I can shatter to dust not only these walls with the stones from my gun, but the very walls of Babylon itself'*." Mehmed ordered him to make the gun.

"Orban's gigantic canon made the difference. It was named, *Basilica*. He used copper, tin, saltpeter, sulfur and charcoal. A monster... 27 feet long, barrel walled with 8-inches of solid bronze, 30-inches in diameter. It could accommodate a stone shot weighing half a ton; could hurl a stone ball over a mile. It was also called the *royal gun*. This super gun inflicted psychological trauma to the nth degree on the Byzantines.

"Prior to the main attack, Mehmed II, later called The Conqueror, told his soldiers, *'My friends and men of my empire, you all know very well that our forefathers secured this kingdom that we now hold at the cost of many struggles and very great dangers and that, having passed it along in succession from their fathers, from father to son, they handed it down to me. For some of the oldest of you were sharers in many of the exploits carried through by them— those at least of you who are of maturer in years—and the younger of you have heard of these deeds from your fathers. They are not such very ancient events nor of such a sort as to be forgotten through the lapse of time. Still, the eyewitness of those who have seen testifies better than does the hearing of deeds that happened but yesterday or the day before'*.

"I must end this now, saying that the fighting was brutal... hand-to-hand combat. Fierce. However, the Fall of Constantinople brought forth émigrés; Byzantine migration of poets, lecturers, musicians, academics, artists, astronomers, printers, and scientists to Western Europe—which furthered the knowledge-based richness of Europe." Lars stood up, shook his arms and touched his toes. Team members tapped on the table, showing their appreciation for his great session.

Anita refilled their coffee and teacups. Tiger asked for another side of the crispy bacon. He and Lars talked about the Nationals. The women huddled together, talking about current fashions. They planned a threesome trip to Tysons II—the Galleria, Nieman Marcus. Followed by a *gals only* lunch at Entyse Bistro.

Lars closed it out, as Alpha Team leader with, "Next time, we tackle the Titanic. Olivia has the lead. Her grandfather drowned on that ship, so she is very close to the historical event. See you next Friday."

All—high fives. On the way out, Tiger stalled—gaping at the dessert ensemble.

Painting depicting the sinking of the
RMS Titanic by Willy Stower

CHAPTER 28

RMS Titanic—Doomed By A Cascade Of Events

"It was great," jostled Tiger. "I had the Bulldog Steak and Cheese with trimmings. Doc had the Bow-Wow Garlic Chicken Breast Sandwich."

Lars added, "Yup, and we washed it all down with a draft IPA-Lost Dog Café Rescue Ale."

"Being a *Big Easy* guy, I also downed the Key Lime Pie," added Tiger.

"And I had the Carrot Cake... after Tiger twisted my arm."

Both were wearing colorful Lost Dog T-shirts. The team members were grinning. The team knew that, a few days ago, the two stud veterans had lunch at the Lost Dog Cafe in Westover.

Olivia clicked her tongue, an indication that she was ready to roll. She was grateful that Lars let her lead the Titanic discussion. She wanted to do this for three main reasons: (1) Her grandfather drowned, going down with the

Titanic. He was the ship's bosun, or petty officer, in charge of rigging anchors, sails, cables... all the work on the ship's deck. Hard working... very proud man, like most of his crewmates. Olivia loved him dearly. (2) Even though she grew up in Yorkshire, England, she was born in Belfast. The Titanic was built there in Harlord and Wolff's Shipyard on Queen's Island, Belfast, Ireland. She remembered that it cost $7.5 million and was launched in 1911. And... (3) She covered the Titanic in her Pulitzer Prize winning book, *Mistakes That Changed History*. So she already had a wealth of research material on-hand. A good head start for the team discussion.

On this Friday morning the temperature was 32°, wind 29 mph. The temperature for the past three days was in the 20s with heavy winds. This morning held a slight relief, but everyone was bundled up with winter coats.

Olivia commenced the discussion. "First of all, there are many research materials on the Titanic. Essays, books, documentaries, movies, articles, survivor interview reports and well, you name it! For example, I know of two expert researchers who have devoted their lives to studying the Titanic disaster... one for 20 years, the other a writer for 30 years. Compared to my humble research... materials stacked about three foot high, I'm sure theirs is immense. Even the National Archives is loaded to the till on Titanic material.

"In all the research I've done, I have not found anyone who has prioritized the mistakes made that caused the iceberg collision. I have done that. But I have had to tackle this blunder in two ways: (1) the mistakes made that caused the collision, and (2) the mistakes made that caused the unnecessary loss of 1,517 lives. Those are two separate slants.

"None of the mistakes should have ever occurred, thus the Titanic should have arrived in New York, Pier 54, with all 2,224 passengers and crew intact. Safely.

"Let me begin with (1) what I mean by prioritization, in this case, is that if the first mistake had not been made then the probability of the collision occurring would be less. If the first mistake could not be avoided, then the second major mistake if not made, should have caused the ship to sail on. Then, there's the 3d, 4th, and 5th major mistakes. I think you all get my drift!

"In short, what I'm trying to say is that avoidance of any one of these five mistakes would have avoided the catastrophe."

Team members nodded, indicating that they understood Olivia's point. Tiger shot up a thumbs up.

"Before I kick off, I must say that many writings on the Titanic are in disagreement and controversial. Controversy, conflict, and arguments amongst Titanic experts *still* persist to this day. What I will cover here is my best take after a thorough research effort. Much of what I cover is unknown to most of our general population... even to some historians!

"Let's look at the five major mistakes, in priority order, that could have prevented this terrible collision: (1) fire in the coal bunker, (2) ignored iceberg warnings, (3) lack of key navigation tools, (4) excessive speed, and (5) wrong turn.

"Here goes...

"FIRE IN THE COAL BUNKER: There was an

enormous fire in a coal bunker that started ten days before the ship's departure. FYI—coal bunkers are 3 stories high. According to stokers in stoke holes 9 and 10 the blaze was *'a raging hell'*. There were 150 stokers *(firemen)*.

"Twelve stokers tried to control the fire to no avail. A 30-foot black streak appeared on the outside of the hull... starboard side, in front of boiler room 4. The Titanic was reversed in its berth at South Hampton so passengers could not see the damage caused by the on-going fire. The fire was about 1,000°.

"According to Senan Molony, a journalist who has researched the Titanic for 30 years, *'The fire was well known about, but it was played down. She should never have been put to sea. Bruce Ismay, President of the company that built the Titanic, gave strict instructions to officers to not mention the fire to passengers'*.

"Ray Boston, a well-known Titanic expert, said, *'Fires could have caused serious explosions below decks before reaching New York'*.

"I discovered that on April 7, 1910, the British steamer *Cairnrona* incurred a terrific explosion. One child was killed and 70 were injured. It carried 900 passengers, mostly immigrants.

"The explosions occurred in the coal bunkers. It was ruled that the ship *'should not have gone to sea with fire in its bunkers'*.

"On a side note, a coal fire in a mine in Centralia, Pennsylvania has been burning for 58 years.

"I know that fires occur frequently, due to spontaneous combustion of coal. But a major fire should be properly controlled prior to departing a port. The fire on the Titanic was an enormous, uncontrolled fire. The bulkhead was seriously damaged and warped. Upon hitting an iceberg, the bulkhead would be the main defense against sea water coming in."

Brenda pointed out, "It is good that you choose this unwarranted mistake as your first one, in priority order. If the Titanic had delayed due to the fire, it may not have hit the iceberg. Also, it would have given the captain more time to pay attention to iceberg warnings."

"Thanks, Brenda," Olivia said. "That's a good point. It isn't mentioned in any of the research materials I've checked on. Now, my second priority.

"IGNORED WARNINGS: In the evening before the Titanic hit the iceberg, Jack Phillips, the senior wireless officer, was extremely busy handling a backlog of messages due to a Marconi wireless breakdown. Harold Bride was helping.

"Both of them were sending out passenger messages via the Marconi wireless. Thus, he failed to respond to six warning signals about icebergs.

"Many ships sent messages: the Mesaha, SS California, La Touraine, Caronia, Amerika, Baltic/Athinal, Prinz Frederick Wilhelm, and the La Bretagne.

"ALL warnings were ignored. Phillips body is one of the 1,160 still missing. Phillips was 25 years old. A decent looking lad. He failed to pass on the last iceberg warning. He felt that it was non-urgent because it didn't have the prefix MSG *(Master Service Gram)* markings to indicate that it requires the captain to acknowledge receipt.

"Smith himself ignored seven warnings. The Marconi wireless telegraphy was innovative, new... not many people knew how to operate and receive Marconi messages.

"NAVIGATION SHORTCOMINGS: David Blair, a merchant seaman, was reassigned from his post on the Titanic three days before the voyage. He took the keys to the crow's nest locker which housed binoculars. Blair's forgetfulness could have caused this blunder. Fred Fleet, a lookout, said that binoculars would have helped since he *'might have seen it a bit sooner. Well enough to get out of the way'*.

"No searchlights onboard. Incredible shortcoming. The electrical arc searchlight is called the *guardian beacon of light*. Second Officer Charles Lightoller said, *'I think a searchlight would have assisted us, under these peculiar conditions, very probably. The light would have reflected off the berg, probably'*.

"Searchlights do provide for safe navigation. Some believe that icebergs are hard to spot in a calm sea, little light, no break at the iceberg's water line. Clear and starry skies, no moon. But come on, that iceberg was 50-100 foot high and 200-400 foot long! How could you miss that!

"There were only two lookouts for a ship heading into a field of huge icebergs. My goodness, there should have been 5-6 lookouts on all sides of the ship... not just in the crow's nest. Up to this point, if the fire, ignored warnings and navigation mistakes weren't enough to avoid the disaster... how about the speed?

"SPEED: Because of the navigation failures, there was only 37 seconds from sighting the iceberg to hitting it. The ship was travelling at 22.5 knots, which is 0.5 knots below its top speed of 23 knots. So... there was not enough time to avoid the iceberg. The ship should have been traveling at about 15 knots or less in a field of icebergs. A speed of 11 knots would have cut the impact in half. Bruce Ismay, Director of the White Star Line, and Captain Smith, known to be a speed demon, both wanted to beat the time of the sister ship, Olympic. They were almost... paranoid about it.

"First class passenger, Elizabeth Lindsey, overheard Smith and Ismay about lighting the last of Titanic's boilers to beat the crossing time of the Olympic's maiden voyage. Ismay said, *'We will beat the Olympic and get into New York on Tuesday'*. That meant one day early.

"Again, Smith loved speed. It was felt, secretly, that speed was essential to arrive at port before the fire in the coal bunker exploded. Remember, passengers were unaware that a fire was raging below deck."

All team members squirmed in their seats. Olivia was really pouring it on. Refills by Anita on coffee and hot tea were timely.

"Let me wrap up this part with the 5th mistake," said Olivia, bottom lip trembling.

"WRONG TURN STEERING ERROR: Robert Hitchins, Steersman, hit the panic button and turned the ship the wrong way. The granddaughter of Charles Lightoller, 2nd Officer said, *'They could have easily avoided the iceberg if it wasn't for the blunder. If the Titanic had stood still, she would have survived at least until the rescue ship came and no one need have died'*.

"The command was *'hard a starboard'*. It was

misinterpreted. This made the ship turn right, rather than push the tiller right to make the ship head left.

"Another error was the engine room was told to reduce and then reverse thrust. This reduced the turning *ability* of the Titanic."

"Unfortunately, the ship hit the iceberg on the starboard side where the fire had damaged the steel, warping it and making it brittle. The fire inside the coal bunker had weakened this segment of the hull. The level of temperature, 1,800°, against the steel reduced its strength by 75%.

"If it had hit the stern straight on, it would have been better off, since that is the strongest, reinforced part of the ship. The Titanic was made of low grade and high impurity steel... which is easier to damage. Remember, icebergs have 80% of their true mass below water level.

"If it had hit head-on, only two compartments would have been breached. It was built to survive the breach of four compartments. All passengers would have been safe because the Titanic would have stayed afloat. Rescue ships could have picked up all passengers and crew.

"It was definitely a chain of events leading up to the calamity. Or you might say... a cascade of events. I've covered the mistakes that caused the crash into the iceberg.

"Now, I'll quickly cover all the errors that caused the unnecessary loss of 1,517 lives. Let's begin.

- Shortage of lifeboats. Designed for 64; carried only 20. Ismay, in his infinite wisdom said, *'I'll not have so many little boats, as you call them, cluttering up my decks and putting fear into my passengers'*. It appeared that Ismay wanted to use the decks for more passenger friendly, luxury activities. Twenty lifeboats would only hold 1,178 individuals. Yet, they had 3,560 life jackets. Crazy thinking;

- Allowed lifeboats to leave ship partially filled.
    - The first lifeboat launched had 27 passengers, though it had room for 65.
    - Elizabeth Shutes, a survivor, said, *'There were only 36 people in my lifeboat; only half full'*.
    - An officer shot six passengers who were rushing to lifeboats. Proper lifeboat procedures would have saved at least 500 passengers— 53.4% could have survived with the number of lifeboat spaces available. There were no lifeboat drills. A lifeboat drill was cancelled the day of the sinking;
- Everyone was under the assumption that the Titanic was unsinkable. Thus, a complacent attitude prevailed. Yet it sunk in just 2 hours and 40 minutes;
- No immediate rescue resources available;
- Poor quality, low-grade iron rivets; unzipped the hull at the seams as a result of the impact. This allowed an ingress of seawater;
- Passengers left portholes open. This caused a surge of seawater to fill the ship. There were 1,110 portholes. The hull had 12-feet of damage to it. It would take only 12 open portholes to double the rate of the Titanic's sinking. No effort was made by the crew to ensure passengers closed their cabin portholes. Many passengers opened their portholes to see what was

happening;

- Many sailors and firemen had never handled an oar before. And they didn't know how to launch the lifeboats. Again, due to not having a lifeboat exercise. It was a farce—complete disorder and chaos;
- Water temperature was 28°. A person will last about 15 minutes before freezing to death in that temperature. The US Coast Guard believes that you probably won't survive in 32.5° water more than 15-45 minutes. If below 32°, you will reach exhaustion and unconsciousness in less than 15 minutes. You will undergo shock within the first two minutes. So, you can see that many lost their lives due to the freezing water. Those in lifeboats did not try to rescue anyone else for fear of being overturned by them. One passenger survived for two hours in the water. He lasted that long only because he was *drunk as a skunk*. His alcohol level raised his body temperature. A rare case indeed.

"Now, I also want to make it clear that those that died and survived are not the *only* victims. There were, according to my own formula, 5,625+ family and relatives affected deeply by the catastrophe. Let me explain. This is in no way scientific. My final results are not without error.

"These statistics are derived from sources such as: Psychiatry Advisors, Mental Health Surveys, Medical Networks, Statistical Manuals of Mental Disorders, Veterans Administration, Journals, and other appropriate writings. An unexpected death is a stressful life event for many of the kin connected to those that died and survived. My point is that a part of those left behind dies with them. I'm referring to husbands, wives, sons, daughters, uncles, aunts, grandparents... will have the haunting effect *forever.*

"Chances of developing PTSD for loss of spouse is 9.6%; son/daughter is 8.7%. Women are three times more likely to get PTSD than men. There are many studies, with sample sizes in the thousands, with varying results. For example, one study declared that of 64 deaths, 3,004 people are affected.

"This information is just to let you know that the Titanic sinking affected a large number of people. If you equated this to Titanic's 1,517 deaths it would be that 74,020 other people would be affected in some way due the tragedy. However, I'm referring only to close kin.

"Shock, sadness and disbelief sets in stronger with those that continue on with this traumatic death realization until they reach the PTSD level. I have chosen to take the results of several studies that state 5.2% are at high risk of getting PTSD following the unexpected death of a loved one or when someone close to you dies suddenly.

"Also, in my own mind, not scientifically, the lowest number of kin affected deeply by the loss is 3 for those missing (1,177); 2 for those whose bodies were recovered (340); and 2 for survivors (706).

"Just eyeballing this, it would seem more kin would be affected by a missing passenger/crew member since there is no closure. There is some closure for those kin whose loved one's body is recovered. And for survivors, it would be the survivor himself/herself and one other kin. These numbers are low, but again my point is about the *total impact* of the Titanic disaster on masses of people.

"Here's my formula: 3 x 1, 177 + 2 X 340 + 2 X 706 = 5,623 will have psychiatric disorder episodes. But for PTSD, I multiply 0.052 X 5,623 = 292 who may suffer from PTSD. Research is not clear, but I know at least 15 or more victims of the dead related to the Titanic episode committed suicide.

"Some true examples *(no name):* 5—shot themselves in the head, 1—cut wrists, 2—drug overdose, 1—hung herself, 2—jumped from a high story building, 1—died of shock in an asylum. Madeleine Astor shot herself over JJ, the wealthiest passenger on Titanic who drowned. John J. was worth $87 million ($2.3 billion in today's money).

"I might end this with a quote from Robert Louis Stevenson: *'I have been made to learn that the doom and burden of our life is bound forever on man's shoulders; and when the attempt is made to cast it off, it but returns upon us with more unfamiliar and more awful pressure'.*"

With a haltering voice, Lars intercedes, "I'm so proud of you, Olivia—*the researcher's researcher!* To even try to put peoples' minds to understand that many are affected by this traumatic event is a wonder in itself.

"Of the tons of Titanic research materials, no writer has ever stepped back and thought about this in the way Olivia approached it." Lars stands up and yells, "Bravo, Olivia!"

Everyone stands up and cheers. The blood leaves Olivia's face, but she holds back tears. Doris' eyes filled up, red and puffy. Same for Brenda, make-up smeared. Lars and Tiger with pinched faces.

Captain Edward Smith

Finally, now composed, Olivia says, "Doris researched interview reports from survivors. I thought this would be a good idea... to make you feel what they were feeling. Getting closer to it, Doris?"

"It's best to hear from survivors and others via their own words. Rather than from Monday morning quarterbacks who weren't even there. These comments put a face on the episode. I couldn't interview survivors because they have all passed on. The last survivor was Millvina Dean. As a baby, 2 months old, wrapped in a sack and lowered into a lifeboat. She died in 2009.

"Here are a few quotes:

'The dead came up holding children in their arms. The

poor people never had a chance'. (Mary Wilburn)

'I am sorry to say there were more bodies than there was wreckage'. (Joseph Scarrot, Able Seaman, survivor)

'And it wasn't until we were in the lifeboat and rowing away; it wasn't until then I realized that ship's going to sink. It hits me there. The sounds of people drowning are something I cannot describe to you, and neither can anyone else. It's the most dreadful sound and there is a terrible silence that follows it'. (Eva Hart, Survivor)

'The partly filled lifeboat standing by about 100 yards away never came back. Why on Earth they never came back is a mystery. How could any human being fail to heed those cries'. (Jack Thayer, survivor)

'Striking the water was like a thousand knives being driven into one's body. The temperature was 28°, four degrees below freezing'. (Charles Lightoller, 2nd Officer)

'As the ship sank we could hear screaming a mile away. Gradually it became fainter and fainter and died away. Some of the lifeboats that had room for more might have gone to their rescue, but it would have meant that those who were in the water would have swarmed aboard and sunk her'. (Mrs. D. H. Bishop, Eyewitness from lifeboat)

'...the shrieks of the terror-stricken and the awful gasping for breath of those in the last throes of drowning, none of us will ever forget to our dying day'. (Colonel Archibald Grace)

'...I swam around for about half an hour, and was swimming on my back when the Titanic went down. I tried to get aboard a boat but some chap hit me over the head with an oar. There were too many in her. I got around to the

other side of the boat and climbed in'. (Henry Senior, fireman)

'When I came to the surface the baby in my arms was dead. I saw the woman strike out in good style, but a boiler burst on the Titanic and started a big wave. When the woman saw that wave she gave up. Then, as the child was dead, I let it sink, too'. (Henry Senior, Fireman)

'... The agonizing suspense lasted for many hours until at last the Capathia appeared. We shouted 'Hurrah!' and all the boats scattered on the sea made towards her'. (Paul Chevre, French Sculptor)

"I feel that these comments, out of hundreds I reviewed, will make you feel as though you are there experiencing it with them. I know I do."

Doris wipes a tear streaming down from her left eye onto her cheek. Brenda's lip has been trembling as she listened intently to Doris's true passages from selected survivors. Doris is extremely sensitive to the feelings of others. You may remember, as do the team members, that Doris's mother slipped off the cruise ship Royal Caribbean at 1:40 a.m. when Doris was only 14 years old. The ship had been on the way to the Bahamas. Doris has had PTSD ever since. Lars helps in many ways to support her.

Lars states strongly, "It seems as if the officers were not running a *tight ship*. Lack of communication and discipline across-the-board on the ship were tantamount to contributing to the Titanic's demise. And the fateful circumstances, covered so well by Olivia, sailed her into doom."

"By God, Doc, she was traveling too damn fast!" uttered

Tiger.

Doris agrees, nodding her head. "I think Ismay was more interested in passenger comfort than safety. 20,000 bottles of beer, wine, champagne and hard liquor; 8,000 cigars. Designated rooms for first-class men to congregate for smoking."

Lars stood up again. "One thing about Captain Smith was he went down with his ship. His last words were, *'Well boys, you've done your duty and done it well. I ask no more of you. I release you. You know the rule of the sea. It's every man for himself now, and God bless you'*.

"This was a tough one for all of us. Next week Tiger leads us in a discussion of Napoleon's invasion of Russia, which began on June 24, 1812. See you then!"

All team members hug Olivia on the way to the exit.

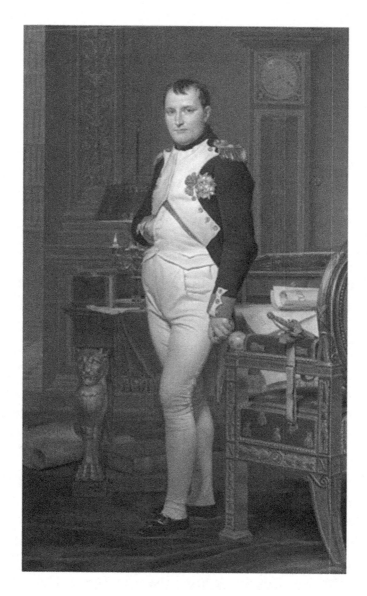

Emperor Napoleon

CHAPTER 29

Napoleon's Invasion Of Russia:
The Greatest Upset In Military History

Tiger filled everyone in on background before diving into Napoleon's mistakes. This is a summary of Tiger's leadoff remarks. Napoleon, *le petit corporal*, was the Emperor of France—the greatest military leader in the world. A military genius. A man of action, full of energy. He controlled most of Europe, just prior to launching the invasion of Russia on June 24, 1812. His Grand Armee, 685 thousand strong, was the largest military force in the world.

Tiger then emphasized that the popular belief is that Napoleon invaded Russia and marched as a hero into Moscow.

Totally wrong. He called Russia the Colossus of the Barbarian North. He did not trust their imperialist intentions. As I said, Napoleon had control of Europe from Spain to Russia. He saw Russia as a gateway to India. He wanted to pound them into submission via his Grand Armee. Instead, it turned out to be a tale of misery and defeat.

"So how did his invasion of Russia become the greatest upset in military history?" Tiger squirmed in his chair, took a sip of coffee. "I'll tell you how!"

"The errors could have been avoided. However, since it turned into a colossal blunder, it changed the landscape of Europe forever. Some, and not in priority order: faulty logistics, strategic miscalculations, fragmented Army, invading in winter months, lack of teamwork, inability to control typhus, poor choice of subordinates, retreat miscues, and poor discipline.

"Napoleon once said, *'Never interrupt your enemy when he is making a mistake'*. Well, in this *Patriotic War of 1812*, he made the mistakes, not the Russians.

"Now, I'll add some beef to the screw-ups I've noted. The Russians adopted a *Scorched Earth* tactic and continually withdrew, drawing the *Grand Armee* deeper into Russia's difficult heartland. This overall strategy was devised by General Field Marshall, Mikail Kutuzov, Commander-in-Chief of the Imperial Russian Army. It was approved by Czar Alexander I, who recruited Kutuzov to take this Command.

"The roads were in terrible condition, thus supply wagons had a tough time. The peasants burned their fields of crops. Based on the advice from his officers on July 28th, Napoleon was agreeable to ending the Campaign. Then, two days later he changed his mind telling them, *'The very danger pushes us on to Moscow. The die is cast. Victory will justify and save us'*.

"Hoping to resupply troops upon taking Moscow,

instead, he found 3/4 of it burned. The Russians were employing an orderly delaying strategy. Very smart on their part. It was sort of like Muhammad Ali's rope-a-dope boxing tactic. The Grand Armee troops couldn't resupply themselves as they marched deeper into rough Russia territory. The cold weather froze thousands of troops to death—horses, too. There were great losses even before entering Moscow, which included ten thousand horses. Basically there was no supply or distribution network.

"Here's a big point that most people are unaware of... the Grand Armee was fragmented. Only 1/2 were French—the other half was composed of Dutch, Italian, Spanish, and Polish soldiers. As they retreated from Moscow in chaos, Cossacks, peasants, and regular Russian troops used guerilla warfare tactics to snip at them.

"In the first week alone, six thousand fell to typhus. Lice were a big factor in the illnesses of thousands of the Emperor's troops. Corps Commanders being from different countries, had rivalries and hatreds. Unity of Command broke down. It became everyone for himself. Earlier on, Napoleon had fragmented his troops in an attempt to control key strategic spots. Remember how Custer divided his forces at Little Big Horn? Not a good outcome."

Lars breaks in. "Tiger and I lived by the US Army's 9 Principles of War. It is the core of our Army's strategy and tactics. This is a good time to bring it up because Tiger just mentioned how unity of command broke down and Napoleon fragmented his forces. That's a violation of our 6th principle—Unity of Command. Actually, listening to Tiger's point has made me realize that Napoleon violated all

9 Principles: 1—Objective, 2—Offensive, 3—Mass, 4—Economy of Force, 5—Maneuver, 6—Unity of Command, 7—Security, 8—Surprise, 9—Simplicity. The *military genius* was off base on this invasion, the failure of which led to his being exiled to Elba. Two more future defeats secured the island of Elba for him... a 2-year stay. They didn't cave in to the invading forces as assumed by the *small corporal*. Instead, they attacked, burned their produce, and harassed Napoleon's troops."

"Good copy on that, Doc. Thanks." Tiger asked Anita for a second cup of Joe (coffee). "Napoleon didn't understand the peasants or citizenry of Russia. The Ruski is a tough dude. They love their country. I never knew it before about the amalgamation of European nationalities that made up half of the Grand Armee. I always thought of it as being 100% French. In the end, out of 685 thousand troops, only 20 thousand were left and less than one thousand were able to return to duty."

Olivia jumps in to point something out. "Don't forget that Napoleon had all of Europe in his hands. He said, *'A leader is a dealer in hope'*. Until the 1812 blunder, that's what he gave everyone. Also, let me add this bit of trivia, Tiger. The victory and celebrations went to the Russians, who celebrated in grand style with Tchaikovsky's 1812 Overture. Tchaikovsky's musical score ends with the roar of canons and bells clanging. But to accurately record Napoleon's defeat, the soft crunching sound of lice munching on soldiers' flesh would've seemed more appropriate."

"Ugh," said Doris with her face in her hands. "What a

disgusting thought!"

Tiger is *really* fired up now. "Not to repeat myself, but Napoleon kept trying to get the Russians into battle. But they kept withdrawing. Early on, battles would have been won by the Grand Armee, which outnumbered the Russian forces by more than 3 to 1. One scholar said '...*if that had been the case, French would be our first language today'*.

"Some of his subordinate commanders were from other countries, commanding at Corps level. He appointed his stepson, Prince Eugene, to a major Command. The Prince, unfit to command, allowed the Russians to retreat, whereas Napoleon wanted to force battles. This would have changed the invasion's outcome to be more favorable for the French. By the way, that Prince couldn't find his ass with both hands!" Tiger pounds the table and yells out *"HOOAH!"*

"And... I didn't mention this before, but he failed to commit the elite Imperial Guard, left in reserve, to finish off the retreating Russians. Lots of mistakes that shouldn't have happened, thus causing the monstrous blunder.

"Another point: Napoleon took the wrong retreat route out of Russia. He had two options: the one he didn't take had very little snow; the one he took had severe winter storms. Many troops froze or starved to death. Some soldiers' wandered in search of food and supplies. Some never returned. A total breakdown of discipline.

"As they journeyed from Moscow, it became a situation of every man for himself. Many horrid instances occurred. Too many to elaborate here. But one stuck in my mind. The burning barn incident.

"Hundreds of men were burned to death inside a barn where they had sought shelter. Other soldiers warmed themselves outside. It is said that some soldiers ate the cooked flesh from those burned to death. They shot their own horses to eat horsemeat. But often, they could not eat the frozen meat, so they sucked the horse blood which was mixed with snow. A bloody popsicle. Anything to survive."

The women shuddered hearing this.

"Twenty thousand horses died from lack of water and fodder, plus the extremely cold weather. Soldiers developed high fever and a bluish tinge on their faces—died rapidly. After one month into the Campaign, 80 thousand soldiers were incapacitated or died from typhus. One eyewitness said all of his companions were swarmed with lice. Clothing was taken off dead comrades. Confusion prevailed as enlisted men wore officers clothing—refusing to obey orders. Attacks were made by Divisions of different nationalities against one another.

"Napoleon left his troops to head back to Paris. The Grand Armee completely broke down because of his departure. The order of the day became, *'Se sauver qui peu'* or *'Save himself who can'*.

"And, here's my last point. Even though the Russians were pushed back, you might think that they were downhearted. Instead, they had spirit. That was their *grand design*. Let Napoleon outrun his worn out logistics tail—use Scorched Earth. Russians, to this day, have a lot of national spirit. Napoleon did not figure a lot of these things in his strategic invasion equation. It was utter misery for Napoleon's soldiers."

"Beautiful work, Tiger," said Lars. "This reminds me of a quote by Albert Einstein: *'Everyone is a genius. But if you judge a fish by its ability to climb a tree, it will live its whole life believing that it is stupid'*.

"Next time, Brenda is going to lead the discussion pertaining to the Triangle Shirtwaist Factory Fire in New York City, 1911—the deadliest industrial fire in history. Her mother worked in a munitions factory during WWII. Looking forward to it, Brenda. See you all next Friday."

High-fives and they all scooted out. Tiger winked at Anita.

Triangle Shirtwaist Factory fire, March 25, 1911

CHAPTER 30

Triangle Shirtwaist Factory:
Deadliest Workplace Fire In History

Friday, 8 a.m. –A nice sunny day. Breakfast was all set up as usual by *Automatic Anita*... as the team fondly calls her. Brenda leads off. "You mentioned last week that my mother worked in a munitions factory, Lars. Actually, it was my grandmother who was one of 5,050 workers who worked in the Torpedo Factory in Alexandria, Virginia during World War II. She was very proud of their work, producing 10,000 torpedoes, which sank 1,500 enemy ships. Now it is an Art Center, as you all know. Let's get right to it because I know Tiger has a funeral service at Murphy Funeral Home at 10 a.m. this morning.

"March 25, 1911 was a sad day in New York City. The fire killed 146 workers out of 500; 49 burned to death, 36 died in the elevator shaft, and 58 jumped to their deaths out of the windows—in total there were 123 women and 23 men.

"Many inexcusable mistakes were made causing the huge blunder to happen. It shouldn't have ever happened, of course! I will list some of the errors. Many are unknown to the public as well as some historians.

- Wooden boxes of highly flammable scraps of fabric scattered about;
- Both exit doors were locked. Unfortunately they opened inwardly. Workers piled up against the doors trying to escape;
- Entire Company floors *(8th, 9th, 10th... 27,000 square feet)* filled with highly flammable materials;
- No emergency fire protection sprinkler system;
- Fire escape in disrepair. Poorly designed—20 of the workers fell to their deaths when it collapsed;
- Firefighters had a ladder that only reached to the 6th floor. Useless—the fire was on the 9th floor;
- Only one of the four elevators were working properly and it held just 12 people. Cecilia Walker Friedman recalled, *'The girls at the machines began to climb up on the machine tables, maybe because they were frightened or maybe they thought they could run to the elevator doors on top on the machines. The aisles were narrow and blocked by the chairs and baskets. They began to fall into the fire'*. She also mentioned that everyone started to scream and holler, but most couldn't get away. Cecilia was only able to escape by wrapping a muff around her hands, grabbed the elevator cable, and slid down all the way to the bottom. She had to leap into the elevator shaft to grab

the cable. She broke her arm and a finger;

- Hose on fire floor was old and rotted so the valve rusted shut—it was of no use;
- Buckets of water made available for emergencies— most were empty. Mary Domsky-Abrams said, *'On that particular morning, the day of the tragedy, I remarked to my colleagues that the buckets were empty, and that if anything were to happen, they would be of no use'.*

"I also have some general mistakes that contributed to this catastrophe:

- Management greed and lack of oversight. Guilty are the two owners: Max Blanck and Issac Harris;
- Garment workers organized in a chaotic tight-fitting group;
- No fire drills ever conducted, which reminds me of the Titanic;
- No emergency instructions for workers;
- Management cut corners on everything to grow the business, thus workplace safety was a low priority;
- Deplorable working conditions. What everyone calls a *sweat shop;*
- Negligence and indifference by owners, Blanck and Harris... the *Shirtwaist Kings.*

"This incident was close to me since my grandma, Nana, worked 12-hour days and weekends. She always said it was *'Rush, rush, rush'.*

"The women, ages 14 to 48, mostly teens and in their 20s, worked twelve 1/2-hour to 14-hour days plus 7-hour days on Saturdays and Sundays. And in just 15 minutes, 30% of the workers died.

"Evidently a box of fabric scraps caught on fire. Perhaps due to a cigarette or cigar by some male worker. Men smoked—women didn't smoke in 1911. By the way, the shirtwaist garments were ready-to-wear blouses of lightweight fabric representing modern womanhood.

"Bessie Cohen, a 19-year old seamstress and a survivor, was warned by her foreman, *'Bessie, save yourself'*. She wanted to help her friend Dora, but Dora jumped out a window to her death. I might add that it was quite gruesome for onlookers below to observe 58 young women jumping out of windows on the 8th, 9th, or 10th stories, to their death.

"It was difficult to recognize bodies. I researched all 146 victims. Some were identified by various means. Examples: a darn in her stocking, two identified by a ring, gold-capped tooth, heel of a shoe. Many could not be identified.

"The Triangle girls were mostly Jewish and Italian immigrants working hard to earn $2 per day to support their families and those relatives in the old country. Just think, a 14-year old girl working in a sweatshop to support her kin.

"Of the teenagers who died: two 14-year olds, three were 15, eleven were 16, thirteen were 17, twenty-two were 18, seventeen were 19, as well as 65 in their 20s. My God! No chance to marry or have children. These youngsters should have been taken good care of... instead, they died a horrible, frightening death. Undeserved and completely unnecessary.

Burned to death, jumped out of windows, fell down elevator shaft, fell from flimsy fire escape, crushed under pile of bodies, locked door exit, and caught in jammed narrow staircases. It just brings tears to your eyes."

Olivia responded. "When I think of those girls my throat tightens up and I feel like I want to vomit. This is so disgraceful and why I have a hard time dealing with some people. They *know* better."

Doris pipes in next. "People need to be more respectful of each other. Recognize the beauty of life."

"I know what I would have liked to do to those that let these girls down," said Lars. It gave him a bitter, coppery taste in his mouth... the same feeling as he had when facing off against the Viet-Cong.

Tiger is the only one who knows about Doc, his wartime partner and hero. When imminent enemy contact was near, Doc used to paint his face like a football player, black under the eyes, but also black streaks down his cheeks. The war paint. Bring 'em on. Many notches on Lars .45 holster.

"OK, gang, excellent discussion. But we have to cut it short today. Next week we'll discuss Pickett's Charge. I'll take the lead on this one."

High-fives. Moving out.

Doris saw Anita give Tiger a seductive wink. "Hey, Tiger, I think Anita wants to get into your brand new Levi jeans!"

"You think?" Tiger blushes, cheeks burning, face looking like a red-hot tomato... even though he is black.

All hit the exit quickly... on to their regular workplaces.

Confederate Major General George Pickett

CHAPTER 31

Pickett's Charge: Turning Point Of The Civil War

Since Lars studied the Civil War battles at West Point, he volunteered to lead this blunder discussion on Pickett's Charge. A rainy Friday morning. Reminded Lars and Tiger of the monsoons in South Vietnam.

Everyone was in place, food served, compliments of Automatic Anita.

Lars explained that there are hundreds of historians that have written about the Civil War; one has studied it for 50 years. He said that his research results may differ from about half of the 500 historians. Lots of them differ from each other. But he emphasized that he was sticking only to Pickett's Charge, the 3rd day of the Gettysburg battles—June 3, 1863.

It is amazing, Lars told them, that in fifty minutes, the duration of the *Charge*, it became the turning point of the battle of Gettysburg.

He stressed that the loss by the Rebels at Gettysburg put

the North as Civil War victors. The entire Civil War depended on the Gettysburg outcome.

"And that's why Pickett's Charge was the biggest blunder of the war." Lars scratched his left ear and took a swig of coffee.

"Some historians call it *Longstreet's Grand Assault* because, unknown to some, it wasn't only Major General Merritt's division charging forward. He had the lead assault on the right, but Brigadier General Pettigrew's division was on the left, with Major General Trimble's two brigades behind him. And actually, two other Brigades were behind and to the right of Merritt, commanded by two BGs (Brigadier Generals), Wilcox and Perry.

"There are four major foul-ups that were made:

1. Maneuvering, or rather marching, across about one mile of open ground against well-entrenched Union Forces at the top of a hill. Winfield Scott Hancock, on surveying his position on Cemetery Ridge, said, *'I think that this is the strongest position on which to fight a battle that I ever saw'*. The Confederate troops were open to cannon fire and small arms fire. A total massacre.

2. Lack of artillery support. Most of the cannons fired over the heads of Union soldiers. Inferior shell fuses. Delayed detonation. Inept artillery leadership. Cannons short of ammunition due to mix up of supply wagons. If they had been squared away, the cannon fire would have doubled the firepower.

3. Failure of cavalry to attack Union rear to disrupt lines

of communications. So Lee did not effectively operate his cavalry. Huge mistake on his part.

4. Having Pickett's division make the main effort. It was weak; two Brigades were absent. Many were young soldiers; never been under fire before.

"Those are the four main mistakes that shouldn't have occurred. Before I go on any further, let me mention that most of this entire Gettysburg debacle rests with General Robert E. Lee. He told Pickett after the *Charge*, *'The fault is entirely my own'*.

"Next, most of these fall into Lee's lap:

- Lee overestimated his Army's ability and underestimated the power of Major General Meade's Army of the Potomac;
- Lee's total disregard of new information—thus he lacked timely enemy intelligence;
- Failure to commit reserves *(five Brigades)* in main attack. Instead, they were held back;
- Fighting in unfamiliar territory, rather than drawing the Union forces south to fight on known Virginia ground;
- Inability to create a functioning, competent staff. Did not control subordinates. Logistics was a mess;
- Poor at strategic offense so... faulty strategic vision.

"As you can see, this turned out to be a catastrophe for the Confederates. Many officers thought Lee was *off his rocker*. Longstreet told Lee before the battle, *'No 15,000 men who ever lived could take that position'.* According to Richard Garnett and Lewis Armistead, *'This is a desperate thing to attempt'.* Both were Brigadier Generals!

"According to authors Scott Bowden and Bill Ward, *'Lee must have known that an attack was a calculated risk that had to be taken'.* Bowden and Ward are experts, however I disagree with that statement—it was a high risk that *didn't* need to be taken. A more thought-out, strategic plan is what they really needed.

"Lee's attack plan was complex and Longstreet's plan was a mistake in itself. In short, Lee and Longstreet didn't have their act together. However, Lee called Longstreet *'my old warhorse and the staff in my very right hand'.*

"There were some inspiring incidents, however. Hays, Union Division Commander, rode back and forth along the battle lines encouraging his troops. *'Hurrah, boys, we're giving them hell'.* He had two horses shot out from under him. That reminds me of Custer, who had 11 horses shot out from under him.

"Pickett's men were forever known as the *flower of Virginia manhood.* Pickett never spoke to Lee again. He never got over losing half of his division and all three of his Brigadier Generals during the Charge.

"Major General George Pickett wrote this letter to his fiancée:

'My brave boys were full of hope and confident of victory as I led them forth, forming them in column of attack, and though officers and men alike knew what was before them— they knew the odds against them—they eagerly offered up

their lives on the altar of duty, having absolute faith in their ultimate success.

'Well, it is all over now. The battle is lost, and many of us are prisoners, many are dead, many wounded, bleeding and dying. Your soldier lives and mourns and but for you, my darling, he would rather, a million times, rather be back there with his dead., to sleep for all time in an unknown grave...

'Even now I can hear them cheering as I gave the order, Forward. I can feel the thrill of their joyous voices as they called out along the line, We'll follow you, Marse George; We'll follow you—we'll follow you.

'Oh, how faithfully they kept their word—following me on—on—to their death, and I, believing in the promised support , led them on—on—on. Oh, God!'

The team members were obviously shaken up after hearing him read the letter aloud, some wiping at their eyes with their napkins.

Olivia broke in on the sobering moment. "Here's a bit of trivia to lighten things up a bit. It is interesting that in the Civil War, West Pointers fought against each other. Imagine that!

"Everyone brags that Lee was first in his West Point *Class of 1829*. But there were only six in his Class, the 22nd Class since 1802... the beginning of West Point. Longstreet was in the *Class of 1842*, next to last in his Class; only eight in the Class. Pickett was in the *Class of 1846*, last, *a goat* of 59 in his Class. Since Custer was mentioned earlier, he was last in his *Class of 1861*, with 34 in Class. Another *goat*, meaning last or ranking low in Class."

Lars said, "Just think—if the South had won, the capitol might be in Richmond. Some historians say Montgomery, Atlanta, New Orleans, or Philadelphia. To me, Lee would not have chosen New Orleans... too far south. Montgomery was already the capitol of Alabama. Atlanta... a little too far south. Philly would be a decent choice or keep it in Washington, D.C. But my bet would be on Richmond. Scholars argue back and forth on this matter. It would be called the Confederate States of America. Not sure about the National Anthem. By the way, right now Switzerland is a model for a Confederate Europe.

"I'd like to end this with William Faulkner's quote about Pickett's Charge. This is from his book, *Intruder In The Dust*, 1948:

'It's all you see. Yesterday won't be over until tomorrow and tomorrow began ten thousand years ago. For every Southern boy fourteen years old, not once but whenever he wants it there is the instant when it's still not yet two o'clock on that July afternoon in 1863, the brigades are in position behind the rail fence, the guns are laid and ready in the woods and the furled flags are already loosened to break out and Pickett himself with his long oiled ringlets and with his hat in one hand probably and his sword in the other looking up the hill waiting for Longstreet to give the word and it's all in the balance, it hasn't happened yet, it hasn't even begun yet, it not only hasn't begun yet but there is still time for it not to begin against that position and those circumstances which made more than Garnett and Kemper

and Armistead and Wilcox look grave yet it's going to begin, we all know that, we have come too far with too much at stake and that moment doesn't need even a fourteen-year-old boy to think This time. Maybe this time with all this much to lose and all this much to gain.

'Pennsylvania, Maryland, the world, the golden dome of Washington itself to crown with desperate gamble, the cast made two years ago; or to anyone who ever sailed a skiff under a quilt sail, the moment in 1492 when somebody thought This is it: the absolute edge of no return, to turn back now and make home or sail irrevocably on and either find land or plunge over the world's roaring rim'."

"Wow, that guy Faulkner was something else, Doc," said Tiger. Everyone nodded in agreement.

Lars added, "Robert E. Lee's decision-making on July 3rd was rigid and fragile. His usual intuition, reasoning, and battle-wise cognition failed him. It could be attributed to his recent heart attack and that he had strep throat. The standard decision-making process was disregarded by Lee and Longstreet. I teach it to Executive MBAs at George Washington University. Here it is.

1. *Identify the purpose of the decision;*
2. *Gather relevant information;*
3. *Identify all alternatives;*
4. *Brainstorm different choices;*
5. *Evaluate alternatives;*
6. *Choose the best alternative;*
7. *Take action; execute the decision.*"

Lars saw that every Alpha member was using their iPhones to take notes. He told them that he would email appropriate information to each of them. Lars added that this process can be used by anybody, regardless of their field of endeavor. Team members fired up high-fives.

"Failure to conduct an orderly retreat and keep the entire Army intact to gear up for another battle was an additional shortfall. Lee's overall plan lacked sound strategy and good ground tactics.

"Flawed leadership style? Giving vague orders. Poor Operational Commander. On the world scale of leaders, he was far below the level of Napoleon, Alexander, and Hannibal.

"He was also poor at supplying troops with food and clothing. For example: thousands of troops had no shoes.

"Longstreet did not care for Lee's plan whatsoever and deliberately undermined it. He opposed the Charge. Frankly, this had a psychological effect, as this attitude drifted down to the troops. Pickett asked Longstreet, *'General, shall I advance?'* In his memoirs, Longstreet wrote, *'The effort to speak the order failed, and I could only indicate it by an affirmative bow'*.

"That wraps it up for today folks. Next Friday I'll cover the Battle of Gallipoli. A real World War I slaughter. Worst ever in WWI. Caused Churchill to be fired. Terrible planning."

High-fives. Then Lars reminded them that they would meet for dinner next Tuesday night.

March 1915 Gallipoli Campaign Montage

Top: Australian War Memorial, Middle left: British and French Battle Fleet at the entrance to the Dardanelles, Middle right: V Beach Helles Gallipoli, Bottom left: Australian War Memorial, Bottom right: Australian War Memorial

CHAPTER 32

Battle Of Gallipoli—Churchill's Fiasco.... A Slaughter

"Sorry to hold you guys up." Brenda was hoarse, gasping for breath. "I ran from the parking lot," she added, taking her seat.

"Tell that Hitler song you sang to us while we were waiting," said Olivia.

"Yeah! OK! This is a flashback to Hitler again. Remember the lyrics to Colonel Bogey's March song? It was covered in our Hitler Blunder discussion. I just came across another one that the Brits sang in 1939-1940... a novelty song, written by Toby O'Brien in August, 1939."

Tiger clears his throat, gargling with coffee. "Here goes:

Hitler, he has only one ball
Goering, he has two but very small
Himmler had something simmler
But poor old Goebbels had no balls at all.

Then Tiger whistles the chorus. Customers that heard him at nearby tables cracked up laughing... as did team members. Brenda laughed so hard that she started choking.

"Great stuff," said Doris. "But, I know Lars is fired up about this blunder, so my dearrrrr *(stretching out the dear)*, let's roll."

"OK, my dearrrrr," mimicked Lars. "You might want to ask the best question—WHY? Why did the Brits want to tackle Gallipoli anyhow? Well, I'll explain why they planned for this insane battle. I have uncovered 8 reasons:

1. To provide Russia, Brit's ally, with a supply gateway linking the Black Sea with the Mediterranean. Their entire naval fleet was landlocked in the Black Sea;
2. The Western Front was at a stalemate... a mindless slaughter. There was a need for a new Front;
3. To seize an opportunity to have Balkan countries *(Greece, Bulgaria, Romania)* join the Allies;
4. To get Turkey *out* of the war;
5. To end the weary Ottoman Empire, which had ruled the Middle East and parts of Europe for 600 years;
6. Capture Constantinople *(Istanbul);* Give to Russia's Tsar as a gift;
7. Divert Turkish forces from fighting in the Caucasus, thus relieving Russia from that pressure;
8. A success would allow an invasion of Austria via the south leaving Germany isolated.

"Frankly, what kicked this off was due to Winston Churchill, the First Lord of the Admiralty, who asked the

Prime Minister, *'Are there not other alternatives than sending our armies to chew barbed wire in Flanders'?*

"The Brits and French had suffered a million casualties in the first four months of the war on the stalemated Western Front. Now are you ready, gang? This is my *attention step.*

"Battle of Gallipoli results. Totals: 392,856 casualties; 130,842 deaths; 262,014 wounded. Some historians have different numbers, but this is close. This is another one of my fact-based analyses. Remember, KIA means killed in action.

"Breaking it down further for the Allies: Great Britain and Ireland—41,148 KIA; Australia—8,709 KIA; New Zealand—2,779 KIA; France—9,789 KIA; India—1,358 KIA; Newfoundland—49 KIA.

"Most people thought the Allies were composed of just Brits, Aussies, and Kiwis *(New Zealanders)*. But... the Turks had 86,692 KIA.

"In short it was the bloodiest, most ghastly battle of WWI. And *nothing* was gained by it. The Allies retreated all forces from the peninsula.

"When we chose blunders for our discussions, you all sort of let me have my way on the *worst* military battle. I've studied various battles in detail. Some military historians might disagree with me. But I analyzed 20 of the seemingly worst battles and narrowed it down to five. Either of these might win a historian's vote, but I gave the Battle of Gallipoli five stars for being the worst. These got four stars: Custer at Little Big Horn; General Ambrose Burnside—The Battle of Fredericksburg; General Henri Navarre—Battle of Dien Bien Phu; General Oreste Baratieri—Battle of the

Adaia (Italians vs. Ethiopians).

"Pickett's Charge at Gettysburg could be added to this list. But of course, that was Lee's mistake. Also, the Battle of Moscow, Stalingrad, the Somme, plus others. However, from the standpoint of the 4 P's, I believe Gallipoli was the worst of the worst. Tiger, tell them what the 4 P's are!"

"Sure, Doc. The 4 P's are **P**iss **P**oor **P**rior **P**lanning. It's used a lot in military jargon."

Lars continues. "Before I list several of the gross errors, I'd like to inform you of something very key. The head of the Royal Navy, First Lord of the Sea, Admiral John Fisher, 74 years old, told Churchill, a mere 40 years old, that his plan *'was doomed to failure'*. Fisher resigned in protest and told Churchill, *'You are bent on forcing the Dardanelles and nothing will turn you from it--nothing. I know you so well'*.

"Churchill should have stuck to his sensible words he wrote in 1911, four years earlier: *'It is no longer possible to force the Dardanelles, and nobody would expose a modern fleet to such peril'*.

"OK, now some mistakes that should have been avoided. Mistakes galore... too many to list them all. I may repeat some. Don't forget that this was more of a campaign, lasting from February 19, 1915 to January, 16 1916—260 days.

"Here goes:

- Not a coherent strategic plan. Too complicated. Not enough men and munitions. For example: Brits had 75 thousand troops, Turks—500 thousand. A doomed plan... never should have started. Reminds me of the Bay of Pigs plan;

- A lack of realistic goals;
- Inexperienced troops;
- Poor intelligence and maps. Lack of good reconnaissance. Navigational errors. Some troops were let ashore in the wrong places;
- Underestimated the Turks *will* to fight. They had high ground, machine guns, artillery, well dug in;
- Little artillery support;
- Incompetent commanders. Division commanders ignored orders from their commander, General Sir Ian Hamilton;
- Naval attack failed. Gave away surprise for invasion to follow. Combined attack *(Navy and Army)* failed. Poor working relationship between Royal Navy and the Army. No combined arms training. Stormed beaches in rowboats. Amphibious operations were new to the British... no guidance;
- Failure to effectively clear mines;
- Inadequate medical services. Disgraceful sanitation: unburied bodies, body waste, swarms of flies, lice;
- Very little water for troops. Difficult to get desalinated water to them;
- Brits confidant of success at the beginning; extremely arrogant.

"Also, Mustafa Kemal, Commander of all Turkish forces, was a superior Commander. Unknown to Brits. For example, he went into no-man's land whispering commands and leading a bayonet charge. He was an astute and ruthless leader, telling his men, *'I don't order you to attack; I order you to die'*. He told them this when they were about to retreat. Whereas the Brits had Hamilton, a *lovy-dovy* nice guy, who let his incompetent underlings make decisions. Lord Kitchner, Britain's Secretary of State, made the mistake of picking Hamilton to command the 1915 Gallipoli invasion. He was known as a bumbling *Ferdinand the Bull.* He treated his Brigadiers as his nephews... he being the uncle.

"I read many diaries and interviews of Gallipoli veterans. Too many to discuss here, but here are a few to give you a feel of how it felt on the ground. Picture yourself there.

"Sergeant D. Moriarty wrote: *'They crept right up to our trenches (they were in the thousands) and they made the night hideous with yells and shouting 'Allah, Allah' and '... the devils used hand grenades and you could only recognize our dead by their identity discs'.* Sergeant Moriarty was killed in France on September 1, 1918. A real hero.

"Lt. Colonel Percival Fenwick, New Zealand Medical Officer observed, *'Everywhere one looked, lay dead, swollen, black, hideous, and over all a nauseating stench that nearly made one vomit'.*

"Captain Guy Nightingale, 1st Battalion—Royal Munster Fusiliers, told his mother, *'Our headquarters was very heavily shelled and then the fire surrounded the place and we thought we were going to be burned alive. Where the telephone was, the heat was appalling. The roar of the flames drowned the noise of the shrapnel, and we had to lie flat at the bottom of the trench while the flames swept over the top... The whole attack was a ghastly failure. They generally are now'.*

"A Gallipoli veteran said, *'There were colossal swarms of these pests which had bred in the dead bodies not buried in no man's land, where it was impossible to recover them without incurring fresh casualties'.*

"There are many more grim stories, but you get the main idea... this was a total slaughter of very fine young men. An insane undertaking.

"Ok. That's it. Churchill was fired from within the War Cabinet a month after the ending of this horrifying Campaign."

"Sorry to interrupt," uttered Tiger. "But I have to ask you how many major, glaring blunders were on Churchill's watch? Gallipoli, bombing of Dresden, Luisitania sinking, and other mistakes. At Gallipoli, while his men were low on water and food, Churchill was probably having his favorite meal. Roast beef with potatoes and brussel sprouts followed by Yorkshire pudding."

Suddenly Tiger let out a thunderous belch. "Excusez-moi." The loud blast shocked the team and those at the three neighboring tables. Silence. After five seconds everyone burst out laughing.

Tiger calmly added, "And he probably had raw oysters as an appetizer... his favorite starter. Because he thought that oysters put lead in his pencil." Again, silence, then everybody snickered.

As you know, Tiger is the *real thing.* A *rubber-meets-the-road* type of guy.

Alpha Team members stood up and applauded Lars for doing such a great research effort.

Lars announced that next week, "Olivia has volunteered to take the lead, backed up by Tiger and Brenda. It is about the famous Battle of Changping in 265 BC."

Olivia added, "Quite a battle; over 450,000 soldiers were buried alive. More next Friday."

High-fives and out the door quickly.

Left: Portrait of Lieutenant-General Tomoyuki Yamashita, of the Imperial Japanese Army
Right: Lieutenant-General Percival arriving by aircraft in Singapore in 1941 as the new General Officer Commanding Malaya

CHAPTER 33

Fall Of Singapore—Worst Disaster In British History

Olivia was glad that Lars chose her to lead the Singapore Blunder. Being a Brit, she knew her British history quite well.

All set at Metro 29, Olivia licked her lips, smearing her Revlon Super Lustrous Lipstick, a sign that she was ready to *have at it*.

"Before I grind this out, let me clear up a few things. Most people have never heard of the Malayan Campaign, in the Far East, that took place from December 8, 1941 to January 31, 1942. It climaxed with the Fall of Singapore, the invincible fortress, on February 15, 1942... a 7-day battle. The Allied Forces surrendered to the Japanese.

"Much to the embarrassment of the British government, the Japanese Rising Sun flag was hoisted over the Cathay Building... the tallest building in Singapore.

"Now, a tiny bit of history here. Singapore dates back to the second century. It was called Sabana—an important foreign trade center. But modern Singapore was founded in 1819. A rich history... too much to relay to you here."

Olivia crunched on her Lox Eggs and a pile of onions. Taking a swig of her herbal tea, she continued. "According to Churchill, the fall of Singapore was *the worst disaster and largest capitulation in British history'*.

"Singapore was important, as British forces were required on the Malayan mainland to prevent the Japanese from establishing forward bases. Singapore, the *Gibraltar of the East,* was the British *Gateway to the Pacific.*

"As Lars would say, here's the bottom line. In 73 days, 30 thousand Japanese troops drove 650 miles and defeated three times as many British/Allied troops. As the Japanese moved through Malaya towards Singapore, General Yamashita ordered his commanders: *'I don't want them (the enemy) pushed back. I want them destroyed'*. He was able to gain the psychological advantage, since the top Brit commanders were dead on their feet. Near zero morale.

"Now... let me zoom forward to the mistakes. There are too many to cover in great detail and these are in no particular order. Keep in mind that General Arthur Percival was the Commanding Officer of the British Empire forces— US, India, Malaya, and Australia.

"Ok, here we go, gang:

- Inexperienced Commonwealth troops;
- Under-equipped;
- Shortage of RAF (*Royal Air Force)* aircraft; relied on volunteer air force and commercial planes;
- Percival had never commanded an Army Corps;

- Extreme shortages of water and ammunition;
- Brits had zero tanks. Japanese had 200;
- Outnumbered the Japanese by a lot—85 thousand to 30 thousand, yet they still lost;
- Allied defenders were not trained to fight against tanks. Lack of anti-tank guns, proper communications, and decent maps. Panicked at the sight of Japanese tanks. Called them *'monsters'*;
- Failure to build entrenchments on Singapore Island;
- Battleship *Prince of Wales* and Battlecruiser *Repulse* were without air cover or an escort. A reporter wrote, *'Blown clean away at one fell swoop was one of the main pillars on which our sense of security rested'*;
- No training on orderly withdrawals. Troops did not know how to retreat. One officer observed, *'One of the mistakes made in our training was that they never let us do withdrawal exercises'*;
- Underestimated the Japanese will and military prowess;
- Poor strategy from the very beginning;
- Percival's failure to counter the Japanese *pincers* movements *(double envelopment; both flanks of an enemy formation attacked)*;
- Brits failed to unload much of the equipment that accompanied the troops. Rather, it was sent back to England or to other theaters. Furthermore the RAF was ordered out of Malaya and Singapore;
- Misjudgments on the part of Percival in regards to location of point of major attack by Japanese;

- Failure of commanders to *jack-up* troops' morale. General Iwane Matsui wrote, *'The enemy troops have no fighting spirit... they are glad to surrender... they are relieved to be out of war'*;
- Terrible defensive strategy.

"That wraps up most of the glaring mistakes." Olivia scratches her chin and continues. "A renowned historian, Arthur Swinson, summarized this debacle nicely: *'Seldom in the history of war can there be such an unbroken skein of muddle, confusion, and stupidity'*.

"This is a very disappointing mark in British world history. Results: 5,000 killed or wounded, 80 thousand captured; Japanese—1,714 killed; 3,378 wounded.

Tiger blurts out wildly, "Sorry to interrupt Olivia, but I discovered a diary notation via the *Peoples' War Memories:*

'Our wildest guesses did not take into account the possibility of abandoning Singapore to the enemy'.

"Excellent. Thank you, Tiger," Olivia replied.

Doris squeezed Olivia's shoulder. "I have something, too. I stumbled upon General Percival's Special Order of the Day on December 10th, which was rather stirring, yet ineffective: *'In this hour of trial the General Officer Commanding calls upon all ranks Malaya Command for a determined and sustained effort to safeguard Malaya and the adjoining British territories. The eyes of the Empire are upon us. Our whole position in the Far East is at stake. The struggle may be long and grim but let us all resolve to stand fast come what may and to prove ourselves worthy of the great trust which has been placed in us'*."

Top: Prince of Wales, Bottom: Repulse
departing Singapore on 8 December 1941

"Well done, Doris, thanks!" Olivia continued. "Churchill, along with many historians did not dig deep enough, like we do, to check out the true, accurate facts. They just use information gathered, repeat it, and thus the errors continue over and over.

"Churchill's cable to General Archibald Wavell, Commander of the American-British-Dutch-Australian Command, on February 10, 1942 showed these errors:

'I think you ought to realize the way we view the situation in Singapore. It was reported to Cabinet by the CIGS (Chief of the Imperial General Staff, General Alan Brooke) that Percival has over 100,000 (sick) men, of whom

33,000 are British and 17,000 Australian. It is doubtful whether the Japanese have as many in the whole Malay Peninsula... In these circumstances the defenders must greatly outnumber Japanese forces who have crossed the straits, and in a well-contested battle they should destroy them. There must at this stage be not thought of saving the troops or sparing the population. The battle must be fought to the bitter end at all costs. The 18th Division has a chance to make its name in history. Commanders and senior officers should die with their troops. The honour of the British Empire and of the British Army is at stake. I rely on you to show no mercy to weakness in any form. With the Russians fighting as they are and the Americans so stubborn at Luzon, the whole reputation of our country and our race is involved. It is expected that every unit will be brought into close contact with the enemy and fight it out'.

"It really was 85 thousand Allied troops *(British, Aussies, Indian Army)* versus Yamashita's 30 thousand troops... about a 3-to-1 ratio.

"However, unknown to most of the historians and Churchill, the Japanese had thousands in reserves. 25th Army—83 thousand; 5th Division—20 thousand; 18th Infantry Division—28 thousand; Imperial Guards—38 thousand. This is seldom mentioned.

Lars spoke up. "Here's a side-bar for you, Olivia. Yamashita, *the Tiger of Malaya,* said: *'My attack on Singapore was a bluff—a bluff that worked. I had 30,000 men and was outnumbered more than three to one. I knew that if I had to fight for long, for Singapore, I would be beaten. That is why the surrender had to be at once. I was very frightened all the time that the British would discover our numerical weakness and lack of supplies and force me into disastrous street fighting'. "*

Brenda tossed in her two bits. "In regards to General Percival... he was the British government's scapegoat. However, most of the blame goes to Churchill and the Cabinet.

"You had a shy general versus a mean tiger. Percival was described as: *'slim, soft spoken'; 'something of a damp squib'; 'tall, bucktoothed, and lightly built'.* He was so shy that it took him seven years to propose to Betty MacGregor, from North Ireland."

Everyone chuckles. Tiger apologizes for farting. The chuckles turned to laughter.

Doris chips in with a few survivor stories. "This will make us feel like we were with them undergoing this horrific crime against humanity... which is what I call it. These are some of the survivors stories.

"Joseph Conceicao was 17 years old, and said, *'We saw limbs, peoples' heads, hands, legs lying about. There was a (British) soldier standing at the edge of the crater, and when my cousin went over to touch him—he fell into the crater; he was dead'.*

"Under the cruel Japanese occupation, Chia Sick Hew's family took drastic measures to survive, with his four sisters hiding in a fake ceiling in the house and only coming down for meals. *'It was a tough time. We had no food. My sister had to carry me to queue for fish and even then, it was rotten fish'.*

British Soldiers Surrender to Singapore 1942

"One example of Japanese viciousness was on February 14, 1942. They entered the Alexandra Barracks hospital. A British Lieutenant approached the Japanese forces with a white flag. He was bayoneted. Inside the hospital, the Japanese killed 50 soldiers, doctors, nurses. Two-hundred male staff members were bayoneted the next day.

"A survivor named Gwee said he *'had to grow up in the worst possible way—no food, living in constant fear of being executed and being forced to drop out of school'*.

"*Peoples War Memories* reported, *'Our wildest guesses did not take into account the possibility of abandoning Singapore to the enemy'*."

Lars popped in at that point. "Frankly, Churchill and his government betrayed thousands of Allied soldiers by declaring the Middle East and the USSR as the highest priorities. Thus, the forces of General Percival were deprived of the equipment and armaments necessary to win the Malayan Campaign. That's it in a nutshell! You know, I teach a term unknown to most: *responsible prioritization.* The Malayan strategy was flawed from the very beginning as we have mentioned. Few solid priorities. You have to be responsible for setting your priorities and indicate what actions are to be taken to nail each of these priorities. This was not done in the case of this worst Brit disaster."

Tiger grunted. "Another gem of wisdom from the Doc!"

Brenda gargled with her tea and pipes in. "Lieutenant General Percival and Lieutenant General Yamashita signed the surrender documents at the Ford Motor Plant at Bukit Timah Hill. Percival became a POW *(prisoner of war).* Just a piece of trivia."

Lars chimed in. "Let me add another. We used the pincers movement against the Viet Cong many times. Tiger remembers. This maneuver was first used by Athenian general Miltiades in the Battle of Marathon in 490 BC. And General Patton used it by trapping the German army in the Falaise pocket in August, 1944. Just a tidbit of history for you all."

Olivia takes over again. "A good way to put this blunder to sleep today is a writing from Winston Churchill's personal physician, Lord Moran: *'The Fall of Singapore on February 15 stupefied the Prime Minister. How came 100,000 men (half of them of our own race) to hold up their hands to inferior numbers of Japanese? Though his mind had been gradually prepared for its fall, the surrender of the fortress stunned him. He felt it was a disgrace. It left a scar on his mind. One evening, months later, when he was sitting in his bathroom enveloped in a towel; he stopped drying himself and gloomily surveyed the floor: 'I cannot get over Singapore',* he said sadly."

"Good job, Olivia!" Lars said, rolling down the long sleeve of his Eddie Bauer polo shirt.

"Hey, Doc... anymore gems of wisdom before we all cut out?"

"Well, Tiger, this blunder does remind me of one. In life... everything is the *before* and *after*. The problems lie in the *middle gray area*."

Tiger blurts out, "Man! I'm going to remember that one."

Doris quickly injects a key comment. "Churchill certainly didn't handle the *middle gray area*, since the Brits got battered from beginning to end."

"That's an excellent analogy, Doris," said Lars. Then he wrapped it up saying, "Next time—Tiger tackles the last blunder, the Battle of Changping, which changed the course of European history." Then Lars surprised the Alpha Team with a piece of Black Forest cake for each.

Ming Dynasty Portrait of Bai Qi
General of Qin State

CHAPTER 34

Battle Of Changping: Changed The Course Of European History

All Alpha Team members were 15 minutes early arriving at Metro 29 at 7:45am. Raring to go, realizing this was the last blunder discussion. Tiger started off providing background so everyone had the same frame of reference. He made it clear that we are only discussing Ancient China, 1600-221 BC. That China was the oldest country in the world with 3,500 years of written history. But its true history goes back to 400,000 BC—Peking Man of Zhoukoudian. Can you imagine that?

He explained how China was made up of seven states: Qin, Wei, Chu, Zhao, Yan, Qi, and Han. From the 26th Century BC to 221 BC there had been 24 major battles. This was called the Warring States period. The largest battle was the Battle of Changping in 260 BC when the Qin State defeated the Zhao State which ultimately led to a Unified China. It was the biggest battle and changed the course of history. The State of Qin had developed a gigantic war machine, which Tiger will be covering.

Very excited to kick it off, Tiger said, "I'm glad we chose the biggest battle in history to be our swan song."

"I covered this Changping battle in my book," declared Olivia. "Actually, to be honest, I feel that writing about this amongst other blunders is what swayed the jurors to give me the Pulitzer Prize three years ago. Most of them had never heard of it and were totally astounded. Plus, I believe they realized the difficulty of researching Ancient China."

Brenda interrupted. "I looked up the Pulitzer Prize. Joseph Pulitzer left money in his will to Columbia University to establish the Prize. Quite an honor, Olivia. Olivia is being very humble, gang."

Olivia sighs, takes in a deep breath and looks down at her plate in a shy manner. "They have 102 jurors, so they really put the entrants through the mill! I'm glad to help you on this last blunder."

"Me, too. We've really dug deep... all three of us," said Tiger with an unexpected belch. Sheepishly, he looked down to his French toast. Gargling his coffee, he began.

"This is a complicated blunder. I must be honest, Olivia helped me a lot. And I got help from Sam Gibson, an old buddy from New Orleans. We met last week at the Fish Market in Alexandria. We shared calamari and had the awesome clam chowder. We washed it down with a Rotating IPA."

Rather impatient, Lars broke in. "So... are we starting, Sergeant?"

"Whoops, sorry, Sir. But Sam did fill me in big time on

Changping, which helped me to prepare. He studied ancient history at the University of Oxford... the number one University for Classics & Ancient History. Gotta' give him and Olivia credit, Doc." All Alpha Team members give a thumbs up!

Tiger jumped in with, "Before I start, let me list some of the worst mistakes in military history. I'm doing this because some people might wonder why we chose the Battle of Changping over these:

- Battle of Cannae, 216 BC;
- Battle of Carrhae, 53 BC;
- Battle at Teutoburg Forest, 9 AD;
- Battle of Agincourt, 1415;
- Battle of Karansebes, 1788;
- Napoleon's Invasion of Russia, 1812, which we've covered;
- Charge of the Light Brigade, 1854;
- Battle of Little Big Horn, 1876;
- Hitler's Invasion of Soviet Union, 1941;
- Japanese Attack on Pearl Harbor, which we covered earlier;
- Battle of the Somme, 1916;
- Battle of Leipzig, 1813;
- Battle of Stalingrad, 1942-1943.

"These were big screw-ups, but after studying all of these and 45 other battles in world history, we realized that the Battle of Changping was the most colossal of all. Probably the biggest blunder in world history. I know we say that a lot, but where do you find a battle resulting in 450,000 enemy soldiers buried alive? By the greatest general ever... Bai Qi from the Qin State. A fierce guy. The most feared person in China."

"I'll explain more about this later." Olivia swigged her herbal tea. "It might be good to set the stage even more by covering a few numbers. Like China's total population was about 20 million during this period of time. That is according to Ge Jianxong, a very famous scholar in Fudan University, Shanghai.

"The book *Zhanguo Ce (Stratagems of Warring States)* provides military strength of the seven Warring States: Qin—several million soldiers *(infantry),* a thousand chariots, and ten thousand cavalries; Chu—one million men (infantry), a thousand chariots, and ten thousand cavalries; Zhao—several hundred thousand soldiers *(infantry),* a thousand chariots, and ten thousand cavalries; Han—several hundred thousand soldiers *(infantry);* Wei—200,000 soldiers *(infantry);* 200,000 men with blue band wrapped around their head; 100,000 servants; and 600 chariots; Qi—210,000 troops in capital Linzi; and Yan—several hundred thousand men *(infantry);* 700 chariots; and 6,000 cavalries."

Tiger jumped back in. "Seems as if, back in those times the Armies were organized as follows:

- Division: 12,500 men—commanded by Minister-Commander;
- Regiment: 1,500 men—Ordinary Grand Master;
- Battalion: 500 men—Junior Grand Master;

- Company: 100 men—Senior Serviceman;
- Platoon: 25 men—Ordinary Serviceman;
- Squad: 5 men—Junior Serviceman.

"There are many fabulous Chinese scholars who have studied the complexities of Ancient China. Most have agreed that the four best generals in Ancient China were Li Mu, State of Zhao; Bai Qi, State of Qin; Lian Po, State of Zhao; and Wang Jian, State of Qin. I found a survey that rated Bai Qi as the best, giving him over 80% of the votes; next was Wang Jian with 10%. Their ratings might have been the result of Bai Qi's record of having won over 70 battles with no defeats. And he seized more than 73 cities and captured 83 castles. He was called the *God of War* and the *Killing Machine.*

"He was responsible for killing over 900,000 people in battles. His tactics were: *'Mors Tua, Vita Mea'*, or *'Your Death, My Life'*. And, *'All is fair in slaughtering the enemy'*.

"At the Battle of Yique in 293 BC, his troops slaughtered 240,000 enemy soldiers of Wei and Han. In other battles, he had 100,000 drowned; in another, he threw 20,000 Zhao soldiers into a river. It goes on and on. Bai Qi was considered the ancestor of *annihilation war*. He calculated the outcome of the battle before it started. He used his soldiers to analyze the enemy situation, and then adopted the correct strategies and tactics to launch devastating attacks. Kill all to prevent a rebellion later on. A *Legendary Warlord.*

"Soon, I will discuss foolish mistakes made by Zhao in

the Battle of Changping. But first, it is important to understand that Zhao She, a well-respected general, told his wife to not let their son, Zhao Kho, command an Army. When Zhao She died, Lian Po was given command of the Army as directed by the King of Zhao. In 259 BC, the Army of Qin invaded Zhao; a stalemate—lasted three years, April 262 BC to July 260 BC. Zhao held a strong defensive position under Lian Po's command.

"Finally, the wise Bai Qi sent over two spies to spread a rumor that Lian Po was old, senile, and a coward; not wanting to fight. And that they feared Zhao Kho taking charge. All falsehoods, but it worked.

"Zhao Kho thought he was *hot stuff,* because he studied Sun Tzu's *The Art of War* and understood everything about strategy. Immediately, he disregarded Lian Po's strong defensive strategy, and launched an attack against the Qin State, commanded by the fearless Bai Qi.

"Thus, the real Battle of Changping began in 260 BC. Actually, most Chinese scholars and historians will agree with me that this should be called the War of Changping, lasting 3 years, rather than a battle. Most of the 3 years, like the Battle of the Somme, was a stalemate. Sort of a... military campaign."

"I spent a lot of time studying Bai Qi," said Olivia. "Most generals had goals of capturing castles. Let me go off on a tangent here. Glad we are rather casual. This reminds me of Thomas Custer, younger brother of General George Custer. Thomas won two Medals of Honor in one week. First two-time Army Medal of Honor recipient in the Civil War—Battle of Namozine Creek and Battle of Sailor's

Creek. Both times he seized the enemy's colors. In one war, castles; in another, colors *(flags)*. Bai's goals were *'...to annihilate the enemy. Kill as many as possible. When you've done that, kill more. Take no prisoners. Can't feed them anyway and they will haunt you by returning to attack you. Pursue the enemy with vigor'*. These are Bai Qi's words that I have paraphrased.

"He was good at luring enemies out of fortresses. As mentioned by Olivia, he predicted the outcome of the battle before it started. It reminds me of Adrian Peterson, of the Minnesota Vikings, who has the most rushing yards, 296, in a regular NFL game. I'll never forget when he was asked how were you able to rush for so many yards as a fullback?

"He said that he *'played the game over and over in his mind the night before. Each movement'*. Gosh! I'll never forget that. General Bai Qi must have done the same thing because let's face it... he wiped out a lot of people!" Olivia asked Anita for another cup of herbal tea.

"Thanks, Olivia," said Tiger. "The toolkit of most Armies consisted of crossbows, shields, pole axes, which were 9-18 feet with spears having slashing blades. Most of the infantry were drawn from ordinary farmers. The big business in those days was agrarian. Universal conscription: 15 to 60 years old; some as young as 11 years old. Brenda will cover some of the mistakes made by Zhao that should not have been made. Brenda! You're up!"

"Hey! Thanks. This is so fascinating. I could hardly sleep last night in anticipation of our discussion this morning. My first two have been missed by many scholars. Here goes. The King of Zhao refused help from other States *(Qi, Chu, and Wei)*. Instead, he asked for peace negotiations with Qin. Later, these States would not help Zhao because they were told that Zhao was negotiating peace with Qin. A severe strategic mistake. The King of Zhao commanded Zhao Khu to have a defensive battle with Qin to end the war immediately. Another terrible strategic mistake, especially since Qin soldiers were fierce fighters and outnumbered them. Of course asking Zhao Khu to be in charge of this important battle was a dire mistake. Here's why choosing him as commander was bad:

1) Inexperienced;
2) Made many changes in a short time. Troops confused;
3) Changed flag signals;
4) Changed subordinates familiar to line soldiers with his own inexperienced soldiers;
5) Known as a *paper commander*. It became a popular Chinese idiom that warned against *fighting a battle on paper*. They made a fool of Zhao Khu;
6) Poor strategy and tactics in action;
7) Poor logistic plans. The Army allowed itself to be cut off from supplies for 46 days. Soldiers ate one another due to starvation. Specifically, Bai Qi led 25,000 cavalries to cut off the retreat of Zhao's Army. And sent 5,000 soldiers to cut off main supply lines;
8) Zhao Khu led the whole Army deep, from main fortress, to attack Qin; left rear to be cut off from supplies, as I mentioned before. Totally incompetent;
9) Failure to breakout from Qin entrapment. Just stayed in place until attrition wiped them out. Had to

surrender.

"You're back on, Olivia," ended Brenda.

"Merci, Brenda... that was *heavy*. Well done! OK. The end result was 449,760 soldiers of the State of Zhao buried alive and the State of Qin losses were 250,000.

"Many Chinese and American scholars believe these numbers were exaggerated. That is probably true. Many generals wanted to report high numbers to impress their superiors. Also, they exaggerated numbers to impress enemies of their own forces strength. Soldiers would exaggerate because they were paid for the number of enemy dead. Sometimes proven by showing heads of enemy soldiers."

"Sorry, got to butt in here," said Lars. "Reminds us of the body count in Vietnam, right Tiger?"

"That's right, Doc. It was a sorry mess. Generals and other commanders wanted to look good by high body counts."

Lars added, "And in most cases they were false."

"Right on, Doc," agreed Tiger. He whispered to Lars, "You know, Sir... the problem with dying is that you're dead too long!"

All team members heard Tiger's rather loud whisper. Most were grinning. They all were thinking *thank God for our Tiger!*

Doris informed Tiger, "If you fill your soul, you are better off than others; those with empty souls." Everyone on the team knows about Doris' expertise in mediumship. She continued. "In a cemetery, after midnight, you can hear some of the dead talking. It's sort of a low murmur. Ask any grave digger who works late in the night about this. They'll substantiate this phenomenon. When it occurs, it is a nonpareil event."

Tiger blurted out, "Yow, you got me there, Doris! Maybe the dead get restless."

The team knows that Doris visits her fraternal twin, Andrew, at Arlington National Cemetery and talks to him at great length at his gravesite, Section 60, #5551. All team members have visited the site with Doris. Andrew was murdered.

Olivia remarked, "This was quite a research project for the three of us. The result of the Battle of Changping caused the unification of China in 221 BC. It changed the world."

"Before we close I want to mention something that is just plain logic," injected Tiger. "You have to consider that food and water for men and horses would be quite an undertaking for that many soldiers. Can you imagine that? Nearly impossible. So again, these numbers mentioned could be higher than are realistically possible. However, it is true that Qin had about a 550,000 population and Zhao about 450,000. All of these numbers are up for grabs, as Jeff Probst says on the TV show, *Survivor*. It depends on what research Brenda, Olivia, and myself were studying."

"Well gang, I can't believe it... we're done!" Lars scratches his left ear, eyes sort of filled. Then he stands up and Tiger leads the Alpha Team in a *"HOOAH!"* yell, which startles the dining crowd. But they cheer, loving it. Many are regulars who are used to seeing the team at table #98 in the rear area on Friday mornings.

Lars composes himself and says, "Hey, we're going to

have a wrap-up of these blunders' bottom lines next Wednesday at the Carlyle restaurant in Shirlington. Everyone think of three main things you got out of our discussions. It'll be a celebration."

All departed on a high. Tiger whispered to Anita on the way out, "I shall return." She giggled.

"A clever man commits no minor Blunders."

Johann Wolfgang von Goethe

AFTERWORD

The day after the last blunder discussion on Changping, Lars sent this email to the Alpha Team.

To: AlphaTeam04&@gmail.com
Cc/Bcc: LAlphaTeam01&@gmail.com
Subject: Dinner Meeting, Wednesday 7pm

ALL: I'll meet you at the Carlyle soon. Instead of three main things you got out of our blunder discussions, let's make it five each. Your top priorities. It will be a good wrap-up for us. I'm looking forward to it. And I will have a surprise for you all.

Best, Lars

They were all seated at the upstairs dining room at the Carlyle Restaurant in Shirlington on Campbell Avenue. It was a moonlit, clear Wednesday evening. Five days after the last blunder discussion. The Carlyle is Lars and Doris's go-to place. Upscale atmosphere... a Picasso sketch, Chagall print, turn-of-the century posters, stained glass art, etched glass, marble—a decoesque décor. Classy, yet cozy and casual.

Lars made reservations at this American 5-star Brasserie because he wanted to celebrate the magnificent job done by all team members. He reminded everyone about the team's definition of blunder: a result of a series of mistakes that should not have happened, therefore a blunder is a cluster of mistakes.

As a Business School Professor, Lars declares a blunder as being the macro element, or umbrella, over the microelements—the mistakes. He praised them for their great work over the past year.

Lars ordered starters for everyone... Lobster Bisque and Crab Fritters. The hungry team scanned the menu. Gabriel took their orders: Lars—8 oz. Filet Mignon *(Pittsburgh Style),* Doris—Pecan Crusted Trout, Brenda—Smoked Salmon Filet, Tiger—New Orleans Shrimp and Creamy Grit Cakes, and Olivia—Jambalaya.

Lars ordered a bottle of Pinot Grigio and a Cabernet Sauvignon. For desert, Olivia had the White Chocolate Bread Pudding; Tiger, the Key Lime Pie, and the others had the Deep-Dish Apple-Pecan Pie. Then, they settled back... drinking their coffee or tea... ready for the wrap-up discussion.

Tiger waved his hand to go first. But Lars stopped him saying that he wanted to say a few words before Tiger kicked it off.

"There are those that are looking up at us from the depths of the ocean. Others are looking up at us from earthly pits.

Forgotten by many, but not by our Alpha Team. The dead live forever as long as you don't forget them. They have life everlasting. A toast to them."

All eyes were flooded as they raised their glasses. "I really mean that with all my heart. And for each of you, never forget your loved ones because they live inside you. Go ahead Tiger, you're up!"

"Before starting I want to make my strongest point, that ya'll are tired of by now. Unfortunately it is true. The wealthy get treated like royalty; the regular people get treated like dirt. Most of the rich let the poor do all the fighting. Specifically, our lower class (29%) and middle class (52%) do the fighting. While most of the upper class (19%) shirk military service."

"How do they get out of it," piped in Doris.

"Several ways, Doris. Well connected with a family doctor who writes up a phony medical issue (bad back, foot, neck, eyes, etc.); enlist in National Guard; draft deferment since wealthy families send kids to college; buy their way out; flee to Canada... All of this is very sad and it browns my fanny."

Olivia injects, "Most of those are cowards. Or as we say in Old English (Englaland), they are sods or cheeky people."

Everyone gives Tiger a thumbs up!

Lars adds, "However, none of this is in God's eyes, my comrades."

"Thanks for the reinforcing comment, Doc. Most of these guys in our blunders did not deserve to die due to poor leadership."

Silence at the table. Solemn faces. Doris breaks the

silence.

"There needs to be more Nathan Greene's in this world." Doris prefers to call Tiger by his proper name. All nod in agreement.

"Ok, here's mine, Doc."

- Failure to act in a timely manner;
- Lack of coordination;
- Disregard for human life;
- Dysfunctional management/leadership;
- Underestimating the enemy; overestimating own strengths.

Doris followed:

- Self-centeredness; selfish;
- Ego, coupled with being macho;
- Stupidity and ignorance;
- Greed;
- Carelessness; thoughtless.

Olivia is next:

- Misguided judgment, inaccurate, not listening to advice;
- Covering up;
- Lack of common sense;
- Failure to perceive consequences of decisions;
- Over-confident.

Then Brenda:

- Failure to react in a timely manner;
- Not providing feedback; poor communications;
- Failure to use oversight;
- Poor execution;
- Goals not clear.

Lars batted cleanup with these, excusing himself for exceeding 5 points:

- Lack of strategic and tactical sense;
- Not delegating effectively;
- Leader is too hands-off; far from action;
- No clean plan;
- Failure to share intelligence;
- Inability to anticipate; doomed optimism;
- Lack of focus on day-to-day tactics;
- Forgetfulness; sleeping at the switch.

Lars continued. "What some of the leaders, who blundered, didn't realize is that your decisions shape your destiny. This was a good wrap-up, gang. Would everyone like to meet say... the last Friday of every month for breakfast at Metro 29?" Everyone cheered. Thumbs up!

"OK! Great. My surprise is that our sabbatical with the local Police Department may be over. They have a case that has them clueless, the Police Chief told me."

"Hey! Doc, that's when *we* enter the game, right? I

mean, after all, we've helped them solve *five* cases so far!"
Tiger popped up his chest.

High-fives and they all departed in high spirits.

"All truths are easy to understand once they are discovered; the point is to discover them."

Portrait of Galileo Galilei, 1636

AUTHOR'S CLOSING COMMENT

"My whole purpose is to bring out the truths to the general public. They deserve it... by understanding blunders that should not have occurred in world history."

C.Toftoy, 2020

These truths may open your eyes to realize that our lives might be different today if certain people had made better decisions and faced the truth. Instead, many unnecessary blunders occurred.

I spent six years of research and study to unearth many unknown facts and to bring them to light. I feel that you must look to the past if you want to see into the future.

The Alpha Team, used in my previous three books, was perfect to use as a discussion group. I didn't want the research material to be one-sided, me to you only.

I don't pretend to be an expert historian, rather a writer in a quest to uncover missing links to better explain certain aspects of world history.

Feel free to contact me at charles.toftoy@gmail.com.

"Knowledge is in the end based on acknowledgement."

***Portrait of Ludwig Wittgenstein being awarded
a scholarship from Trinity College, 1929***

ACKNOWLEDGEMENTS

"First, I want to thank you for reading Blunnders. Hopefully it opened your eyes to many missing facts that are still shaping our destinies.

My acknowledgement list is too long, but those that contributed know who they are. I'm eternally grateful to them and all the historians and scholars whose research allowed me to delve deep into each of these blunders.

Actually, 'I lived this book'. I suffered somewhat doing this because I feel for those who lost their lives unnecessarily due to the blundering fools who were careless, ignorant, or negligent. Writing this book was harder than I thought, yet very rewarding. None of this would have been possible without Cindy Bauer, my Editor in Chief and go-to person. She kept the pace right with me during this six-year journey.

Charles N. Toftoy

Some specific acknowledgements:
- Editor in Chief, Cover Design, Interior Formatting Brainstorming: Cindy Bauer
- Creative Thinking And Sharing Ideas:
    - Jeff Duvall, Sergeant E-5, USA (Retd. 100% Disabled. Combat Vietnam Veteran (1st Cavalry Division)
    - Wil Danielson, Librarian (Retd.)
    - Bradley J. Johnson, Colonel, USA (Retd.) Combat Helicopter Pilot, Vietnam

- Tony Padilla, Policy Analyst, National Commission on the BP Deepwater Horizon Oil Spill and Offshore Drilling (2010-2011)
- John Oscar Bagot Sewall, Major General, USA (Retd.) Strategy and Policy Formulation Expert
- Ben Herring, Writer/Editor, Washington, D.C.
- Mack Brooks, former Advisor—Vietnamese Airborne Division and former West Point Admissions Officer
- Patricia N. Toftoy, Author's Wife

Research Support And Cooperation:
- One-on-one live interviews, small group live discussions, journal articles, books, articles/writings on internet, archives, diaries, posts, and blogs. And those living and dead whose quotes and sayings I selected.
- Because of them much was uncovered that is not apparent to our average citizen.
- Of special note is Robert Youngson, who wrote the book: *Scientific Blunders*.

Other support:
- I'd like to acknowledge Wikipedia (hosted by the Wikipedia Foundation). I respect them for bringing free education globally.

Special Support:

- My two Yorkshire Terriers, Sasha and Zoe who supervised me. Especially Zoe, who would lie down on top of my desk, less than two feet away from where I was writing... watching me with one eye open. And Sancho, my African Grey Parrot, who would play around in my lap with his toys during break time.
- Lastly, it would be only fair to bestow my gratitude to Enya and Tchaikovsky, whose music played continuously as I wrote.
- Finally, as mentioned previously, this book could never have been completed without the extraordinary efforts of Cindy Bauer.

"Books are for nothing but to inspire."

American writer Ralph Waldo Emerson in 1857

THE BOTTOM LINE

These blunders form shadows for the future. And we have unfortunately inherited these shadows formed by the past blunders. Shame on those responsible for the filling of graves of indispensable, respectable people. May those people who passed on, *all of them,* forever rest in peace.

- The Author

SPECIAL CLOSING COMMENT FROM THE ALPHA TEAM TO *YOU*... THE READER

Aristotle said: *'The whole is greater than the sum of its parts'.* Our team members, the parts, have been connected together during this extremely earnest research journey. That has allowed us to more effectively, as a whole, to provide the real truths to you as part of the deserving public.

Hopefully, we have imparted this to you, the reader— who counts the most.

Respectfully,
Lars, Doris, Tiger, Brenda, Olivia

ABOUT THE AUTHOR

 Charles N. Toftoy has five books published. He has worked in the military, corporate, and academic sectors.

A highly decorated US Army Infantry Officer. Served two one-year Vietnam tours as a Ranger/Paratrooper. Awards include two Purple Hearts.

Graduate of West Point and has an MBA and Doctorate in strategic planning. He taught in The Business School, George Washington University, for 17 years and is now emeritus from GWU. He has received numerous academic, corporate, and military awards and honors. Currently, he serves as a business advisor to several local companies in Northern Virginia.

Charles lives in Arlington, Virginia with his wife, Patricia, two Yorkshire Terriers, Sasha and Zoe, and an African Grey Parrot, Sancho.

Dr. Toftoy is available for readings, lectures, group discussions and signing sessions. Learn more by visiting: www.charlesntoftoy.com.

A portion of the proceeds will be donated to the Wounded Warrior Mentor Program. The author is a mentor.

MORE BOOKS BY THIS AUTHOR

How CEOs Set Strategic Direction For Their Organizations
by Charles Toftoy 1987
(Non-Fiction Business)

This practical book evolved from Toftoy's doctoral dissertation. Based on a survey of 100 companies via personal interviews with top CEOs.

The role CEOs perceive for themselves in the strategic planning system. Responsibilities of different managers in the development of plans. Shows how setting strategic direction is the principal job of the CEO.

IT'S IN THE EYES
by Charles Toftoy 2009
(Thriller)

A Psychopath Is Stalking Co-Eds In Washington, DC

It's spring in Washington, DC - a beautiful time of year in the nation's capital, yet its citizens are uneasy. Their heightened restlessness is reminiscent of the recent 9/11, sniper, and anthrax scares. But this time the enemy is a psychopathic killer responsible for the deaths of four local university co-eds - raping and murdering them using rituals practiced by the Thuggees, killers for the Goddess Kali who were responsible for the deaths of more than two million travelers in India in the 17th and 18th centuries.

It's up to Lars Neilsen, a college professor and part-time sleuth, and his highly skilled Alpha Team to find out who is committing these atrocious murders. But Lars and his team are in for a few nasty surprises along the way...

EYES OF COLD CASE KILLERS
by Charles Toftoy 2011
(Thriller)

Cold Case Killer Haunts Washington, DC Metro Area

Lars Neilsen, a professor-sleuth, and his highly skilled Alpha Team put their lives on the line to catch the cold case killer of twenty victims.

Taurus, nickname for the killer, has a track record of murders from Buffalo, Albany, Philadelphia to the Washington, D.C. Metro area. His modus operandi is mostly strangulation—placing a plastic bag over the head of his victims.

D.C.'s heightened restlessness is reminiscent of the post 9/11, snipers, and anthrax scares. Everyone is walking on pins and needles, particularly in the Northern Virginia region. The entire nation watches.

AMAZING FIRESIDE TALKS
Intriguing Thoughts to Awaken YOU
by Charles Toftoy 2014
(Motivational Self-Help)

Based on extensive research, Dr. Toftoy provides practical, rubber-meets-the-road thoughts to INSPIRE us. The ALPHA TEAM, characters from his first two novels, gathers weekly to discuss important topics of life.

This book is written TO you and FOR you, the reader, providing insights to help you cope with personal difficulties, make self-improvements, and assist or care for others. It will be beneficial to teenagers, young adults, seniors, men and women. A portion of the proceeds will be donated to the Wounded Warrior Mentor Program.

Note: These books are available at Amazon and most major online bookstores.

PHOTO ATTRIBUTIONS

To the best of my knowledge, all photos used are public domain. Most were obtained from Wikipedia Commons Public Domain.

*****

COVER:

Native Americans painting – Wikipedia Public Domain
  – *attribution: Karl Bodmer 1832-1834*
Kennedy in car – Wikipedia Public Domain
(Copyright expired in 1991 without renewal. First published November 24, 1963)
  – *attribution: President Kennedy in the limousine in Dallas, Texas, on Main Street, minutes before the assassination. Also in the presidential limousine are Jackie Kennedy, Texas Governor John Connally, and his wife, Nellie*
Challenger Crew – Wikipedia Public Domain
attribution: NASA
Adolph Hitler – Wikipedia Public Domain
attribution: Bundesarchiv
Chernobyl
attribution: Hone/Gamma-Rapho (Getty Images)
Indianapolis – Wikipedia Public Domain
World Trade Center – Wikipedia Public Domain
  – *attribution: WTC smoking - Michael Foran*
Katrina – Wikipedia Public Domain

Hubble – Wikipedia Public Domain
Napoleon
  – *Believed to be public domain; copyright unknown*

INSIDE:

- *attribution: United States Department of the Interior advertisement offering Indian Land for Sale; the man pictured is a Yankton Sioux named Not Afraid Of Pawnee.*

Page 79 – Indianapolis – Wikipedia Public Domain

Page 85 – McVay – Wikipedia Public Domain
- *attribution: Bettmann Archive (Getty Images)*

Page 91 – Whipped Slave – Wikipedia Public Domain

Page 99 – Slaves – Wikipedia Public Domain

Page 106 – WWI Montage – Wikipedia Public Domain

Page 119 – Pizzaro – Wikipedia Public Domain

Page 127 – Climate Change – Wikipedia Public Domain
- *attribution: NASA*

Page 136 – Chinese Poster
- *Believed to be public domain; copyright unknown*

Page 144 – Bay of Pigs – Wikipedia Public Domain
- *attribution: Rumlin*

Page 159 – Lusitania – Wikipedia Public Domain
- *attribution: Bundesarchiv*

Page 180 – Challenger Montage – Wikipedia Public Domain
- *attribution: US Gov-NASA*

Page 185 – Challenger Crew – Wikipedia Public Domain
attribution: NASA

Page 191 – Tay Bridge – Wikipedia Public Domain

Page 200 – Piltdown Chicken – Wikipedia Public Domain
- *attribution: Photograph on left taken in May 2004 by Kyle Butt and Eric Lyons of the Apologetics Press staff*

Page 205 – Mars Climate Orbiter – Wikipedia Public Domain

Page 211 – Hubble – Wikipedia Public Domain
Page 216 – Cold Fusion – Wikipedia Public Domain
  – *attribution: Photo taken on 2/18/2005 at the United States Navy SPAWAR Systems Center in San Diego, CA; Photo Credit - Steven B. Krivit*
Page 221 – Chernobyl – Wikipedia Public Domain
  – *attribution: Soviet Authorities*
Page 236 – Hitler – Wikipedia Public Domain
  – *attribution: Bundesarchiv*
Page 241 – Chart – Wikipedia Public Domain
Page 271 – JFK – Wikipedia Public Domain
Page 278 – Katrina – Wikipedia Public Domain
Page 289 – Oil Spill
  – *Believed to be public domain; copyright unknown*
Page 304 – Constantinople – Wikipedia Public Domain
Page 310 – Titanic – Wikipedia Public Domain
  – *Attribution: Willy Stower*
Page 323 – Captain Smith – Wikipedia Public Domain
  – *Attribution: Photograph was taken aboard the Olympic by author unknown and was published following the sinking, in 1912*
Page 327 – Napoleon – Wikipedia Public Domain
Page 335 – Firetrucks – Wikipedia Public Domain
Page 341 – Pickett – Wikipedia Public Domain
Page 350 – Gallipoli – Wikipedia Public Domain
Page 359 – Yamashita, Percival – Wikipedia Public Domain
Page 364 – Two Ships – Wikipedia Public Domain
Page 367 – Soldiers – Wikipedia Public Domain
Page 370 – General – Wikipedia Public Domain
Page 382 – Goethe – Wikipedia Public Domain

Charles N. Toftoy

Made in the USA
Monee, IL
24 January 2022

89770942R00223